ROUSSEAU'S CONSTITUTIONALISM

Despite Rousseau's legacy to political thought, his contribution as a constitutional theorist is underexplored. Drawing on his constitutional designs for Corsica and Poland, this book argues that Rousseau's constitutionalism is defined chiefly by its socially directive character. His constitutional projects are not aimed, primarily, at coordinating and containing state power in the familiar liberal-democratic sense. Instead, they are aimed at fostering the social conditions in which a fuller sense of freedom—understood broadly as non-domination—can be realised across all social domains. And in turn, since Rousseau views domination as being deeply embedded in complex social practices, his constitutionalism is aimed at fostering a radical austerity—social, economic and cultural—as its foil. In locating Rousseau's constitutional projects within his social and political theory of servitude and domination, this book will challenge the predominant focus and orientation of contemporary republican theory. Leading republican thinkers have drawn on the historical republican canon to articulate a model of constitutionalism which is, on the whole, 'liberal' in focus and orientation. This book will argue that the more communitarian orientation of Rousseau's constitutionalism—that is, its socially directive focus—stems from a sophisticated and compelling account of the sources of unfreedom in complex societies, sources which are ignored or downplayed by the neo-republican literature. Rousseau embraces a communitarian social politics as part of his constitutional project precisely because, pessimistically, he views domination as being deeply embedded in the social relations of the liberal order.

Rousseau's Constitutionalism

Austerity and Republican Freedom

Eoin Daly

·HART·
OXFORD · LONDON · NEW YORK · NEW DELHI · SYDNEY

HART PUBLISHING
Bloomsbury Publishing Plc
Kemp House, Chawley Park, Cumnor Hill, Oxford, OX2 9PH, UK

HART PUBLISHING, the Hart/Stag logo, BLOOMSBURY and the Diana logo are
trademarks of Bloomsbury Publishing Plc

First published in hardback, 2017
Paperback edition, 2019

© Eoin Daly 2017

Eoin Daly has asserted his right under the Copyright, Designs and Patents Act 1988 to be
identified as Author of this work.

All rights reserved. No part of this publication may be reproduced or transmitted
in any form or by any means, electronic or mechanical, including photocopying,
recording, or any information storage or retrieval system, without prior
permission in writing from the publishers.

While every care has been taken to ensure the accuracy of this work, no responsibility
for loss or damage occasioned to any person acting or refraining from action as a
result of any statement in it can be accepted by the authors, editors or publishers.

All UK Government legislation and other public sector information used in the work is Crown
Copyright ©. All House of Lords and House of Commons information used in the work is Parliamentary
Copyright ©. This information is reused under the terms of the Open Government Licence v3.0
(http://www.nationalarchives.gov.uk/doc/open-government-licence/version/3)
except where otherwise stated.

All Eur-lex material used in the work is © European Union,
http://eur-lex.europa.eu/, 1998–2017.

A catalogue record for this book is available from the British Library.

Library of Congress Cataloging-in-Publication data

Names: Daly, Eoin, author.
Title: Rousseau's constitutionalism : austerity and republican freedom / Eoin Daly.
Description: Portland, Oregon : Hart Publishing, 2017. | Includes bibliographical references and index.
Identifiers: LCCN 2017006466 (print) | LCCN 2017008742 (ebook) | ISBN 9781509903474 (hardback) | ISBN 9781509903481 (Epub)
Subjects: LCSH: Rousseau, Jean-Jacques, 1712–1778. | Constitutional law—Philosophy. | Constitutional law—Poland—History. | Constitutional law—France—Corsica—History.
Classification: LCC K457.R6 D35 2017 (print) | LCC K457.R6 (ebook) | DDC 342.001—dc23
LC record available at https://lccn.loc.gov/2017006466

ISBN: HB: 978-1-50990-347-4
PB: 978-1-50993-313-6
ePDF: 978-1-50990-349-8
ePub: 978-1-50990-348-1

Typeset by Compuscript Ltd, Shannon

To find out more about our authors and books visit www.hartpublishing.co.uk.
Here you will find extracts, author information, details of forthcoming events and
the option to sign up for our newsletters.

ACKNOWLEDGEMENTS

I first encountered Rousseau as an undergraduate student in the Department of French at University College Cork. Coming from the relatively sterile world of doctrinal legal analysis, the field of eighteenth century political thought opened new horizons. While I remember the opening chapters of the *Social Contract* as a revelation and an awakening, equally I remain grateful to those who introduced me to the history of French political thought—teachers like Paul Hegarty, Grace Neville and Patrick O'Donovan.

The ideas and arguments in this book first began to take shape around 2011, not long after I began teaching constitutional law, and during a period in which I began to turn away from liberal doctrines about individual rights and looked back to Rousseau in particular. Over this period, I was fortunate to have had the company and the support of colleagues and friends in three very different university departments—in Dublin City University, University College Dublin and NUI Galway. I particularly thank those who encouraged and accommodated me both in research and teaching. In no particular order, I thank John O'Dowd, Donncha O'Connell, Conor O'Mahony, Joe McGrath, Siobhán Mullally, Mairead Enright, Liam Thornton, Colin Scott, Gavin Barrett, Iseult Honohan, Imelda Maher, Olivia Smith, Kevin Costello, Robert Elgie, John Danaher, Ioanna Tourkochiriti, Dan Carey, Niall Ó Dochartaigh, Daniel Savery, Yaniv Roznai Cathal Curran, Philip Pettit and Tom Hickey. I am especially appreciative towards those who read and commented on draft chapters of this book—Aoife O'Donoghue, Daniel Savery, Tom Daly, Mairead Enright, Paul O'Connell, Anne Neylon, Tom Hickey, Gerard Sadlier and Robert Knox in particular. I also thank the many anonymous peer reviewers who helped to focus my thinking on Rousseau through various journal articles, elements of which I draw on and develop in this book.

I thank Bill Asquith and Hart Publishing for their support during the publication process. Finally, I thank my wife, Eilionóir Flynn, especially for all her encouragement as a colleague, and my parents, Tom Daly and Ann Sheehan, for all their support.

A note on translation

In general—and except where stated otherwise—I have used my own translation from the French language editions of Rousseau that are cited.

CONTENTS

Acknowledgements v

Introduction: Rousseau's Austerity and Rousseau's Constitutions 1
    I.   Rousseau as a Constitutional Theorist 1
    II.   Rousseau's Constitutional Projects 4
    III. Outline of Chapters 10

1. The Constitution of Freedom 13
    I.   Introduction 13
    II.   Freedom and Domination in Republican
         and Liberal Traditions 14
         A.   Domination and Unfreedom in Hobbes and Rousseau 18
    III. (Re)constituting Freedom 21
    IV. Situating Rousseau's (Un)freedom 27
    V.   Rousseau as a Republican Outlier 29
    VI. Constitutionalising Rousseau's Freedom 36

2. The Constitution of Autarky 37
    I.   Introduction 37
    II.   Commerce and Autarky in Corsica and Poland 38
    III. Commerce, Virtue and Corruption 44
         A.   Republican Politics for the Moderns 47
         B.   The Morality of Commerce: Constitutional
             Translations, Republican Adaptations 49
         C.   Rousseau's Rejection of the Republican
             Compromise with Commerce 52
         D.   The Destructive Force of Commercial Society 53
    IV. Rousseau's Concept of Constitutionalism 62
    V.   Autarky between Realism and Utopia 66
    VI. Conclusion 71

3. The Constitution of Symbol and Ritual 73
    I.   Introduction 73
    II.   Symbolism and Ritualism in Contemporary
         Constitutional Thought 74
    III. Rituals and Symbols in Corsica and Poland 76

IV.	The Political Function of Symbols and Rituals	78
V.	The Radical Scope of Rousseau's Civic Ritualism	83
VI.	Culture and Domination in the Early-modern World	85
VII.	Culture and Aesthetics under Austerity	90
VIII.	Civic Ritualism and Constitutional Design: Contemporary Problems	96
IX.	Conclusion	102

4. The Constitution of Deliberation 105
    I. Introduction 105
    II. Rousseau on Deliberation, Dissensus, Dissent 106
    III. Deliberation and Non-domination 108
    IV. Deliberation as Domination 111
        A. Rousseau as Critical Discourse Theorist 114
    V. Deliberation under Republican Austerity 119
    VI. Deliberation and Difference 123
    VII. Neo-republican Blindspots 125

5. The Constitution of Judgment 131
    I. Introduction 131
    II. Legislation and Judgment in Rousseau's Constitutional Projects 132
    III. The Paradox of Judicial Power under the General Will 134
    IV. Principled Adjudication and the General Will 137
    V. Adjudication under Republican Austerity 139
    VI. Complexity, Differentiation and Symbolic Power 143
    VII. Conclusion 146

Bibliography 149
Index 157

Introduction: Rousseau's Austerity and Rousseau's Constitutions

I. Rousseau as a Constitutional Theorist

It may seem anomalous, or at least awkward, to use the phrase 'Rousseau's constitutionalism'. Jean-Jacques Rousseau is celebrated for his brilliant philosophical anthropology of servitude and domination, and for the highly abstract theory of political freedom—and of the republican state—that he outlines in the *Social Contract*. Yet there has been little discussion of Rousseau's distinctive contribution as a constitutional theorist, or indeed little sense of him having originated a specific concept or project of constitutionalism. No doubt this is due in part to the fact that Rousseau strongly rejected any constitutional constraint on legislative power, and therefore seems at odds with the dominant substantive concern of contemporary constitutionalism—that is, the idea that legally defined individual rights, defined and codified in advance, should constrain and limit the exercise of constituted popular sovereignty.

Yet the problem relates to the concept as much as the substance of the Constitution. *Constitutionalism* most often refers to an idea of government being bound by a higher law, usually in the form of an entrenched legal document that cannot easily be amended. And this is a concept of government that Rousseau decisively rejects, while the legalistic tradition of constitutionalism—originating rather late with thinkers like Thomas Paine—is one he lies clearly outside. His concept of a Constitution is more organic, understood roughly as the structure and principles that define the whole polity and its components. In this light, I use the term constitutionalism in a slightly wider sense, referring to the purposes and aims of Constitutions (of varying forms). And in this adjusted sense, Rousseau sketches an idea of constitutionalism—related to, yet distinguishable from, his political theory per se—which still speaks and relates to our contemporary ideas and concerns.

On the one hand, Rousseau's most famous work of political theory—the *Social Contract*—sketches a Constitution, in a sense, for a highly abstract, non-specific state, or what he calls an 'ideal Republic'.[1] However, in this book I will argue that it is largely in his projects of constitutional design for specific, historically situated states—namely, Corsica and Poland—that we can discern a distinctive

---

[1] Jean-Jacques Rousseau, *Du Contrat Social: Principes de Droit Politique* (first published 1762, Paris, ENAG, 1988).

understanding of constitutionalism. Rousseau's constitutionalism, I will argue, is characterised mainly by its socially directive character, thus offering a contrast to the standard liberal-democratic and republican concepts that are focused on the dispersal and containment of state power. In turn, this distinctive concept of constitutionalism stems directly from—and simultaneously, does a great deal to clarify—his theories of freedom and unfreedom. Particularly, it illustrates Rousseau's sense of the sources and constitution of unfreedom and domination in early modern societies. In short, then, Rousseau's constitutionalism can be read as an institutional response, albeit under peculiar historical conditions, to the problem of servitude and domination that he sketched at an abstract level in the second *Discourse* in particular.

Of course, the 'Constitutions' Rousseau wrote for Corsica and Poland were not legal Constitutions in the sense the phrase is now widely understood. These are projects for systems of government in the broad sense, interspersed with a good deal of social criticism and polemic. But in their content and focus, these Constitutions speak to particular concepts of freedom—and indeed of unfreedom—in a sense that is equally true of contemporary, written Constitutions notwithstanding their very different structure and shape.

The constitutional devices and mechanisms that Rousseau recommends for Corsica and Poland are not aimed *primarily* at what we might understand as the fundamental task of Constitutions—that of coordinating and establishing political institutions. That is to say, they are not concerned primarily with structuring and containing state power, or indeed with limiting its reach over individuals. Indeed Rousseau's recommendations in terms of institutional design are inconclusive, permissive and contextually flexible; he relaxes, for example, the insistence on 'direct democracy' or direct popular legislation that he affirms in the *Social Contract*. Instead, the distinctiveness of Rousseau's Constitutions lies in their socio-economic, cultural and symbolic focus. Their main purpose, I argue, is to foster and sustain *austerity* in its broad sense—social, economic and cultural—as the basic framework of republican politics. And specifically, his constitutional projects are aimed at maintaining cohesive, autarkical and relatively unified societies, against the forces of cosmopolitanism, liberalism and commerce. Rousseau's idea of a Constitution is interlinked with a certain vision of organic social order. Yet despite its communal character, the political function of his austerian Constitution is not to integrate citizens within a shared way of life or a particular conception of the good, or indeed to realise any specific vision of human excellence. I will argue, then, that Rousseau's socially directive constitutionalism should not be mistaken for any 'communitarian' philosophy in this sense. Instead, Rousseau's austerity is resolutely aimed at (re)constituting individual freedom, albeit understood in a very particular way.

Like other republican thinkers, Rousseau equates unfreedom or servitude with domination—roughly understood as the condition of being dependent upon arbitrary power, or the will of an alien other. And insofar as Rousseau embraces austerity as a constitutional antidote to the pervasive servitude he identifies in the second *Discourse*—and thus as the social horizon of republican freedom—this, in turn, tells us a great deal about his understanding of the structure and source of domination and servitude. And crucially, since austerity is envisaged specifically as a foil to the ills engendered by social complexity and social differentiation, this tells us a great deal about Rousseau's sense of how domination is experienced and inflicted in increasingly complex and differentiated societies in the early modern context. Thus his austerian constitutionalism gives institutional and political expression to Rousseau's scepticism concerning the emancipatory effects of cultural, artistic and scientific progress in the Enlightenment period. Indeed in this sense, Rousseau presages certain aspects of much later critical thought concerning the insidious forms of domination that are latent in liberal social orders.

In summary, then, Rousseau's austerian constitutionalism confirms and concretises the view he sketches at a more abstract level in his *Discourses*[2]—effectively, that domination, both social and political, is constituted, inflicted and reproduced in ostensibly mundane and benign social practices—not only in language and discourse, but also in culture, taste and symbolic exchange. In contrast with other republican thinkers—including contemporary neo-republicans—his insight, in part, is that domination is irreducible to the alien control of individual *choice*: rather, it is inflicted and experienced largely through symbolic forms, being rooted in our need for external recognition. And it is embedded, in particular, in the production and exchange of social, symbolic and cultural capital. This pessimistic view concerning the intractable and insidious character of servitude in liberal social orders does much to explain the socially radical scope of his constitutionalism compared to other republican thinkers. And it suggests that for Rousseau, the central problem of politics—and thus, the central concern of constitutional design—is not our disagreement concerning questions of the good, or the conflict between our 'comprehensive doctrines', to borrow John Rawls' phrase.[3] Rather, the starting point is the corrupting self-love wrought by humans' need for external recognition—their need to live in the eyes of others—once they enter society. The challenge of politics is how it is possible—notwithstanding our corrupted *amour-propre*—to constitute an authentically shared and coherent universe of symbols and meanings in which not only discourse and political communication, but social practice generally, can assume transparent and non-dominating forms. Thus for Rousseau, the challenge of political theory—and by implication the motivation of his constitutional endeavour—is to create a society in which political communication, in particular, can be rescued from obfuscation, befuddlement and symbolic violence.

Rousseau's austerian constitutionalism aims in part, then, at stemming social complexity and at foiling the various, insidious forms of domination that flow

---

[2] Jean-Jacques Rousseau, *Discours sur les sciences et les arts* (Paris, Livres de Poche, 2012/1751) (hereinafter *First Discourse*); Jean-Jacques Rousseau, *Discours sur l'origine et les fondements de l'inégalité parmi les hommes* (Paris, Flammarion, 1755/2008) (hereinafter *Second Discourse*).

[3] John Rawls, *Political Liberalism* (New York, Columbia University Press, 1996).

from it. In this light, he challenges the central preoccupations and normative assumptions of our dominant contemporary, liberal-democratic account of constitutionalism. Since he identifies servitude and domination at a foundational social level—as being intractably embedded in ostensibly innocent social relations—this means that the object of constitutionalism cannot lie simply in the containment and coordination of state power. Rather, the republican Constitution must effectuate transformation across all social domains, fundamentally re-configuring our social relationships generally.

Accordingly, this book will argue that the socially directive orientation of Rousseau's austerian constitutionalism is explained largely by his pessimistic understanding of domination as being deeply pervasive and insidious. But conversely, the substance of this constitutionalism—the specific devices and mechanisms it encompasses—can, I argue, give us a more complete picture of Rousseau's complex theories of servitude and freedom. And in addressing constitutionalism to all dimensions of servitude and unfreedom, by the same measure it poses an important challenge for the contemporary liberal-democratic account. This inquiry is all the more pertinent given that, in many senses, Rousseau anticipates the political problems of our world much more presciently than his more optimistic contemporaries of the European Enlightenment—particularly our problems of intractable, complex inequality, alienation, and the disintegration of the public sphere—in the face of unprecedented material abundance and scientific progress.

II. Rousseau's Constitutional Projects

Constitutional theories and indeed constitutional projects can be understood as attempts to institutionalise particular understandings of freedom—say, a concept of freedom as political self-government, one of national dignity or collective emancipation, or simply a concern to limit state power over individuals. And this is equally true of Rousseau. As I will outline in chapter one, Rousseau offers a particular understanding of servitude or unfreedom, and conversely, an understanding of freedom that resides not only in political self-government but also a radical politics of social transparency. Social domination, he argues, originates largely in *amour-propre*—that is, our need for external recognition and distinction. However, he also outlines a redemptive project of republican politics in which *amour-propre* can be reconfigured and manipulated, such that it is consummated and exercised in appropriately transparent and benign ways, and ultimately harnessed to promote republican ends. Indeed in the second *Discourse* Rousseau suggests it is the very 'frenzy for distinction'—that is, *amour-propre*—to which we owe 'the best as well as the worst' of ourselves.[4]

---

[4] *Second Discourse*, above n 2, 140.

It is widely accepted that Rousseau's austere social politics are aimed at manipulating and re-orienting *amour-propre* towards transparent and benign forms that are consistent with freedom as non-domination, understood in a suitably broad sense.[5] My aim in this book, however, is to show how Rousseau's distinctive understanding of the source of unfreedom, in social complexity and differentiation, and of its cure—austerity—is given expression in a specific concept of constitutionalism. While most analyses of Rousseau's constitutional thought focus primarily on the institutional mechanisms that are intended to effectuate the 'general will' in legislative form, I will aim to show that Rousseau's constitutionalism is overwhelmingly oriented towards economic, cultural and social concerns—and in turn that this stems from his sense of the pervasive character of domination in ordinary social life. It is a truism that any given theory of constitutionalism—for example, the liberal-democratic concept that dominates contemporary thought—stems at least implicitly from a particular set of assumptions concerning the source and character of unfreedom (assuming that constitutionalism is a response, at least in part, to the problem of freedom). At the very least, for example, it reflects assumptions concerning the relative importance of different kinds or sources of domination or unfreedom. And the central focus of liberal-democratic constitutionalism—on checking and constraining popular sovereignty for the sake of individual rights—squarely identifies arbitrary governmental power as the central problem of politics and as the most important threat to individual freedom and individual flourishing. Conversely, the socially directive focus of Rousseau's constitutionalism reflects a different sense of the sources and constitution of unfreedom—and indeed in this respect it poses an important challenge to the core normative assumptions of the liberal model.

This emphasis on the socially directive orientation of Rousseau's constitutionalism is not to discount the importance and centrality of the general will in his thought generally, but rather to suggest that the central function of the Rousseauan Constitution is to foster the social, economic and cultural conditions within which the general will—a political will that citizens can internalise as their own—may successfully be effectuated in political life. As I will show, strictly institutional devices and mechanisms, such as legislative process, etc, in some senses occupy a secondary importance in this light: in turn, the fact that Rousseau is willing to discard apparently central institutional prescriptions (such as direct popular legislation) says a good deal about the central preoccupations of his political thought, and especially concerning the social horizons of republican freedom.

I will argue that Rousseau's understanding of austerity as the social horizon of republican freedom is given expression in his two works of constitutional design for historically situated states—*Constitutional Project for Corsica* and

---

[5] Frederick Neuhouser, *Rousseau's Theodicy of Self-Love: Evil, Rationality and the Drive for Recognition* (Oxford, Oxford University Press, 2010); Frederick Neuhouser, 'Freedom, Dependence and the General Will' (1993) 102 *Philosophical Review* 363; Nicholas Dent, *Rousseau* (London, Taylor and Francis, 2005).

Considerations on the Government of Poland. In contrast with the *Social Contract*—his seminal and more abstract political work—his writings on Corsica and Poland, being concerned with real-life polities, reveal a great deal concerning his understanding of how a suitably wide sense of freedom as non-domination could be realised under peculiar and specific political circumstances. Counter-intuitively, therefore, they demonstrate an underappreciated pragmatism and realism in Rousseau's political thought—despite their radical and often eccentric content. More generally, these writings give us a greater understanding both of Rousseau's sense of the sources of servitude and unfreedom in increasingly complex and differentiated early-modern societies, and of the emancipatory function of constitutional devices across broad swathes of social life.

Rousseau's first project of constitutional design was for Corsica, a sparsely populated and historically obscure island in the north-western Mediterranean.[6] In 1762, in the *Social Contract*, Rousseau made a passing but admiring reference to the island:

> There is still in Europe a country capable of [true] legislation: the island of Corsica. The valour and resolve with which this brave people recovered and defended its liberty is such as to warrant that some sage should instruct them how to maintain it. I have a premonition that someday, this little island will astonish Europe.[7]

Indeed, Corsica was an object of fascination for Enlightenment Europe. In the 1750s and 1760s, it enjoyed a brief interlude of independence following an insurrection against Genoa—until it was annexed, in 1769, by pre-revolutionary France.[8] During its independence, it implemented a republican system of government that reflected many of the political themes of the Enlightenment, anticipating the revolutions of later decades.[9] Its short-lived republican experience stoked intellectual imaginations further afield: Pascal Paoli, Corsica's revolutionary

---

[6] The entry for Corsica in Diderot's *Encyclopedia* reads: 'a considerable Italian island, in the Mediterranean, belonging to the Republic of Geneva. The inhabitants are restless, vindictive and bellicose', cited in James Boswell, *An Account of Corsica, the Journal of a Tour to That Island, and Memoirs of Pascal Paoli* (Bolton and McLoughlin eds, Oxford, Oxford University Press, 2006).

[7] *Social Contract*, above n 1, Bk I, Ch X.

[8] For an historical account of revolutionary Corsica, see Boswell, above n 6. In Boswell's contemporary account, 'a nation of brave and liberty-loving islanders had endured centuries of tyranny but were now poised to make good their independence under a heroic and charismatic leader ... Not only did [Boswell] bring a remote and unvisited island to public consciousness in Britain and the other countries where it was rapidly translated. [He] also offered a portrait of the congenitally quarrelsome Corsicans as heroic freedom fighters in a truly Spartan mould, who had chosen as their general a martial but modest and judicious paragon of leaderly virtues. It was a script which the Americans and George Washington would make their own in the next decade.' See William Doyle, 'An Account of Corsica, the Journal of a Tour to That Island, and Memoirs of Pascal Paoli (review)' (2007) 61 *French Studies: A Quarterly Review* 227.

[9] Dorothy Carrington, 'The Corsican Constitution of Pasquale Paoli' (1973) 88 *The English Historical Review* 481.

figurehead, was feted in Europe's literary salons, seen as the first political figure to have attempted implementing the ideas of the *philosophes* in politics.[10] William Pitt the First excitedly described Paoli as 'one of those men no longer to be found but in the *Lives of Plutarch*.'[11] Saul describes a cult-like devotion following Paoli's exile to England; as he crossed Europe, 'he was greeted as the great hero of political reason.'[12] The Corsican revolution influenced republican thought in the American colonies, and presaged the constitutional ambitions of the French revolutionaries three decades later.[13]

In 1764, Buttafoco, a Corsican aristocrat, invited Rousseau to devise a new Constitution for the young Republic, despite him never having visited the island. The existing Corsican Constitution of 1755, devised by Paoli, reflected many of the political themes of the Enlightenment and encapsulated rudimentary liberal-democratic as well as republican ideas.[14] Ultimate authority vested in the people, with the preamble proclaiming the Corsican people 'legitimately master of itself'; legislative power was vested in an indirectly elected national assembly or 'Diet', which appointed functionaries and the head of government.[15] Thus it echoed

---

[10] John Ralston Saul, *Voltaire's Bastards* (New York, Vintage, 1993) 55.
[11] ibid 56.
[12] ibid.
[13] 'When Paoli was called from exile in London across to Paris ... he was cheered by the entire national assembly, from moderates to revolutionaries, as the first man to have fought the kings and governed under the sign of reason ... Corsica played a key role in the rise of the republic ideal within the thirteen colonies. ... when the revolution came, the rebels used him same a s a rallying cry during charges against the English troops. And in later years the old revolutionaries throughout the American republic raised their glass in his honour on the night of Paoli's birthday ... the modern equivalent of Paoli's popularity among the intellectuals and young of 18th century Europe and America is perhaps that of Dubcek's Czechoslovakia or Allende's Chile in the 1960s. In popular terms his impact was like that of John Kennedy.': ibid 56–57. See also Thadd E Hall, 'The Development of Enlightenment Interest in Eighteenth-century Corsica' *Studies on Voltaire and the Eighteenth Century* vol 64 (Geneva, Institut et Musee Voltaire, 1968) 166.
[14] See generally Carrington, above n 9.
[15] Robert Chesnais, in preface to Jean-Jacques Rousseau, *Projet de Constitution pour la Corse* (Paris, Nautilus, 2000) 12–13. Carrington wrote: 'Paoli [as general of the nation] had no seat in the assembly; he was merely president of an executive council which the Diet appointed. The Diet moreover, being the national legislature, had power to modify the constitution of which, in theory, it was the author. Paoli's role in shaping the constitution of November 1755 is unquestionable; yet in the relevant document the constitution is presented as emanating from the Diet, representing the sovereign people. The Diet 'decreed' the establishment of the executive council, the Council of State, 'conferred' on it supreme authority in political, military and economic affairs. The Diet appointed Paoli 'chief and director' of the Council and elected all its members ... The Corsican Diet was then an unusual and very powerful institution. It was remarkable, in its period, by its mere existence: most of the great European nations were governed without a representative legislature: such was the case in France, Russia, Prussia, Spain. The Diet made laws and regulated taxation; these prerogatives, of course, were also exercised by the English parliament. But the Corsican Diet also nominated the heads of the executive, whereas in England the appointment of ministers belonged to the sovereign. Moreover by the terms of the Corsican constitution the Diet could censure and depose any member of the executive, Paoli not excepted.': Carrington, above n 9, 492, 495.

Montesquieu's prescriptions in separating legislature and executive 'into two distinct but interdependent bodies, operating in equilibrium.'[16]

However, Rousseau's *Constitutional Project for Corsica* fell completely out of this mould. Whereas others looked upon revolutionary Corsica as perhaps presaging a form of republican constitutionalism for the European powers, Rousseau instead viewed its revolution as an opportunity to revive—with a radical autarkic twist—the rugged virtues of the ancient republics. Thus his project was to differ dramatically from the patrician republic, along Genoese or Venetian lines, that Paoli advocated.[17] And decisively, eschewing commercial development, he advocated a 'total autarky'.[18] The content of his project—focused on sustaining Corsica's rustic insularity and its peasant virtues, reflected his scepticism towards the emancipatory claims of progress, reason and Enlightenment, as expressed so forcefully in his earlier *Discourse on the Sciences and Arts*. In fact, it contains little by way of institutional prescriptions and focuses almost entirely on constitutional rules and devices—especially in the area of family and property law—that are designed to sustain agrarian autarky on the island and stem the development of corrupting social practices. He advocates a 'total autarchy excluding all luxury and superfluous goods, based on traditional agriculture and crafts'.[19]

Mocked by intellectual adversaries for his efforts, Rousseau abandoned his project in 1765, unpublished. It had no influence on Corsican politics or intellectual life. It was eventually published posthumously, as a fragmentary work, in 1861.[20]

Rousseau attempted his second and final project of constitutional design in the early 1770s at the invitation of a Polish noble. He attempted 'to devise concrete political and cultural measures that, by taking into account the specific circumstances of eighteenth-century Poland, aim to set [it] on a path that will

---

[16] ibid 482. For James Boswell it was 'the best model that hath ever existed in the democratical form.' Cited in Carrington, above n 9, 491. Referring to the Corsican Constitution's preamble, Carrington notes: 'Here we see a concentrated statement of some major doctrines of the Enlightenment which must astonish in view of its early date', citing 'concepts of liberty as a natural right ... of the happiness of the nation as the proper aim of government, of the nation as the aggregate of the sovereign people ... in line with the celebrated texts of the American and French Revolutions Independence.' Yet Paoli drew not only on cosmopolitan Enlightenment influences, but also 'Corsican political traditions, rooted in the distant past ... Elective institutions had been known in the Corsican villages at least since the Middle Ages.' ibid 492–94. Carrington concludes: 'His regime can be usefully evaluated only within the context of its day. Its defects, as a democracy, are now obvious. The judiciary was incompletely separated from the executive. The Diet was only partly elected by manhood suffrage, and after 1766 in theory not at all; it was always invaded by members of the executive and judiciary, and from 1763 was overweighted by the clergy. On the other hand Paoli, who according to the original constitution of 1755 possessed less power than any monarch of his time.'; ibid 500.

[17] See further Jean Marie Arrighi, 'Textes théoriques de la révolution corse' in JM Arrighi et al (eds), *Pasquale Paoli: Aspects de son Oeuvre et de la Corse de son temps* (Albiana, Universita di Corsica, 2009).

[18] Chesnais, above n 15, 17.

[19] ibid 15.

[20] ibid 20.

bring it closer to realising positive philosophy's ideals.'[21] Again, he was overtaken by political events, and especially the invasion of Poland in 1772, which ended its independence. This was his last work of political theory. Compared to his work on Corsica, *Considerations on the Government of Poland* contains a good deal more detail concerning institutional design and constitutional structure in the more familiar sense. Along with many of the same eccentric autarkical and communitarian ideas present in *Corsica*, his Polish project reveals a surprising degree of pragmatic flexibility on institutional matters, especially compared to his earlier, abstract work. In particular, confronted with the extensive size of Poland compared to the idealised city-state of the *Social Contract*, Rousseau is prepared to countenance a degree of representative government, albeit with strict qualifications. Compared with the plenary citizen legislature envisaged in the *Social Contract*—with power distributed vertically downwards from an indivisible popular sovereign—effectively he devises a 'mixed' Constitution more in keeping with the classical orientation of republican thought.

However, *Poland* also places strong emphasis on non-institutional matters, particularly cultural and social practice. It sets out a range of eccentric prescriptions for public rituals, ceremonies and symbols, with a strong emphasis on cultivating an austere republican aesthetics. His main concern, as in Corsica, was to 'preserve and revive among your people simple customs and wholesome tastes.'[22]

Thus Rousseau's constitutional projects for Corsica and Poland are aimed at fostering and sustaining austerity—social, economic and cultural—as the horizon of republican freedom. Taken together with the social criticism contained in the *Discourses* and works like *Letter to D'Alembert*, they illustrate his sense of the relationship between domination and social practice. They show that for Rousseau, the central concern of republican constitutionalism is not simply to control arbitrary state power, but to sustain the social conditions under which a wider sense of domination, in all of its insidious guises, can be foiled within a suitable— and attainable—form of political community. These works illustrate his fear that in increasingly complex and differentiated societies, domination would assume highly encoded and symbolic, yet potent forms. And correspondingly, they illustrate how, for Rousseau, constitutionalism is aimed not only at permitting citizens to legislate their common interests in the more obvious republican sense, but also at ensuring transparency in social practice generally.

Compared to his more famous abstract work, Rousseau's projects of constitutional design show that although he is often typecast as a political utopian, he

---

[21] Frederick Neuhouser, *Rousseau's Theodicy of Self-Love: Evil, Rationality and the Drive for Recognition* (Oxford, Oxford University Press, 2010) 7.

[22] Jean-Jacques Rousseau, *Considérations sur le Gouvernement de Pologne et sur sa réforme projetée* in *Collection complète des oeuvres* (Genève, 1780–89) vol 1 Ch XI; for a translation see 'Considerations on the Government of Poland' in Frederick Watkins, *Jean-Jacques Rousseau: Political Writings* (New York, Thomas Yelsen, 1953).

is in fact distinctly preoccupied with the question of how principles of political right might successfully be implemented under real social conditions. Austerity, as he envisages it, is intended as a response to the problem of domination under eighteenth century conditions. Therefore, I do not argue that the *content* of his austerian constitutionalism has much to offer in contemporary debates on constitutional design. Rather, the argument is that the socially directive orientation of his constitutionalism is in one sense a peculiar expression of a more enduring radical challenge to the normative assumptions of liberal-democratic constitutionalism and the limited concept of freedom it enshrines.

III. Outline of Chapters

Chapter one, *The Constitution of Freedom*, outlines the distinctive understandings of domination and freedom upon which Rousseau's constitutional projects are based.

Chapter two, *The Constitution of Autarky*, illustrates how Rousseau's famous ambivalence concerning commerce and wealth is given expression in his constitutional thought. It will argue that while wealth gives *amour-propre* perhaps its most obvious expression, Rousseau's apprehension of commerce stems mainly from his rejection of the social differentiation it engenders. It will consider how Rousseau's promotion of autarky reflects his sense of the dominating effects of social differentiation.

Chapter three, *The Constitution of Symbol and Ritual*, explores the role of ritual, ceremony and symbolic power in Rousseau's constitutional projects for Corsica and Poland. It will argue that Rousseau envisages republican rituals and symbols as supplanting, and not merely as supplementing, the private rituals and practices of liberal society. Thus republican ritualism pervades the whole of social life. It will argue, in turn, that the symbolic and ritualistic focus of Rousseau's constitutionalism stems from his apprehension of the symbolic violence and thus, the domination latent in differentiated and complex forms of cultural practice and cultural consumption.

Chapter four, *The Constitution of Deliberation*, offers a similar argument in relation to Rousseau's treatment of political deliberation. It will argue, on the one hand, that austerity—the desire for a transparent social universe—stems in one sense from Rousseau's famous rejection of complex political deliberation as a source of deception and corruption. While he aims to stem social complexity so as to ensure transparency in social practice generally, transparent political communication can only be realised under republican austerity.

Many of these arguments are drawn together in the final chapter five, *The Constitution of Judgment*, which considers Rousseau's approach to lawmaking and adjudication. An enigma of Rousseau's legal thought is that while he defines legislation as the expression of the general will and thus of popular sovereignty, he recommends that it should assume a terse, laconic and open-textured form of the sort that will accord judges a great deal of discretion and indeed, lawmaking power in practice. However, I will argue that Rousseau's theory of judicial power must be understood in light of his broader social politics. And specifically, he rejects any understanding of law as a principled interpretive discourse or as an esoteric expert domain. Instead, he envisages that judicial power will be checked by a more generic sense of republican virtue. In law as in other social fields, republican austerity serves as a check against the dominating effects of social complexity.

1

The Constitution of Freedom

> Dependence on things, since it has no morality, is in no way detrimental to freedom ... Dependence on men, since it is without order, engenders all the vices.[1]

I. Introduction

As I argued in the Introduction, the main purpose of Rousseau's political and constitutional project is to recover or constitute a certain kind of freedom. In turn, his specific constitutional projects are centrally concerned with, and are largely expressions of, a particular understanding of freedom and unfreedom. In later chapters, I will consider how Rousseau's peculiar constitutional devices and prescriptions can be understood as an attempt to institutionalise, under particular historical conditions, such a peculiar—and indeed a highly demanding—concept of freedom. In this chapter, I will sketch the philosophical theory of freedom on which this attempt is grounded. This is drawn from a kind of historical and philosophical anthropology, in which Rousseau depicts the freedom that existed in the hypothetical, pre-social 'state of nature'—and its subsequent loss through various stages of civilisation and social development. Equally, however, Rousseau gives an account of how freedom—understood roughly speaking as an absence of domination or dependency on arbitrary power or alien will—can be recovered or reconstituted within political society. From man's 'fall' into corruption and servitude, there can be recovered the seeds of a possible future redemption, achieved within and through politics itself.

On the one hand, I offer no original interpretation of Rousseau's philosophy of freedom and servitude per se. Rather my aim in this chapter is to contextualise his constitutional projects in light of his theories of freedom and servitude and their relation to social structures and practices. Departing from the familiar republican idea of freedom as non-domination or non-dependency, I will consider, first, the insights that can be gleaned from Rousseau's historical genealogy of *unfreedom*. Specifically, I will outline how his understanding of servitude or unfreedom must

---

[1] Jean-Jacques Rousseau, *Emile or On Education* (A Bloom trans, New York, Basic Books, 1979) 85.

be understood in relation to the problem of *amour-propre*—the corruptible self-love that is consummated through external recognition—and correspondingly, how social domination is rooted partly in symbolic production and exchange. This insight explains key elements of his constitutional project. Second, I will consider Rousseau's understanding of a redemptive path to an alternative freedom—with its own distinctive constitution—through and within politics itself. I will outline how freedom, still understood, roughly, as non-domination or non-dependency, might be recovered or reconstituted, albeit on a different basis, within political society. Dependency on the will of the alien other is, in short, substituted by interdependency in the context of political community, with citizens being subject to a will—the general will—that each can recognise as his own.

In summary, then, this chapter provides the philosophical context for Rousseau's attempt at constitutionalising an ideal of freedom as non-domination, in light of his understanding of the social origins and constitution of unfreedom itself. In turn, this will help to explain how his particular constitutional devices are aimed at stemming particular dimensions of unfreedom that are latent in social power relations—including symbolic as well as economic and political dimensions. While Rousseau's constitutional projects are aimed at fostering austerity as a social framework for republican politics, this must, in short, be seen as a response to his distinctive understanding of servitude and unfreedom. On the one hand, this belongs within a broader republican history of thought that can be understood in part as a response to certain inadequacies in the dominant liberal way of thinking about freedom. On the other hand, Rousseau's radically 'communitarian' politics—a source of unease and opprobrium amongst other republican thinkers—can itself be understood as a coherent response to certain lacunae or blindspots in the mainstream of historical republican thought, and particularly its understanding of the social sources of domination.

II. Freedom and Domination in Republican and Liberal Traditions

It is useful to locate Rousseau's theories of freedom and unfreedom within the wider republican history of thought—even if in some ways the 'republican' classification may be somewhat inadequate (and especially since Rousseau is often seen as an outlier in the republican canon).[2] On the one hand, republicanism is sometimes distinguished from liberalism based on its lesser emphasis on individual

---

[2] For arguments along these lines, see Philip Pettit, *On the People's Terms: a Republican Theory and Model of Democracy* (Cambridge, Cambridge University Press, 2013).

freedom or 'rights', and a greater concern for civic virtue, the common good and so on.³ On the other hand, republicanism is also, and perhaps more often, distinguished from liberalism based on its different understanding of freedom itself. In particular, republicanism is associated with a concept of freedom as an absence of domination, understood broadly in the sense of disparate and unchecked power. Contemporary philosophers who identify as republicans reject any understanding of freedom as an absence of external restraint on individual choices, that is, *freedom as non-interference*. For Philip Pettit—perhaps the most influential contemporary republican philosopher—freedom, in the republican tradition, is best understood as an absence of domination rather than of interference as such. Thus 'the antonym of freedom [is] not interference but rather domination—exposure to the arbitrary, uncheckable power of a *dominus* or a master in one's life.'⁴ And he claims that this neo-Roman concept of freedom—what Skinner describes as 'liberty before liberalism'—runs in various guises through medieval and Renaissance political thought, the parliamentary cause in the English revolution, as well as various historical republican thinkers like Harrington and Machiavelli. Slavery epitomised domination. Even for the slave who is indulged or given licence, freedom is negated by the master's *power* of interference, rather than its actual exercise. A life lived peaceably, but at the grace of a 'kindly master', is not one that is lived freely. Similarly, the licence or toleration we might enjoy at the hands of our political rulers cannot offer freedom if it is enjoyed only at their discretion or good grace. Therefore, only citizens could be considered meaningfully free, irrespective of any tranquillity or security they might otherwise happen to enjoy. We are unfree, then, in the Roman-republican sense, when we are dependent on the goodwill of others, whether at the collective or interpersonal level.

Thus although this historical account is contested, Pettit and Skinner in particular depict a decisive historical *rupture*—one tinged with nostalgia and regret—in which a once dominant republican account of freedom, drawn from Rome, was supplanted by a liberal view from the early modern period onward, and so obscuring important insights. In this account, the relationship between republicanism and liberalism is one of opposition and discontinuity, rather than cross-fertilisation and overlap.⁵ According to one strand of the older republican tradition, freedom was intrinsically *political* in that it required individuals to participate in self-government, and it was silent or agnostic as to what particularised 'freedoms' or rights, in the sense of immunities from legal interference, that

---

³ See, eg, Mortimer Sellers, *The Sacred Fire of Liberty: Republicanism, Liberalism and the Law* (New York, Macmillan and NYU Press, 1998).
⁴ Philip Pettit, 'The Tree of Liberty: Republicanism, American, French and Irish' (2005) 1 *Field Day Review* 30.
⁵ For an alternative view see Richard Dagger, *Civic Virtues: Rights, Citizenship and Republican Liberalism* (Oxford, Oxford University Press, 1997); Andreas Kalyvas and Ira Katznelson, *Liberal Beginnings: Making a Republic for the Moderns* (Cambridge, Cambridge University Press, 2008).

individuals should enjoy. Such questions were fluid and contingent. In classical liberalism, by contrast—or at least in Pettit's reading of it—individuals consent to government in order to enjoy guarantees of private autonomy or non-interference in respect of definite choices or spheres of activity. This concept of freedom usually, although not invariably, emerged within social-contract theories of politics that emphasised legitimacy through consent. In particular, for Thomas Hobbes (although not recognisably a 'liberal' in the typical sense), freedom consists simply of the absence of external restraints on individual actions: 'a free man is he that in those things which by his strength and wit he is able to do *is not hindered to do what he hath the will to do*.'[6] Therefore, freedom is affected neither by our native incapacities nor, crucially, by the form of government per se, but only by the external coercion of our choices, from whatever source—a premise Hobbes used to justify absolutism. Crucially, Pettit argues that beyond and after Hobbes' absolutism, a similar *concept* of freedom—one that came to dominate late-modern thought—was embraced in particular by Bentham and his followers, ultimately providing a somewhat awkward philosophical basis for the later politics of social liberalism.[7] While 'freedom', for Bentham, was simply instrumental to utility understood as net social happiness, most utilitarians assumed this would be best achieved under a regime in which freedom as non-interference was widely observed.[8] It appeals to the value of being 'left alone' generally to pursue one's own happiness or pleasures, subject to the demands of net social utility.

Crucially, freedom defined in this liberal sense is dissociated from any particular form or structure of government. Freedom as non-interference is undermined, at least in an initial sense, by all forms of external coercion, of whatever provenance or constitution. And coercive laws, as Bentham argues, all carry an 'initial cost' for freedom, even where they are justified in overall terms.[9] Conversely, freedom in this sense is not intrinsically connected with any particular form of government.[10] Democracy and freedom are linked in a contingent, but not a conceptual way; democratic government may, depending on circumstance, be more likely to enhance freedom as non-interference, but is not freedom-giving as such.

Freedom, then, acquired quite an individualistic, and somewhat depoliticised understanding which denied any intrinsic significance in politics, citizenship or

---

[6] Thomas Hobbes, *Leviathan: Or the Matter, Forme, and Power of a Common-Wealth Ecclesiasticall and Civill* (Ian Shapiro ed, Yale, Yale University Press, 2010) Ch XXI, emphasis added.

[7] Philip Pettit, *Republicanism: A Theory of Freedom and Government* (Oxford, Clarendon Press, 1997) Chs 1–2.

[8] ibid. See generally John Stuart Mill, *On Liberty* (London, John Parker and Son, 1859); HR West, *An Introduction to Mill's Utilitarian Ethics* (Cambridge, Cambridge University Press, 2004).

[9] Jeremy Bentham, 'Anarchical Fallacies' in *The Works of Jeremy Bentham: Published under the Superintendence of His Executor, John Bowring* Vol 2 (Edinburgh, William Tait, 1843) 503, cited in Philip Pettit, 'Law and Liberty' in Samantha Besson and José-Luis Marti, *Legal Republicanism: National and International Perspectives* (Oxford, Oxford University Press, 2009) 39–59, 39.

[10] Pettit, above n 2, Ch 4.

political community. Freedom, in this sense requires *no more* than the absence of interference: it is silent as to the various aptitudes and resources individuals might need to exercise some measure of directive control over their lives,[11] whether achieved through collective political action or otherwise.

While I resist any neat typography of or opposition between 'republicanism' and 'liberalism'—which in some senses are historically sympathetic and interwoven— certain aspects of republican thought can be understood as a response to the shortcomings of this way of thinking about freedom, whether or not the 'liberal' label is fully warranted.[12] On the one hand, freedom as non-interference might be thought of as unsatisfactory or incoherent from an analytical point of view. As Richard Bellamy in particular has convincingly argued, claims to freedom as non-interference imply triadic relationships ('a three-way relation') whereby the subject of the claimed right calls upon a public authority to prevent 'interference' by a third party.[13] The state, then, interferes to prevent interference, leaving open the question of how competing claims of non-interference are weighted. And the range of interests, activities or choices that are to be especially protected against interference is intractably contested and historically contingent. This cannot transcend some substantive account of autonomy based on a thicker sense of freedom embedded in relations of power—or indeed, which rests on some set of interests or agendas or conceptions of good that inevitably, in itself, violates the supposed 'neutrality' of the liberal state.

On the other hand, the liberal concept might also be understood as an inadequate response to particular, lived experiences of servitude and unfreedom. In particular, republican accounts respond to a sense that the liberal concepts of freedom fail to account for the various, and often subtle forms of servitude, hierarchy and so on that exist in complex human societies. They fail to capture the peculiar injuries and distortions stemming from power imbalances in human relationships— independently of interference per se. There are many dimensions of servitude or unfreedom, republicans insist, that are irreducible to coercive interference.

To summarise, then, freedom, in the reconstructed republican sense, does not consist of an absence of interference as such, but rather an absence of *domination*, where domination is the condition of being subject to alien will. Borrowing Pettit's terminology, domination can be experienced without interference ever occurring, and conversely, some forms of coercive interference do not abrogate freedom, even in an initial sense, but in fact *constitute* it.[14]

---

[11] Isaiah Berlin, *Two Concepts of Liberty* (Oxford, Clarendon, 1958); Pettit, above n 7, 18.
[12] See, eg, Charles Larmore, 'A Critique of Philip Pettit's Republicanism' (2001) 11 *Philosophical Issues* 229; Matt Kramer, 'Liberty and Domination' in Cécile Laborde and John Maynor, *Republicanism and Political Theory* (London, Blackwell, 2008).
[13] Richard Bellamy, *Political Constitutionalism* (Cambridge, Cambridge University Press, 2007) 30.
[14] Pettit, above n 9.

A. Domination and Unfreedom in Hobbes and Rousseau

Pettit and others argue that this way of thinking about freedom has ancient origins, particularly in Roman republican thought,[15] and that it enjoys a certain continuity through early-modern and modern republicanisms. Yet although he lies in some senses at a distance from this tradition, it was Rousseau, in the early-modern period, who offered perhaps the most influential and compelling republican riposte to the emergent early-modern concept of freedom espoused both by the absolutist Hobbes as well as early liberals. Hobbes had famously justified an absolutist sovereign based on a brutal and violent understanding of man's pre-civil state. The civil order, he thought, was justified based on the depredations of the anarchic 'state of nature'. And under the rule of a sovereign, freedom of a kind—at least, freedom as non-interference—would be assured, since man would be spared the unpredictable coercion and violence of his 'natural' state.

Rousseau challenges Hobbes' absolutism by rejecting his understanding of the state of nature itself, and particularly, by refuting his claim that humans are (or were) *naturally* violent and self-interested. In the second *Discourse*,[16] Rousseau suggested that the seemingly rapacious instincts of pre-social man were not 'natural' at all but rather the product of a specific socialisation process; thus, Hobbes' attempt to justify political order based on 'natural' violence and chaos was fundamentally misplaced. Hobbes, in particular, had attempted to construct his political theory by naturalising motivations and dispositions that were, in fact, the product of highly contingent institutional and social influences. For Rousseau, then, 'Hobbes's mistake was to attribute violent passion to natural man that would have developed only as more complex social relations became established'.[17] In a highly speculative genealogy of human development, Rousseau conjectured, instead, that 'natural' humans, in the pre-social state, had developed *amour de soi*—a primal self-love expressed as self-preservation—and *pitié*, an aversion to seeing others suffer based on sympathetic identification. These attributes are 'natural' both because they are antecedent to social development but also because they are 'anterior to reason'.[18] Insofar as 'nature' referred to man's (hypothetical) condition before civilisation and social relations, men were naturally good.[19]

---

[15] Quentin Skinner, *Liberty before Liberalism* (Cambridge, Cambridge University Press, 1998).

[16] Jean-Jacques Rousseau, *Discours sur l'origine et les fondements de l'inégalité parmi les hommes* (Paris, Flammarion, 1755/2008) (hereinafter *Second Discourse*).

[17] Robin Douglass, *Rousseau and Hobbes: Nature, Free Will and the Passions* (Oxford, Oxford University Press, 2016) 59.

[18] ibid 68.

[19] Scott notes: 'We usually brand attributions of "goodness" as moral judgments, even as matters of "value" distinct from those of "fact." Rousseau, however, does not mean "good" in a moral sense, and even takes it in a sense compatible with matters of physics … for Rousseau our natural, physical passions and needs make us ordered or good beings.': John Scott, 'Politics as the Imitation of the Divine in Rousseau's "Social Contract"' (1994) 26 *Polity* 473, 476.

Hobbes, then, had confused two very different species of self-love, one properly 'natural', and the other a product of social conditioning. In contrast with *amour de soi* which relates solely to the self and its survival, Rousseau posits an entirely different, and *relational* species of self-love—*amour-propre*—that is consummated and fulfilled through recognition by others. A crucial feature of *amour-propre* compared to *amour de soi* is its relativity—the fact that it is exercised only though the esteem and recognition of others, whatever this might entail—and accordingly, its *arbitrariness* in terms of say, whatever gestures, appearances, manners or forms or speech that this might require.[20] Obviously, then, this kind of self-love develops only after the fall of the state of nature, and with the development of increasingly complex social relations. Yet for Rousseau, Hobbes' error was to have naturalised *amour-propre* and made it the original centrepiece of human motivation. In Douglass' analysis:

> Rousseau's principle of natural goodness was set out against Augustinian and Hobbesian accounts of man, which he thought depicted man as naturally evil. In opposition to these accounts of man's post-lapsarian state, Rousseau argued that man is naturally good and that his corruption is occasioned only by the development of certain types of social relations.[21]

For Rousseau, then, the social and political order cannot be justified or appraised from the standpoint of Hobbes' rapacious 'state of nature'. Instead—at least for some of his interpreters—it must be judged against the harmony and independence enjoyed by pre-civilised man in the 'Golden Age',[22] before the corruption

---

[20] Charvet notes: 'What Rousseau seems to be saying is that it is in the first place the making of comparative evaluations of each other which psychologically marks the break between natural and social men; that these comparative evaluations create in men a desire to be distinguished in the opinions of others and thus at the same time both a concern for their relative status and a dependence for their self-identity on how they exist in the eyes of others; and finally that this transformation engenders a fundamentally competitive consciousness in men, which is reflected in equally competitive and vicious relations between them': John Charvet, *The Social Problem in the Philosophy of Rousseau* (Cambridge, Cambridge University Press, 1974) 26. This is supported by a passage in the *Second Discourse*: 'Men began to take the differences between objects into account, and to make comparisons; they acquired imperceptibly the ideas of beauty and merit, which soon gave rise to feelings of preference ... A tender and pleasant feeling insinuated itself into their souls and the least opposition turned it into impetuous fury; with love arose jealousy; discord prevailed.': Rousseau, *Second Disourse*, above n 16, 141. Skillen argues that in Rousseau's historical anthropology, he 'makes competition for admired women quite central, creating one dimension of the insecurity that gets the wheels of estrangement moving'—and thus, essentially, that the corruption of self-love spills over into that of love, including romantic love in general. Anthony Skillen, 'Rousseau and the Fall of Social Man' (1985) 60 *Philosophy* 105, 112.

[21] Douglass, above n 17, 10. Similarly, Neuhouser observes: 'Despite its secular and naturalistic presuppositions, the structure of Rousseau's account mirrors that of the traditional Christian conception of human history: an original harmony among humans, God, and world is ruptured by a fall from grace—an effect of human freedom—that corrupts human nature and initiates an era of slavery and misery but that also beings with the possibility of redemption and transcendence.': Frederick Neuhouser, *Rousseau's Theodicy of Self-Love: Evil, Rationality and the Drive for Recognition* (Oxford, Oxford University Press, 2010) 2–3.

[22] Douglass, above n 17, Ch 2.

wrought by socialisation and *amour-propre*.[23] 'Nature', then, remains a normative standard, but it is understood very differently from Hobbes' vision—and not only because it is a positive standard rather than a dystopian counter-factual.

Rousseau is cognisant how an 'array of evils'—vanity, rapaciousness, cruelty and so on—can 'easily appear to be necessary features of the human condition'[24]—and aims instead to illustrate their origins in an historically contingent kind of corruption. Whereas his aim in the second *Discourse* is to 'separate what is artificial from what is natural in the present nature of man', Rousseau's task in part is to clarify the standpoint from which political institutions must be evaluated. But more pertinently, for current purposes, his aim is also to illustrate the full extent to which conditions of servitude and unfreedom are highly contingent historical constructs rather than natural attributes of humanity. And by extension, this account of history as a loss of freedom necessarily broadens the horizons of any redemptive politics and of the vision of freedom or emancipation it offers.

Accordingly, Rousseau illustrates the problem of freedom using both the hypothesis of the state of nature, but also, by speculating as to the historical origins of unfreedom in human society—through the development, first, of basic sociability, followed by the onset of more complex social forms with the development of agriculture and the progressive division of labour. Thus in the second *Discourse*, he 'recounted a secularized version of the Augustinian story of man's fall, with Original Sin recast in terms of the development of entrenched relations of inequality and the onset of luxury.'[25]

Independently, perhaps, of their divergent views of the social contract—or indeed of their different justificatory methods—Hobbes and Rousseau are concerned with very different understandings of *unfreedom*. Hobbes' main concern, in establishing undivided sovereignty, is that we are protected from the violence and coercion that he understands as the main threat to freedom and to human welfare generally. Submission to the sovereign itself or indeed, to the social order, is not, at least, an important sort of unfreedom—nor, crucially, is the servitude or subordination that is experienced within established social hierarchies. By contrast, Rousseau, following the republican tradition, is more concerned with dependency, domination and alienation within social and political relationships that are legally ordered and even consensual. Thus while for Hobbes the central problem of politics is the need for social order so as to forestall violence and chaos, Rousseau's departure point is the servitude that he sees as pervading social relationships generally. He is quintessentially a republican in that he understands servitude or unfreedom, roughly speaking, as the condition of being dependent

---

[23] Neuhouser argues: 'even though private property, material dependence, inequality of wealth, and the division of labor all play significant roles in Rousseau's explanation of war, domination and vice, these economic phenomena are of secondary importance in relation to *amour-propre* ... many of these supposedly distinct causes of human ills in fact depend on *amour-propre* for their existence and development.': Neuhouser, above n 21, 10.
[24] ibid 2.
[25] Douglass, above n 17, 15.

on an alien will; that is, the will of particular others, and where dependency has a much broader sense than coercion, encompassing affective and even psychic, along with material and economic, dimensions. Freedom in this sense likely prevailed in the pre-social state of nature, as man was relatively free of external constraint and indeed of social interaction, and thus free of dependency on any alien will. Unfreedom developed in tandem with our growing dependency on others, especially with the development of property and the division of labour. With the development of complex social relations, *amour-propre* was activated and 'inflamed', as humans became dependent on external recognition.[26] And crucially, as our moral psychology was transformed, we became dependent on others not only for our bodily security and material well-being, but also for our status and recognition as interdependent human agents. Through our need for recognition and esteem, we became dependent on others for our very sense of self—for our 'sentiment of existence'.[27]

To summarise, then, Rousseau's insight is first, that servitude is constituted in the very essence of social relations and is irreducible to coercion, and second, that these power relations are not merely political and economic, but rather assume affective, ritual and symbolic forms. Unfreedom, for Rousseau, does not occur simply where external agents coerce our choices and actions; rather, it is ubiquitous in man's postlapsarian state.

III. (Re)constituting Freedom

While natural freedom was decisively lost with the development of property, social hierarchy and the division of labour, how could it be recovered? On the one hand, Rousseau believed that the 'natural' freedom that pre-social or pre-civilised man hypothetically enjoyed was permanently lost and could never be recovered, given the irreversible and permanent character of social interdependency, and particularly the irreversible changes in man's moral psychology that had been wrought by *amour-propre*. On the other hand, despite this pessimism, the whole thrust of Rousseau's political theory lies in a redemptive horizon—that is, in the possibility, however unlikely—that freedom can be recovered or reconstituted in a new form or guise.[28] This redemption is far from inevitable—it is not man's *telos*. What

---

[26] Neuhouser, above n 21, 1.

[27] David Gauthier, *Rousseau: the Sentiment of Existence* (Cambridge, Cambridge University Press, 2006).

[28] Some have pointed out that Rousseau envisages 'freedom' in radically disparate forms and contexts. Brookes notes: 'Rousseau, like Berlin, described a number of different visions of human freedom and the good life across his various works, from Spartan citizens, to the denizens of Clarens, to solitary walkers ...': Christopher Brooke, 'Isaiah Berlin and the Origins of the "Totalitarian" Rousseau' in Ritchie Robertson and Laurence Brockliss (eds), *Isaiah Berlin and the Enlightenment* (Oxford, Oxford University Press, 2016) 1.

Rousseau sketches, however, is an attempt to recover from *within* man's 'fallen' state the means of such a possible redemption and emancipation—however distant and faint.[29]

What is clear is that freedom in its proper sense cannot be recovered simply by enshrining and safeguarding the 'basic liberties'. Certainly, the freedom of the state of nature was essentially a *negative* freedom, since it consisted of man being left largely to his own devices, free of dependency—whether social, material or psychic—upon others. On the other hand, however, any attempt to recover this negative freedom in a social setting, simply by guaranteeing individuals a limited sphere of non-interference against depredations by government or others, only obscures and entrenches a deeper and insidious social domination. This is one decisive plank, then, of Rousseau's critique of liberal thought: negative liberties under the rule of law offer an impoverished account of freedom, because unfreedom does not consist of coercive interference as such, but rather dependency in a variety of forms—not necessarily material or economic.

Rousseau's apparent pessimism stems from his sense of the intractable and pervasive nature of dependency, which often assumes highly insidious forms. Even if we were to be safeguarded against the most egregious forms of oppression, dependency pervades the whole of our social relations, even (or perhaps especially) in their ostensibly innocent dimensions. The overarching insight of his constitutional projects, explored in later chapters, is that servitude is experienced and inflicted in ostensibly mundane social practices—in everyday manners, tastes and dispositions.

In the second *Discourse*, Rousseau considers not only the historical origins of unfreedom, but also its enduring pattern and form in man's postlapsarian state. In particular, he anticipates the figure of the phoney bourgeois, whose pathologies are a constant preoccupation in his critique of eighteenth century European societies. These pathologies, while intensified under early-modern conditions, have distant historical origins, arising from the very first stages of man's social development and his emergence from the 'natural' state. And specifically, man's moral psychology was transformed by his need for external recognition and esteem. Rousseau hypothesises that when the first societies formed, 'a value came to be attached to public esteem … [to] whoever sang or danced best, [or] was the most eloquent … *and this was the first step towards inequality*.'[30] Man's 'rank and condition' came to depend not only on his 'property and power', but also his 'wit, beauty and talent'—attributes which it became necessary to 'possess or affect'.[31] Thus the need for recognition sowed the seeds of domination, as we began to 'live in the opinion of others'.[32] Consequently, 'each senses his existence not in

---

[29] See Neuhouser, above n 21.
[30] *Second Discourse*, above n 16, 141, emphasis added.
[31] ibid.
[32] ibid.

himself, but in his relationship to those whom he perceives as other.'[33] Rousseau speculates that with the advent of propertied civilisation, our natural 'love of self' (*amour de soi*) is supplanted with a corrupted *amour-propre*—manifested as a craving for external approbation and esteem, compelling us to seek status and distinction relative to others. And since *amour-propre* is consummated in the performance and internalisation of social and symbolic classifications, ultimately it permits the powerful to 'disguise their usurpations'.[34] He describes how, following the emergence of *amour-propre*, the 'great and rich' distinguish themselves and secure their status by creating 'a different symbolic universe' and 'trapping the rest into believing'.[35] And crucially, as societies become increasingly complex and differentiated, *amour-propre* is exercised and consummated in increasingly discrete and specialised, and thus, more insidious forms.

Crucially, *amour-propre* engenders a kind of dependency—a dependency on the recognition and esteem extended by other humans, upon their recognition of our dignity and humanity. This is less visible or obvious than economic or material dependency, but no less potent socially and politically.[36] Bearing in mind the salience and potency of *amour-propre* and the intractability of the dependency it engenders, Rousseau essentially rejects, then, the ideal of bourgeois freedom, understood roughly speaking as a sphere of private autonomy under the rule of law. This would provide only an illusion of security in a universe of insidious social domination. Nonetheless, while *dependency* is intractable and irreversible, this does not mean that *freedom* per se is unrecoverable. Because crucially, Rousseau does not oppose freedom against dependency per se, but only against dependency on a will or a power that is *alien* or *arbitrary*. Dependency on a personal will, he says, is dependency 'without order', as distinct from say, dependency on nature, with its regularity and order.[37] We might remain dependent—yet free—if we are dependent on a power or a will we can recognise as being in some sense our own.

Therefore, while dependency as such cannot be reversed, unfreedom can be redeemed through the horizon of politics. For Rousseau, then, the social contract—essentially his solution to the problem of freedom—would not preserve or partly re-establish natural freedom understood negatively, but rather establish a new type of freedom—'civil' freedom. While natural freedom consists of freedom from dependency upon the will of alien others, 'civil' freedom, and in turn, political freedom, consists in subjection to a will that individuals, as citizens, can identify as their own. It is related to and facilitates 'moral' freedom in that it entails obedience

---

[33] Gauthier, above n 27, 10.
[34] *Second Discourse*, above n 16, 144.
[35] J Patrick Dobel, 'The Role of Langauge in Rousseau's Political Thought' (1986) 18 *Polity* 638, 651.
[36] For a comprehensive analysis see Neuhouser, above n 21.
[37] 'Dependence on men, since it is without order, engenders all the vices, and by it, master and slave are mutually corrupted. If there is any means of remedying this ill in society, it is to substitute law for man and to arm the general will with a real strength superior to the action of very particular will.': Rousseau, above n 1, 85.

to a law 'one has prescribed to oneself', substituting our obedience to passion and impulse[38] (an insight later reflected in Kant's thought).[39]

In turn, this kind of freedom can only be experienced in the framework of a political community.[40] At the early modern juncture, then, man's unhappy condition stems from the *incompleteness* of his social and political integration.[41] Freedom was lost with our partial and incomplete socialisation, with the chains imposed by property and social order, as men became dependent on the powers of alien others. And it could only be recovered, Rousseau conjectures, by transitioning to a fuller or complete phase of social and political integration—and specifically, through a form of mutual interdependency in a self-governing political community.[42] This is the redemptive horizon of republican politics.

More fundamentally, Rousseau's insight is that natural freedom cannot provide a template or model for freedom in the civil state, because it misidentifies the structure as well as the genealogy of servitude. Freedom was lost through the onset of dependency, and since dependency is irreversible, freedom could only be recovered through a transition to a form of dependency that is non-dominating and even emancipating—that is, to a political horizon of mutual interdependency. A simulacrum of 'natural' freedom in the guise of piecemeal negative liberties will only perpetuate and obscure the dependency and thus the unfreedom running through the totality of social relations.

Rousseau's quintessentially republican argument is that freedom is abrogated not by dependency as such, but rather by dependency on an alien or arbitrary

---

[38] Jean-Jacques Rousseau, *Du Contrat Social* (Paris, ENAG, 1988/1762) (hereinafter *Social Contact*) Bk I, Ch VIII. As Neuhouser notes, 'if individuals are fully to realise the promise of the modern world,—if they are to be more than dependent and unindividuated vehicles of the general will of their respective polities—they must also be socialized men, which is to say: educated in accordance with the ideal of a sovereign moral subject, a subject that exercises its own reason and is bound to laws it itself recognises as good.': Neuhouser, above n 21, 24.

[39] Samuel Freeman, *Justice and the Social Contract: Essays in Rawlsian Political Philosophy* (Oxford, Oxford University Press, 2007) 31.

[40] See *Social Contract*, above n 38, Bk 1, Ch VIII:. 'What man loses by the social contract is his natural liberty and an unlimited right to everything he tries to get and succeeds in getting; what he gains is civil liberty and the ownership of all he possesses. If we are to avoid mistake in weighing one against the other, we must clearly distinguish natural liberty, which is bounded only by the strength of the individual, from civil liberty, which is limited by the general will; and possession, which is merely the effect of force or the right of the first occupier, from property, which can be founded only on a positive title. We might, over and above all this, add, to what man gain in the civil state, moral liberty, which alone makes him truly master of himself; for the mere impulse of appetite is slavery, while obedience to a law which we prescribe to ourselves is liberty.'

[41] Patrick Riley, 'A Possible Explanation of Rousseau's General Will' (1970) 64 *American Political Science Review* 86.

[42] In *Emile*, Rousseau notes: 'natural man is wholly for himself; he is numerical unity, the absolute entirety which is relative only to itself or its kind. Civil man is only a fractional unity dependent on the denominator; his value is determined by his relation to the entirety, which is the social body. Good social institutions are those that best know how to denature man, to take his absolute existence from him in order to give him a relative one, and transport the I into the common unity, with the result that each individual believes himself no longer one but a part of the unity and no longer feels except within the whole.': Rousseau, above n 1, 39–40.

will. And while dependency on others, as such, is a permanent feature of human societies, freedom can nonetheless be realised through mutual interdependency in political community. Therefore, the social contract is not an agreement to partly (and conditionally) abrogate natural freedom for the sake of governmental protection, as per Locke's liberal account. Rather, through the social contract we renounce natural freedom completely and constitute a new form of freedom as self-rule in political community.[43]

This is the departure point for the infamous concept of the general will—a will that constitutes political freedom precisely because it is neither alien nor arbitrary to those on whom it is imposed. Rousseau conjectures that 'as long as several men united consider themselves a single body, they have a single will, concerned with their preservation and general well-being.'[44] The general will, then, is the corporate will of a political community directed towards the common interests of its members. It is a will that members of a political community share *qua* citizens and that they can recognise as a form of non-arbitrary power, one that they can internalise as being in some sense their own, being directed at interests they hold in common.[45] It is precisely through the rule of the general will that we replace dependency on arbitrary power with mutual inter-dependency in a framework of political community.[46] Thus individual freedom can be secured only by 'transform[ing] personal dependence into dependence on the Republic.'[47] And this freedom is not experienced as an absence of dependency per se, but rather as dependency on a non-arbitrary, impersonal will, regularised in institutional form. To realise political freedom, each must 'put his person and all his power in common under [its] supreme direction'[48]—this being the only way we can relinquish the natural freedoms of the state of nature while remaining 'as free as before'.[49] The order of the general will, in some interpretations, imitates the regularity and order of nature itself, as a form of 'general providence', with Rousseau aiming to 'refashion our existence by imitating our original position as well-ordered beings within the divine or natural whole, a whole ordered by law.'[50] The order of the general will, then, is a secularised rendition of the benign, and divine providential order of God.[51]

---

[43] Rousseau's innovation, then, was to repurpose and adapt the device of the social contract during a period where 'the ideals of classical republicanism had largely been swallowed up by the rising tide of contractarian political thought.': Quentin Skinner, 'Liberty and Rights' in Michael Rosen and Jonathan Wolff, *Political Thought* (Oxford, Oxford University Press, 1999) 168.
[44] *Social Contract*, above n 38, Bk IV, Ch I.
[45] ibid.
[46] Frederick Neuhouser, 'Freedom, Dependence and the General Will' (1993) 102 *Philosophical Review* 363, 390.
[47] ibid, 390.
[48] *Social Contract*, above n 38, Bk I, Ch IX.
[49] ibid, Bk I, Ch VIII.
[50] Scott, above n 19, 479.
[51] ibid. He notes: 'In our original condition we were spontaneously well-ordered by our immersion in the ordered divine or natural whole. The subjection to the laws the citizens themselves make as

Rousseau's understanding, then, is that mutual, reciprocal dependency on the impersonal rule of the general will can substitute and supplant the asymmetrical dependency that we experience by virtue of being vulnerable to the arbitrary power, or the personal will of individual human agents, whether public or private. On the one hand, to say that a law reflects the general will is merely to say that it possesses certain qualities by virtue of which it can be considered as something other than a purely alien will at work in our lives: 'in a perfect act of legislation, the individual or particular will should be at zero.'[52] On the other hand, the rule of the general will not only ensures non-dominating government in the narrow sense, but reconfigures social relations generally so as to stem power asymmetries across society in general. In other words, it stems private as well as governmental sources of domination. Thus we enter into political society not to guarantee ourselves a sphere of non-interference for unhindered actions, but rather to free ourselves of dependency on any alien will, and this requires that collectively, we exercise authorship and control over our laws. However, the purpose of a political society of this sort is not just to preclude domination in the guise of arbitrary government; it is also aimed at foiling domination in social relationships—that is, domination based on those social hierarchies and classifications that stem primarily from *amour-propre*. While we enter political society to escape dependency on alien will, dependency can exist in many subtle and insidious forms—social and cultural as well as economic and political—and many of which involve no coercion as such. Therefore, the republic must protect citizens not only against coercive invasions of their person or property, but from dependency in all of its dimensions—affective, social and symbolic. Dependency on the general will of an association, of which we are an 'indivisible' part, will 'reinternalise' the 'sentiment of existence' that was alienated with the advent of propertied society.[53] The rule of the general will, then, is not simply a model of government but the cornerstone of a social vision that represents a redemptive horizon for reconstituting freedom within and throughout social relations.

sovereign in the political whole has a similar effect. First, the citizens are ordered in the best possible manner relative to the political whole by their dependence upon it. The sovereign power "must have a universal, compulsory force to move and arrange each part in the manner best suited to the whole"'. Scott, ibid, 495, internal citations omitted.

[52] *Social Contract*, above n 38, Bk III, Ch II. Scott notes: '[Rousseau] does speak of all justice coming from God, but he means this first in a purely formal sense pertaining to order and generality, and, second, he reverses the priority of justice and law. Rousseau raises generality to be the unalterable character of justice. The formal generality inherent to all justice is derived from the general providence of God and patterned after it. Rousseau's elaboration of his concept of law is strikingly secular in a sense, but his indications that politics somehow imitates the divine point to the way in which he appropriates at least the formal structure of divine general will and law. ... Rousseau's reversal of the priority of justice and law alone distinguishes him from many of his predecessors. Aristotle, for example, conceives of law as an imperfect rule or formulation of justice that has to be corrected by the prudent statesman looking to equity ... whereas Kant's moral theory is explicitly universal or cosmopolitan, Rousseau's general will-and his political solution to our ills as a whole-is necessarily confined to a particular community, as is evident from his criticism of Diderot's conception of the general will of the entire human race.' Scott, above n 19, 490.

[53] Gauthier, above n 27, 58.

IV. Situating Rousseau's (Un)freedom

In one sense, Rousseau's work can be read simply as a continuation or variation of a familiar republican argument concerning the relationship between freedom and politics: effectively, that the political and legal order does not *preserve* freedom, but rather *constitutes* it. And conceptually, then, there is a radical discontinuity between the freedom of the state of nature and the freedom enjoyed in political society: the latter is not simply a partial reconstitution of the former but requires an entirely transformed configuration of social relations. In this light, Rousseau simply reasserts the broader view that republican freedom is a 'freedom of the city' rather than a 'freedom of the heath'—that, by its nature, it can only be enjoyed in a participatory political community.[54]

Indeed other historical republican figures similarly insist that freedom consists not of any immunity against interference, however conditioned, but rather collective self-government based on the common good—with unfreedom, correspondingly, consisting in the rule of factional interest or personal will.[55] And 'rights', in this view, are not 'natural'; they are established not despite politics, or prior to it, but rather through and within political society. This theme is emphasised by contemporary republican critics of legal constitutionalism, particularly Richard Bellamy, for whom 'rights' are, quintessentially, 'claims made by citizens on fellow citizens within a social and political setting.'[56] This rejects the more dominant liberal view of 'rights' as representing a moral consensus that can and should be put beyond the reach of ordinary politics, usually through a legally enforceable set of constitutional rights.[57] And this contemporary republican claim echoes a quintessentially Rousseauan insight—that rights stem from the conventional nature of the political compact and have no value or meaning outside of the context of political community. This sets Rousseau apart from theorists of natural right, like Paine, who introduced the notion of 'pre-existing' rights that 'were not present in classical republicanism, where the individual most often was understood not as freestanding, but as integrated within, indeed constituted by, the community.'[58] In turn, this underlines the fluidity and historical-cultural contingency of specific rights-claims, whereas emergent liberal thinkers like Madison had posited individual, 'negative' rights as pre-given and as 'marking the limits of politics'.[59]

---

[54] Anthony Laden, 'Republican Moments in Political Liberalism' (2006) 237 *Revue internationale de philosophie* 341.
[55] Sellers, above n 3. See also Bellamy, above n 13.
[56] Richard Bellamy, 'Democracy as Public Law' (2013) 14 *German Law Journal* 1, 9.
[57] Bellamy, above n 13.
[58] Kalyvas and Katznelson, above n 5, 107.
[59] ibid, 109. Similarly Benjamin Constant, by naturalising rights, 'elevated them into absolute, immutable principles ... normatively circumscribe the realm of politics, thus protecting the private sphere of intimacy, pleasure and freedom from being overwhelmed.' Kalyvas and Katznelson, above

For contemporary republican philosophers like Bellamy, the culture of legalised 'rights' is distorting partly because it distorts the contextual and historical contingency of 'rights' claims, and the reality of widespread social disagreement concerning the ordering and reconciliation of such antagonistic claims on rights.[60] Thus political freedom is identified with the democratic and political process itself—in Bellamy's case, via majoritarian rule—rather than with any definite concept or content of rights, because such concepts fail to decisively place conflicts about rights beyond the 'circumstances of politics'.

This contemporary republican position, sceptical towards rights, has obvious affinities with Rousseau's identification of freedom with political self-rule. On the other hand, however, Rousseau's insight concerning the political character of freedom—and as to how this distinguishes it from 'natural' freedom—is equally reflected in analytical theories of rights that have been formulated by other republican philosophers, such as Pettit, who are more sympathetic to the liberal idea of setting 'rights' apart from ordinary politics. For republicans who are more sympathetic than Bellamy to legal constitutionalism and 'rights' culture, the state and law still assume a central and distinctive role conceptually speaking. According to such theories, coercion, through law, in fact *constitutes* freedom (rather than *causing* it), because it protects citizens from being subjected to domination or alien will—bearing in mind that unfreedom stems, in the first instance, from the *possibility* of arbitrary interference rather than its actual experience. Indeed it is impossible to enjoy freedom as non-domination in the absence of coercive law, because non-dominating interference—that is, the legal interference that is exercised under a system of democratic control—is necessary to prevent domination by private agents.[61] While Pettit ultimately repudiates Rousseau, this view nonetheless has parallels in the role of the general will and its relation to freedom, since the rule of the general will prevents dependency in the context of power asymmetries.

Conversely, and *contra* Bentham, Pettit's definition means there is a necessary connection between freedom and the democratic form of government, even if we reject Bellamy's identification of political freedom with democratic procedure itself. Subjects of non-democratic government, who happen to enjoy non-interference to a seemingly adequate degree, are still subject to a form of 'alien power'—a power in which they have no influence and control—and thus, to a form of domination. And relatedly, republicans like Pettit emphasise the salience of domination that occurs without interference as such ever being suffered—that is,

---

n 5, 162. On the relation between Rousseau and Constant, see ME Brint, 'Jean-Jacques Rousseau and Benjamin Constant: A Dialogue on Freedom and Tyranny' (1985) 47 *The Review of Politics* 323. Brint observes at 324: 'In the works of Constant and Rousseau, a battle is fought between the ancients and the moderns; between two visions of freedom set within two opposing historical models of society. In Constant, we find a champion of individual liberty, an advocate of limited sovereignty and an admirer of modern commercial society. In Rousseau, on the other hand, we find a theorist of absolute sovereignty, a proponent of political liberty and a critic of modern society.'

[60] Bellamy, above n 13.
[61] Laden, above n 54.

the lived experience of individuals who are subject to the whim or discretion of others, and must in particular engage in a kind of self-censorship aimed at 'keep[ing] our master sweet'.[62]

Similarly, while neo-Roman republicans like Pettit are somewhat sympathetic to the culture of juridified constitutional rights as part of a framework of 'checks and balances', equally they tend to be acutely conscious of private sources of domination, in the communitarian and familial realms, that cannot be easily captured as a set of codified constitutional rights. Accordingly, they will typically defend a relatively robust role for the state in checking those forms of domination that stem from inequalities and disparities of bargaining power in the 'private' sphere. Freedom, for Pettit, is a 'function of our *relative powers*.'[63] Republican freedom, understood in this way, will embrace a strong socio-economic dimension and a redistributive state. By contrast, the kind of society envisaged by classical liberalism—with a minimal state and a rigid divide between public and private spheres—will likely be marked by these insidious forms of domination, which are legitimated by ostensible consent.[64] Republicans, Pettit suggests, will be

> more radical in their view of the social ills that the state ought to rectify ... [they are] socially more radical. Their lesser scepticism ... will come of the fact that they do not view state action, provided it is properly constrained, as an inherent affront to liberty.[65]

Republicanism, then, embraces a form of 'status freedom'—one which is acutely conscious of the psychological effects of social inequality and indeed the strategies of self-censorship, the 'fawning and toadying' that dominated individuals may be forced to engage in. In contrast with the social relations that define the laissez-faire liberal state, republican citizens will be able to 'look one another in the eye' in the private as well as public realms.[66]

V. Rousseau as a Republican Outlier

To a certain degree, there is a clear continuity between Rousseau's work and the broader republican canon, simply because it is focused on domination as the central social and political problem. And yet while Rousseau can be located within a broader intellectual republican history conceiving of freedom as non-domination, he is often identified as something of an outlier in the republican history of thought—particularly given his commitment to a bracingly austere social policy, his distrust of science and arts, and his generally romantic view of political order. In writings such as *Letter to d'Alembert*—where he famously decries 'frivolous' and

---

[62] Pettit, above n 7, 134.
[63] Pettit, ibid, 113–14, emphasis added.
[64] Pettit, above n 2, Chs 1 and 2.
[65] Pettit, above n 7, 148
[66] Pettit, above n 2, 3.

corrupting pursuits such as theatre—he advocates a bracing social conservatism that seems inconsistent with the radical, emancipatory tenor of his abstract political theory, and indeed of eighteenth century republicanism in general.

Yet above all, perhaps, Rousseau is considered a republican outlier because of his (apparent) rejection of a longstanding republican model of 'mixed government' in favour of an undivided, unitary sovereign which seems, in particular, to collapse individual freedom with a project of collective self-government.[67] Likes Hobbes, Rousseau assumed it necessary that there should be a singular, undivided sovereign—in his account, the people—as the source of all legitimate governmental power.[68]

Thus both in his social politics and his constitutional model, Rousseau's project is defined largely by a communal and communitarian focus that apparently quashes individuality and thus seems to defy a historical republican concern for providing security to individuals against arbitrary authority. However, I will argue that his seemingly eccentric and severe communitarianism is, in fact, inseparable from the core concerns of his political theory. In fact, it helps to underline and explain the distinctiveness of his idea of freedom relative to the broader republican canon, whether classical or contemporary.

Certainly, there is nothing particularly distinctive or original in Rousseau's idea that unfreedom consists of domination or dependency, understood as subjection or vulnerability to arbitrary power. Quentin Skinner in particular has documented its ancient Roman origins.[69] Both Skinner and Pettit have comprehensively reconstructed a Roman-republican concept in which slavery epitomised domination, and where freedom consisted of citizenship under a resilient rule of law. This emphasis represents an important continuity with the wider republican canon. Yet in terms of substance as well as emphasis, Rousseau undeniably stands apart, in important respects, from the neo-Roman concept as articulated by scholars like Pettit. Indeed, Pettit himself has dismissively described Rousseau as a 'continental romantic' who lies outside the 'Atlantic' tradition of republican thought.[70] The *discontinuity* lies partly in his institutional recommendations—especially his recommendation of something like 'direct' democracy. But more decisively, perhaps, the differences lie in Rousseau's understanding of the sources and social constitution of domination itself.

In particular, Pettit—echoing Benjamin Constant—argues that Rousseau understands freedom in an 'authorial' rather than a negative sense: a free citizen is not one secured against arbitrary public or private power, but rather one who participates directly in the authorship of laws.[71] This is what Constant understood as 'ancient' liberty, inappropriate to the sociology of modern societies and a threat to

---

[67] For Pettit's critique of Rousseau see Pettit, ibid, Chs 3–4.
[68] *Social Contract*, above n 38, Bks II and III.
[69] See generally Skinner, above n 15.
[70] Pettit, above n 2, Chs 1 and 2.
[71] ibid.

the private, negative liberties of modern citizens.[72] Moreover, by adopting Hobbes' account of sovereignty as absolute and undivided, Rousseau's republicanism risks making the 'people' itself a source of domination, in contrast with the 'checks and balances' or mixed constitution that are associated with Roman-republican thought. In short, Rousseau is sometimes understood as somewhat heretical in the wider republican canon because he associates freedom with participation in sovereignty (expressed through legislation) rather than as security against sovereign power (along with other kinds of power). Political freedom is realised through collective identification with, and the rule of, the general will. This means that citizens' subjection to the rule of the general will must be unconditioned and absolute: each must 'put his person and all his power in common under [its] supreme direction', thus becoming 'an indivisible part of the whole'.[73] As in Hobbes' account, the people effectively alienate all their 'natural' freedoms to the collective sovereign: 'the alienation being without reserve, the union is as perfect as it can be.'[74]

The people itself, then, assumes the authoritarian role of Hobbes' sovereign.[75] Thus Rousseau's idea of direct popular rule is understood as defying the mainstream of historical republican thought because it is associated with 'the ultimate form of arbitrariness, the tyranny of a majority.'[76] James Madison, in particular, described this kind of direct popular rule as 'incompatible with personal security or the rights of property'.[77] Moreover, it appears that, in this vision, the question of what personal immunities, safeguards or indeed 'rights' individuals must enjoy is left radically unstable, since political freedom is understood only as participation in the authorship and exercise of a general will against which the individual as such enjoys no ultimate protection. And this is reflected in a broader critique of Rousseau emphasising his disregard, or even disdain, for pluralism and diversity

---

[72] For Constant, ancient liberty consisted in 'the collective, but direct exercise of many aspects of sovereignty, de-liberating in a public place on everything from war and peace to forming foreign alliances, voting on laws, pronouncing judgments, examining the accounts, the acts and the management of magistrates-making them appear before all the people to accuse, condemn or absolve them. This, which the ancients called liberty, completely joined the individual to the authority of the whole.': Benjamin Constant, 'De la Liberté des Anciens Comparée à celle des Modernes' in Benjamin Constant, *Ecrits Politiques* (Paris, Gallimard/Folio, 1997) 495. Indeed Neuhouser observes: 'on Rousseau's view, political cohesion in Rome and Sparta rested on citizens' complete and mostly affective identification with their polity, an identification that was incompatible with having any notion of their own interests or value as individual and any sense of themselves as sovereign sources of moral authority and evaluation.': Neuhouser, above n 21, 22.

[73] *Social Contract*, above n 38, Bk I, Ch IX. Pettit, for example, describes Rousseau's understanding of a 'total subjection' of citizen to sovereign. Pettit, above n 2, 14.

[74] *Social Contract*, above n 38, Bk I, Ch IX.

[75] By way of contrast, Pettit claims that Rousseau's scheme, like Hobbes' account, can tolerate 'no independent centre of power', whether internally or externally—but this overlooks the extent to which the principle of sovereign indivisibility is confined to legislative power specifically. Pettit, above n 2, 226.

[76] Pettit, above n 7, 8.

[77] James Madison, 'Federalist no 10' in John Jay and Clinton Rossiter, *The Federalist Papers* (New York, New American Library, 1961) 81.

as potential sources of discord and instability.[78] In this account, the exaltation of popular sovereignty inevitably diminishes negative, individual freedoms.[79]

Under Pettit's reconstruction of the Roman-republican tradition, political participation is, by contrast, assigned a much more modest role. Wide political participation is still seen as necessary to ensure the rigorous contestation and checking of political power and thus to combat statist domination. However this is simply instrumental to freedom understood negatively, as an absence of domination.[80] Thus unlike Aristotle, Cicero, for example, understood freedom as being guaranteed through citizenship under the rule of law—and specifically the security against arbitrary power this provided—rather than through participation in politics as such.[81] In turn, for contemporary neo-republicans it is more important that citizens have the opportunity to *contest* political power than to necessarily *participate* in its exercise.[82] Much like historical republicans such as Madison, Pettit understands that political participation is not intrinsically valuable in itself, but instrumentally important simply insofar as it will stem political and social domination in various domains.[83] Thus we are free not through our status as participants in collective self-government, but rather through the resilient security offered by the rule of law against any 'alien will'.

Yet while Rousseau's political and social communitarianism may seem unattractive or unfeasible, it is in some senses simply a corollary of his understanding of domination itself—of its sources and its social constitution. While Rousseau, like other republicans, essentially understands political or civil freedom as non-domination, he embraces a communitarian social politics precisely because, pessimistically, he views domination as being radically pervasive and intractable, compared to other republican views. Neo-Roman republicans like Pettit define domination in relation to the external control of *choice*: in short, we are dominated where others enjoy powers of interference in relation to choices that we are in a position to make. Unfreedom, roughly speaking, arises in the subjection of individual choice to alien will. Domination may occur in private relationships marked by disparities of bargaining power, even where no actual interference occurs; and correspondingly, neo-republicans assume public and private domination can be minimised through appropriate systems of rule of law and democratic control which track 'commonly avowed interests'.[84] But the point of

---

[78] See, eg, Margaret Canovan, 'Arendt, Rousseau, and Human Plurality in Politics' (1983) 45 *Journal of Politics* 286; Robert Nisbet, 'Rousseau and Totalitarianism' (1943) 5 *The Journal of Politics* 93.

[79] Thus for Constant, 'Rousseau's vision of the freedom of the ancient citizen is a dangerous myth. Under modern conditions, it provides a justification for the absolute power of the state. By promoting popular sovereignty, Rousseau's vision denies man his individual liberty. It creates the pretext for a tyranny, which allows the sovereignty of the people to exist as long as the people themselves do not demand their individual liberty.': Brint, above n 59, 341.

[80] Pettit, above n 7.

[81] Cicero, *On Duties* (Cambridge, Cambridge University Press, 1999).

[82] See generally Pettit, above n 9.

[83] ibid.

[84] ibid, Chs 4–5.

such remedies is to remove, insofar as possible, the powers that others enjoy to arbitrarily interfere, in a more or less unchecked way, in choices that we are in a position to make. Crucially, however, neo-republican theories of unfreedom occlude any dimension of domination that might arise in certain features of social structure that are irreducible to 'choice' in the narrow sense: say, in the production and reproduction of social norms, in ideology, or in the dispositions and attitudes of dominated agents themselves.

By contrast, Rousseau's bracing communitarianism—for example, his rejection of commerce, luxury and sophisticated arts[85]—stems from his understanding of domination as being intractably embedded in mundane social practice: in affective, symbolic and ritual forms. And this reflects an understanding in which domination cannot be understood solely as the subjection of individual choice to alien control. In general terms, Rousseau rejects any understanding of freedom as non-interference partly because he identifies the latent, insidious forms that domination assumes in complex liberal societies. And compared to the neo-republicans, he views domination as more intractably embedded in the production and exchange of symbolic, cultural and social capital—in systems and structures that are irreducible to agential dynamics of choice and conversely of interference in choice. Domination stems partly from the need for external recognition which 'natural' man experiences once he enters society and develops *amour-propre*. As Gauthier notes, Rousseau's insight is essentially that 'dependence on another person is ... not simply dependence on his power; most deeply, it is *dependence on his recognition*.'[86] His insight is that in complex, differentiated societies, our very sense of self is dependent on social and symbolic classifications that are determined by arbitrary external forces. Thus domination is exercised and experienced through 'positional goods' within complex social hierarchies.[87] In such societies, merit and legitimacy are deeply encoded as social and cultural practices become increasingly complex and specialised. Participation within such societies requires increasingly elaborate yet arbitrary techniques that are unequally distributed, and that befuddle those insufficiently endowed in the relevant forms of human capital—cultural, social and symbolic. Domination, then, cannot be understood in terms of 'choice', and its control, because it is embedded in our sentiment and psyche, in our tastes and manners, in the bodily and linguistic techniques we use to negotiate complex social worlds. Relatedly, Rousseau stands apart from the contemporary neo-republican canon because of the political significance he identifies in the social and cultural domain, and in politics of the mundane.[88] More than for any other republican thinker, perhaps, the personal and the private are political: a republican politics must concern itself in particular with culture, ritual and taste, not only to secure the affective

---

[85] See further ch 2.
[86] Gauthier, above n 27, 30, emphasis added.
[87] ibid, 19.
[88] See further ch 3.

foundations of successful self-government, but more radically, to supplant the insidious domination that arises in complex private social practices. Unfreedom cannot be understood simply as the subjection of choice to alien will, if 'choice' itself stems from a fundamental sort of corruption—that is, if choice itself is the product of dominating social structures. Servitude, in such societies, simply assumes more invisible forms, and is given expression in ostensibly legitimate social classifications.

In turn, it is precisely this sense of the intractable and insidious character of domination that leads Rousseau to embrace austerity, in the broad sense, as a social framework for republican politics. His insight—one, that I will argue, informs his constitutional thought—is that republican freedom (understood as non-domination) can only be realised in a highly unitary and cohesive society, where the dominating effects of social complexity and social differentiation are submerged in a transparent social and civic universe. Austerity, in this sense, will foil those forms of domination that are insinuated in seemingly benign social practices. Thus Rousseau effectively discounts or rejects, whether explicitly or otherwise, various early-modern attempts at reconciling the emancipatory horizons and indeed, the virtues of classical republicanism with the increasingly atomised and dislocated society of the moderns.[89]

It is Rousseau's 'communitarian' orientation that usually leads neo-republicans to reject his legacy.[90] Yet the concerns underlying it may equally point to shortcomings in their more optimistic account as to how a republican vision of non-domination might be realised in our contemporary liberal societies. Pettit's theory of freedom as non-domination appeals to a social world in which, far from the image of the classical liberal society, citizens 'do not have to bow or scrape, toady or kowtow, fawn or flatter', where they are 'their own men and women.'[91] Yet he largely ignores those forms of domination that arise in cultural and social practices, implicitly deeming these relatively trivial or insignificant and focusing freedom as non-domination within the domain of the traditional 'basic liberties'. By contrast, Rousseau's austerian social politics stems largely from his sense that, in the early modern context, increasing social differentiation would give rise to new—and more invisible—axes of distinction,[92] and thus that domination would acquire newly potent, but also, peculiarly insidious forms. This stems, again, from his sense of the pervasive and intractable nature of dependency and domination in social relationships generally—and rejecting the view, associated

---

[89] See further ch 2.
[90] Pettit, above n 2, Ch 3.
[91] ibid 82.
[92] Jean-Jacques Rousseau, *Considérations sur le Gouvernement de Pologne et sur sa réforme projetée* in *Collection complète des oeuvres* (Genève, 1780–89) vol 1 Ch XI; for a translation see 'Considerations on the Government of Poland' in Frederick Watkins, *Jean-Jacques Rousseau: Political Writings* (New York, Thomas Yelsen, 1953) Ch 3.

with Adam Smith in particular, that the transactional world of commerce and exchange would have an elevating moral effect.[93] The challenge Rousseau raises, for contemporary neo-republicans, is that since domination stems in large part from dependency on recognition, it cannot be understood in terms of discrete capacities of interference—and correspondingly, that non-domination must embrace the whole of social relations.[94] In particular, we are beholden to arbitrary power partly by virtue of the insidious status hierarchies that are embedded in ostensibly mundane social practices. Thus republican freedom requires not only guarantees of security from arbitrary power, but a radical and fundamental transformation in our social relationships—precisely of the sort that contemporary neo-Roman republicans tend to eschew. In a sense, then, Rousseau rejects accommodation and compromise with liberal modernity because he brings historical republican insights concerning domination to a consistent, if perhaps uncomfortable conclusion.

We may return, then, to Pettit's critique of Rousseau—that in effect, he advocates the wholesale subjection of the individual to sovereign power in a way that contradicts the historical republican view (as well as being unattractive for independent reasons). We can say, on the one hand, that this confuses the notion of undivided *sovereignty* (which Rousseau embraces) with that of undivided *government*, which he rejects.[95] Indivisible popular sovereignty does not equate with democratic absolutism or undivided rule per se;[96] indeed, the rule of the general will—which Rousseau says applies only to public goods—is in many senses contiguous with the security and protection of 'private' freedom.[97] More to the point, however, while the complete displacement of 'natural' right under the republican social contract appears, initially, as a complete subjection of individual to community, it is in fact simply a way of expressing the pervasiveness of domination and servitude even under the ordered and consensual relationships of liberal society. Man must relinquish 'natural' rights partly because unfreedom and alienation stem from the incompleteness of his socialisation.[98] In a society that is ordered by law but which is not self-governing in Rousseau's full sense, man is poised incoherently between the natural and the civil states, corrupted and oppressed

---

[93] See further ch 2.

[94] Gauthier, above n 27, 30.

[95] Peter Steinberger, 'Hobbes, Rousseau and the Modern Conception of the State' (2008) 70 *The Journal of Politics* 595.

[96] Richard Tuck, *The Sleeping Sovereign: The Invention of Modern Democracy* (Cambridge, Cambridge University Press, 2008).

[97] For discussion see John Rawls, *Lectures on the History of Political Philosophy* (Cambridge MA, Harvard University Press, 2007) Ch 12.

[98] Riley, above n 41. Scott notes: 'is total alienation necessary to ensure fairness? He anticipates this objection and then points to the most important reason why this total alienation is necessary. The political union will save men from the distorting effects of dependence through its very comprehensiveness and legalistic fairness.' Scott, above n 19, 482.

by unhinged *amour-propre*:[99] he has irrevocably lost the freedom of the state of nature, without transitioning to a political community that can be experienced as something other than an alien power.

VI. Constitutionalising Rousseau's Freedom

It is commonplace, perhaps even uncontroversial, to understand constitutions and constitutionalism as a response to the problems of freedom and unfreedom. Freedom represents an overarching horizon and aim, or at least a minimal criterion of constitutional legitimacy and success. And while Rousseau's 'constitutions' assume a very different form compared to our dominant contemporary understanding, we can still view these as offering a response to the problem of freedom. In the chapters that will follow, I will argue that the content and focus of Rousseau's constitutions help to illustrate the social, symbolic and economic dimensions of freedom and unfreedom in his thought.

---

[99] Riley, ibid 86.

2

The Constitution of Autarky

For Rousseau, citizenship is something that only the peasants can lay claim to.[1]

I. Introduction

The central focus of Rousseau's constitutional projects for Corsica and Poland is, arguably, social and economic as much as institutional and political. In essence, many of his constitutional devices and recommendations are aimed at creating and sustaining a radical autarky—defined by economic rusticity and bracing social conservatism—in both societies. Thus, on the one hand, autarky represents one of the cornerstones of the wider austerity that Rousseau understands as the social framework for an authentic republican politics. On the other hand, this autarky is to be promoted and incentivised in constitutional structures.

While his uncompromising commitment to autarky is certainly eccentric, it is not altogether anomalous in terms of the wider republican history of thought. Historically, republicans were centrally concerned with the potentially corrupting effects of commerce, and the challenge of sustaining sufficient civic virtues in liberal, relatively atomised societies focused on commercial pursuits. Indeed many eighteenth century thinkers, including Smith, Ferguson and Hume, were preoccupied with the problem of reconciling commerce with civic virtue, given that ancient republican theories had been premised on virtuous citizens, in slaveholding societies, devoting considerable energy to politics and public life. In particular, they considered whether or not—and how—the competitive and individualist ethos of commercial life could be reconciled with the moral psychology of the republican citizen. Additionally, at the institutional level, republican innovators like Madison attempted to explain how republican practices, virtues and forms could not only survive, but flourish in modern and liberal commercial societies. Correspondingly, republican constitutionalism adopted a liberal bent and eschewed any claim to promote romantic or rustic virtues over commercial life. However, Rousseau—in many ways an outlier in republican terms—adopted

---

[1] Marcel Hénaff (Roxanne Lapidus trans), 'Cannibalistic City: Rousseau, Large Numbers, and the Abuse of the Social Bond' (1992) 21 *Substance* 3, 8.

a more pessimistic view, and argued that an authentic republican politics could thrive only in highly austere, undifferentiated societies, free from the corrupting effects of commerce and luxury. In turn, this scepticism was reflected in his constitutional strategies. In this chapter, I consider how Rousseau's constitutional devices aimed to promote autarkic social forms as a foil against the insidious kinds of domination he identifies in liberal societies. Correspondingly, I use this as a lens through which to consider how contemporary, liberal constitutional thought approaches questions of socio-economic power and particularly the relationship between civic virtue and economic life.

II. Commerce and Autarky in Corsica and Poland

Perhaps the most striking thing about Rousseau's constitutional project for Corsica, in particular—and to a lesser extent his plan for Poland—is his emphasis on economic and social matters. And specifically, many of his particular constitutional prescriptions and recommendations are aimed at maintaining an autarkic, self-sufficient economy, and a virtuous society uncorrupted by cosmopolitan mores and sophisticated tastes.

Rousseau sees Corsica, in particular, as offering fortuitous possibilities for designing a republican constitution, because its relative isolation, rugged topography and rusticity—which he compares to the once-autarkic Swiss cantons—make it feasible to stem the development of commerce and trade. Thus counterintuitively, perhaps, he is optimistic as to the possibilities of republican politics in rural, agrarian settings.

In particular, Rousseau saw Corsica's modest size and island isolation—and correspondingly, its presumed social cohesion—as fortuitous for republican politics. In the *Social Contract*, he had, in typically hyperbolic style, described it as 'the one country' in Europe that was capable of 'true legislation' and thus, of political liberty.[2] While he referred to Corsicans' 'valour' in resisting Genoese rule—and while his preference for small, cohesive polities is well known[3]—Rousseau's *Constitutional Project for Corsica* makes clear that it is the island's isolated and agrarian character that gives it its capacity for an authentic republican politics. It is the

---

[2] Jean-Jacques Rousseau, *Du Contrat Social* (Paris, ENAG, 1988/1762) Bk IV, Ch I (hereinafter *Social Contract*).

[3] In *Poland*, Rousseau melodramatically described the large size of early-modern polities as 'the first and principal source of the misfortunes of the human race'. Jean-Jacques Rousseau, *Considérations sur le Gouvernement de Pologne et sur sa réforme projetée* in *Collection complète des oeuvres*, (Genève, 1780–89) vol 1 C IV; for a translation see 'Considerations on the Government of Poland' in Frederick Watkins, *Jean-Jacques Rousseau: Political Writings* (New York, Thomas Yelsen, 1953). In the *Social Contract* he envisaged 'a very small state where the people is easy to assemble and where each citizen could easily know any other'. *Social Contract*, ibid, Bk III, Ch III. See generally Francisco Herreros, 'Size and Virtue' (2007) 6 *European Journal of Political Theory* 463.

Corsicans' existing 'primitive virtues' that make an autarkic Constitution possible,[4] and the role of the Constitution in turn is to sustain and preserve these virtues.

The purpose of the constitutional devices Rousseau recommends is partly to preserve these fortuitous local specificities within which republican politics might take root—and specifically, to promote and sustain an agrarian way of life on the island. While Poland is a relatively large and heterogeneous state compared to Corsica, in *Government of Poland* he also implores the Poles to 'preserve and revive among your people simple customs and wholesome tastes.'[5] But the 'whole thrust' of his Corsican plan, as Peter France puts it, 'was to preserve the rude virtue of the islanders, to prevent them falling prey to the enervating effects of commerce.'[6] While Pascal Paoli, the Corsican republican leader, had promoted commercial development, Rousseau instead advocated, in Chesnais' terms, a 'total autarky excluding all luxury and superfluous goods, based on traditional agriculture and crafts.'[7] 'Useful', artisanal pursuits would be promoted, but 'idle' arts—associated with luxury, debauchment and affectation—discouraged.[8]

Thus Rousseau's specific constitutional prescriptions are largely aimed at incentivising virtuous agrarian activities and disincentivising commercial activities, with the Constitution promoting agriculture as the primary economic activity. He says 'it will be necessary to have the [Corsicans] actually adopt this system, to make them love the [agrarian] occupation we want to give them, and so to determine their pleasures, desires, tastes ... to guide and set limits to their ambitions.'[9] The Constitution will, accordingly orient all of political and social life around this foundation of political economy.

These seemingly eccentric constitutional aims are, in some sense, a natural extension of Rousseau's broader ideas on commerce, virtue and economic inequality. Indeed in the *Social Contract* he expresses a familiar republican apprehension towards economic inequality as an important source of social and economic domination, insisting 'no citizen shall ever be wealthy enough to buy another, and none poor enough to be forced to sell himself.'[10] And accordingly, what seems initially like a rather standard republican suspicion of economic inequality is given stark expression in specific, radical measures, aimed at sustaining an egalitarian, agrarian economy, in Rousseau's constitutional projects for Corsica and Poland. He directs considerable opprobrium against the corrupting effects of urbanity and of capital cities in particular—describing the capital as 'an abyss where almost an entire nation can lose its morals, its laws, its courage and its liberty.'[11] Indeed his

---

[4] Jean-Jacques Rousseau, *Projet de Constitution pour la Corse* (Paris, Nautilus, 2000) (hereinafter *Corsica*) 48.
[5] *Poland*, above n 3, Ch XI.
[6] Peter France, 'Primitivism and Enlightenment: Rousseau and the Scots' (1985) 15 *The Yearbook of English Studies* 64, 68.
[7] Chesnais, preface to *Corsica*, above n 4, 17.
[8] ibid 61.
[9] ibid 51.
[10] *Social Contract*, above n 2, Bk II, Ch 2.
[11] *Corsica*, above n 4, 41.

apprehension of urbanity has been described as 'quasi-heretical' in the republican history of thought.[12] Accordingly, he recommends that the capital or 'high seat' of the Corsican republic should be the remote, sylvan town of Corte, high in the mountains, rather than a coastal, commercial city like Bastia.[13]

In this vein, the bulk of *Constitutional Project for Corsica*, in particular, is not devoted to institutional matters in the narrow sense—nor indeed is it focused, for the most part, even on economics in the narrow sense. Rather, it is focused on the legal foundations of an autarkic political economy and particularly laws relating to property, family and eligibility for citizenship—and whose main purpose is to sustain autarky and agrarianism as the basis of a republican social order.

Some of the 'constitutional' measures Rousseau prescribes are squarely aimed at suppressing commerce and wealth. In *Corsica*, for example, he recommends sumptuary laws against ostentation and luxury, which should apply more strictly to public officials.[14] However, he says they should play only a secondary role: instead, the Constitution will discourage the vices of luxury and ostentation by promoting agrarian activities and occupations, sustaining agriculture as the mainstay of economic life.[15] Agrarianism, underpinned by the Constitution, will spontaneously promote industriousness and discourage 'idleness', which is the 'source of all vices.'[16] Vices generally, he says, are 'tempered by labour.'[17] In *Poland*, he similarly downplays the role of coercion in fostering austerity, saying:

> [I]t is not by sumptuary laws that luxury can be successfully extirpated; it is from the depth of the heart itself that you must uproot it by impressing men with healthier and nobler tastes ... simplicity of manners and adornment is the fruit not so much of law as of education.[18]

Thus, the bulk of Rousseau's substantive prescriptions in *Corsica*—particularly in the areas of citizenship rights, family law and property—are essentially aimed at incentivising agrarian occupations and correspondingly, at disincentivising the development of commerce. His suggestions concerning citizenship laws are explicitly aimed at incentivising agrarian occupations. For example, Rousseau suggests three citizenship ranks: *citizen*, *aspirant* and *patriot*. The rules for ascendancy

---

[12] Hénaff, above n 1, 8. Rousseau, he claims, resented the 'pretension of the city to incarnate authority', with its 'halo' of 'glory and grandeur'. He says: 'Rousseau is no doubt the first to disassociate city-dwelling and citizenship.' Thus, utopia 'moves to the countryside': ibid, 9.

[13] Statesmen, he envisaged, would occupy modest, temporary dwellings in Corte, which, being 'far from the sea, which will conserve for the longest time possible the habitants' simplicity, their morals, their upstanding character, their national character which was so vulnerable to foreign affluence.': *Corsica*, above n 4, 42–43.

[14] ibid 75.

[15] ibid 90: 'instead of suppressing luxury with sumptuary laws, it is better to foreclose it with an administration rendering it impossible.'

[16] ibid 40.

[17] ibid 40.

[18] *Poland*, above n 3, Ch III.

between them must, he says, be designed so as to 'attach men to the land' and strengthen the family.[19] In recognition of their valour in the independence struggle, all Corsicans then aged 20 and over were to automatically secure citizenship upon swearing an oath. Those not yet that age would instead automatically become 'aspirants'.[20] Aspirants would accede to a higher class—'patriot'—on condition that they marry, and acquire some land other than through a dowry. Then, patriots would become citizens when, if married or widowed, they had at least two children, and enough land for subsistence.[21] Any citizen's daughter who married a Corsican of whatever class would receive a dowry of land by the *pière* (a local administrative unit) from the commons, and this would allow the aspirant-husband to accede to patriot.[22] Each of the *pièves* would retain a substantial commons.[23] Finally, any Corsican unmarried at the age of 40 would lose citizenship.[24]

While citizenship law is designed to incentivise smallholding landownership and the family, much the same motivations underlie Rousseau's proposals for family and property law. In particular, he advocates a fertility policy—families with more than five children will receive a premium of land from the commune.[25] He feared that industrial development would lead to absentee land ownership, and an exploitative, servile landlord-peasant relationship.[26] Thus, he proposed a cap on the land any individual could own, and argued citizenship should be confined to those working on the land.[27] He even suggested currency might be abolished, replaced by a system of commodity exchange which could allow Corsicans 'to live in abundance',[28] while deterring bureaucratic corruption.[29] Thus, he planned a 'republic without financiers'[30]—echoing a tirade in *Poland* against finance's 'venal souls'.[31] In the Roman republic, he claims, public revenue was not claimed in monetary tax but in kind, maintaining a military and public works using civic-labour.[32] Public revenue in Corsica would be raised primarily through civilian

---

[19] *Corsica*, above n 2, 51.
[20] ibid 52.
[21] ibid.
[22] ibid 89.
[23] ibid 69.
[24] ibid 84.
[25] ibid 85.
[26] ibid 53.
[27] ibid.
[28] ibid 57.
[29] The warehouses the Genoese had used to commandeer production were to be used as municipal depots, as centres of exchange where individuals would record their commodity needs and surpluses of production. The comparison and balancing of these registers between the provinces will regulate trade and production, the aim being to prevent the conversion of surplus production as accumulated profit: ibid 58, 60.
[30] ibid 70.
[31] *Poland*, above n 3, Ch XI.
[32] It 'had little revenue but did great things': *Corsica*, above n 2, 66–67. As Chesnais notes in an annotation to this assertion, the Roman monetary system was in fact a good deal more complicated than this.

labour for public works and a citizen militia,[33] and public officials paid primarily in kind, through surplus agricultural produce.[34]

For all their eccentricity, Rousseau's ideas echo some of the prescriptions of early American republicans, in particular, for whom—following James Harrington's influence—republican government presupposed a relative degree of economic equality and a wide distribution of property amongst a broad-based middle class.[35] Noah Webster, a federalist, argued that a 'general and tolerably equal distribution of landed property' was the 'whole basis of national freedom'.[36] Jefferson, in particular, believed that laws around property and inheritance should tend towards equalising land ownership or at least mitigating excessive accumulation.[37]

Yet strikingly, political economy is so central to Rousseau's overall scheme of constitutional design—especially in *Corsica*—that his institutional prescriptions are in fact not only secondary to, but derivative of his concern to maintain autarky and stem commerce. Even more so than *Poland*, what is striking in the work is the sheer level of emphasis or priority that economic matters receive, compared to his relatively scant institutional prescriptions (albeit in the context of a fragmentary work). One of the most interesting implications of Rousseau's enthusiasm for agrarian autarky as the cornerstone of republican politics is that, for obvious practical reasons, it precludes the kinds of political structures that might apply in a city-state, and which he sets out in the *Social Contract*. In particular, it rules out the kind of plenary legislative assembly that is often associated with his model of 'direct' democracy. In *Corsica*, he prescribes a fairly broad dispersal of public power, chiefly through local assemblies—a structure which stems from the pastoral economy. He says rather tersely: 'Corsica needs a mixed government,

---

[33] 'No one is to be a magistrate of soldier by status, but must be ready to be called upon to perform whatever duties the *patrie* might impose. The only permanent status is that of citizen': ibid 86.

[34] ibid 70.

[35] Ganesh Sitaraman notes: 'During the ratification debates in Pennsylvania, Anti-Federalist Samuel Bryan, writing under the pseudonym Centinel, echoed the sentiment in forceful terms: "A republican, or free government, can only exist where the body of the people are virtuous, and where property is pretty equally divided … when this ceases to be the case, the nature of the government is changed, and an aristocracy, monarchy or despotism will rise on its ruin."' Ganesh Sitaraman, 'Economic Structure and Constitutional Structure: an Intellectual History' (2015–16) 94 *Texas Law Review* 1301, 1321, citing Herbert J Storing, *The Complete Anti-Federalist Vol 2* (Chicago, University of Chicago Press, 1981) 136.

[36] Noah Webster, *An Examination of the Leading Principles of the Federal Constitution* (1787) 47 cited at Sitaraman, ibid 1322.

[37] Sitaraman notes: 'Thomas Jefferson famously said that one of his proudest moments was Virginia's abolition of entails (a legal device to pass on property to one's descendants) and primogeniture (a legal rule by which property is passed on to the oldest son). Jefferson believed that while "an equal division of property is impracticable", legislators "cannot invent too many devices for subdividing property." … After the Revolution, Jefferson wrote that one way to "silently lessen … the inequality of property is to exempt all from taxation below a certain point, and to tax the higher portions or property in geometrical progression as they rise." He also advocated that the unemployed should be free to take up uncultivated land, and even proposed that every man who didn't have fifty acres of property be given property so he met that minimum threshold.': Sitaraman, above n 35, 1326 (internal citations omitted).

where the people assembles only in sections rather than as a whole, and where the repositories of its authority are frequently rotated.'[38] Decentralised power, and especially decentralised *legislative* power seems inconsistent with his more abstract political thought, but it is a necessary corollary of an autarkic and agrarian political economy.[39] And in fact, while he is remarkably vague concerning the precise powers and functions of the legislative assemblies,[40] his overarching concern is that a decentralised legislative structure should promote and sustain agrarian autarky. On the one hand, decentralised government helps to prevent any divestment of power to elites—precluding 'the separation of ... the body that governs from that which is governed'[41]—enabling 'all members of the polity' to participate in public authority. More importantly, however, this form of government will facilitate an agrarian and autarkic political economy—it will 'permit [citizens] to spread throughout the whole of the island and to populate it evenly',[42] thus avoiding urbanisation and its associated vices. This echoes his seemingly mysterious recommendation in the preface to *Nouvelle Héloïse*, where he says:

> [M]ake [men] love solitude and peace, keep them at some distance from each another, and instead of encouraging them to crowd together in cities, encourage them to spread themselves equally across the territory so as to vivify it in all areas.[43]

This vision is reminiscent more of the sturdy yeomen of the early American republic, rather than the patrician or aristocratic citizen of antiquity.

Perhaps Rousseau's advocacy of what is essentially a mixed and even decentralised kind of government should not be thought of as all that anomalous. On the one hand, his prescription of decentralised government seems surprising only because his insistence on a singular and indivisible popular *sovereign* is frequently confused with a preference for a highly centralised and undivided form of popular *government*—for a democracy that is 'direct' in all its dimensions.[44] Yet he distinguishes indivisible sovereignty, understood rather narrowly and specifically, from any vision of unitary government.[45] And in *Corsica* in particular, he seems less concerned to preclude political representation as such, as per the usual account, but rather to prevent the emergence of a professional clique of specialised politicians—an aim that might be realised under diverse institutional forms. Furthermore, while the *Social Contract* suggests legislative power is exercised directly by the sovereign people and is indivisible by its nature, it has been argued that Rousseau

---

[38] *Corsica*, above n 2, 34.
[39] Similarly, he tolerates a degree of representative democracy in *Poland*, given the impracticability of plenary assemblies. *Poland*, above n 3, Chs XI–XV.
[40] In particular, in what sense their powers are 'legislative'.
[41] *Corsica*, above n 2, 25.
[42] ibid 35.
[43] Jean-Jacques Rousseau. *Julie ou la Nouvelle Héloïse* (Paris, Ornée de Gravures, 1819) 30.
[44] Peter Steinberger, 'Hobbes, Rousseau and the Modern Conception of the State' (2008) 70 *The Journal of Politics* 595.
[45] ibid.

understood 'legislation' in the unusually narrow sense of foundational laws—with more routine forms of lawmaking being permissibly delegated from 'sovereign' to 'government'.[46]

In any event, and bearing in mind that in *Poland*, Rousseau permits what is essentially a version of representative democracy—what emerges is that the choice of institutional forms is flexible and is effectively ancillary to an overarching goal, that of promoting a certain kind of political economy that, in turn, is understood as sustaining an authentically republican society and politics. The central focus of constitutional design, then, is economic and social. The realisation of the general will depends less on any specific institutional structure than on the social framework which it sustains and by which it is sustained in turn.

III. Commerce, Virtue and Corruption

It is tempting to interpret Rousseau's autarkical utopia as a kind of romantic primitivism, and as stemming from a peculiar conception of the good life based on authenticity and simplicity.[47] However, I will argue, instead, that his autarky must be viewed as an extension of his theory of servitude and domination as outlined in chapter one. The most obvious political motivation for Rousseau's autarkical project in *Poland* and *Corsica* lies in his underlying belief as to the impossibility of sustaining republican virtues in the kinds of complex, commercial societies that emerged in eighteenth century Europe, and that he condemns as irredeemably corrupt. Thus while Rousseau's autarkical politics has been interpreted as a lament for a lost, or disappearing utopia—as an 'archaicizing Romantic rebellion against history, individuation and civilization itself'[48]—in some senses it simply expresses an uncompromising, and not altogether incoherent position as to the social preconditions of republican politics. Yet his main emphasis—as I will develop further below—is not on any specific vision of the good life in autarkic and austere societies, but rather, negatively speaking, on the corrupting effects of commerce and of social specialisation or social differentiation more generally.

It is a truism, of course, that the republican concept of freedom presupposes a sustainable level of civic virtue, understood, roughly speaking, as a commitment to public goods and engagement in public life (whether such virtues are considered intrinsically or instrumentally valuable). In turn, a republican constitution will aim to foster, harness or incentivise the appropriate dispositions—with all

---

[46] See, eg, Joel Colón-Ríos, 'Rousseau, Theorist of Constituent Power' (2016) *Oxford Journal of Legal Studies*, Advance Access, published 12 June 2016, http://ojls.oxfordjournals.org/content/early/2016/06/11/ojls.gqw012.full.

[47] See, eg, France, above n 6.

[48] Asher Horowitz, '"Laws and Customs Thrust Us Back into Infancy": Rousseau's Historical Anthropology' (1990) 52 *The Review of Politics* 215, 216.

the challenges, and indeed risks, this presents. Yet from the early-modern period, many political thinkers argued that a sustainable social framework for republican virtue no longer existed and could not feasibly be revived. They doubted whether anything approximating the ancient sense of civic virtue could ever take hold in mass, diverse societies, in citizenries devoted to the pursuit of commerce and private interest.[49] In a liberal world defined by individualism and the transactional life of commerce, any strong commitment to civic virtue began to seem archaic, unrealistic and perhaps oppressive. In the eighteenth century, Montesquieu already suggested that classical republican virtue was too ambitious for the moderns.[50] Figures of the Scottish Enlightenment like Adam Smith argued that ancient republicanism was 'anachronistic, suited to small, homogenous societies characterised by a lower level of economic and cultural development', and unfeasible under 'conditions of differentiation, heterogeneity and division of labour.'[51] Similarly, Benjamin Constant responded to the Rousseauan inspirations of the French revolution in part by arguing that because the moderns were defined by the pursuit of private and commercial interest, this rendered obsolete the full-throated ancient sense of republican citizenship.[52] For Adam Ferguson, republican practices were unsustainable given the 'variety of pursuits and applications that separate mankind in the advanced state of commercial arts'.[53] It was this very division of labour that distinguished modernity from the 'rude ages.'[54] And in the later liberal thought of the twentieth century, we find an additional objection: that any strong commitment to civic virtue undermines state neutrality towards diverse ways of life and conceptions of the good.[55]

While a number of historical factors, social and religious, weighed against any modern revival of ancient republican virtue, Rousseau's eighteenth century

---

[49] For figures like Adam Ferguson, 'the central hallmark of modernity ... is that the unity of society has been broken into a plurality of professions, skills, economic tasks and social niches.' Thus 'The division of labour, individual self-interest, private accumulation of wealth, luxury and a taste for refinement produced a crisis that had destabilized the republican ideal of active citizenship that fosters the common good.' Andreas Kalyvas and Ira Katznelson, *Liberal Beginnings: Making a Republic for the Moderns* (Cambridge, Cambridge University Press, 2008) 53. See also Adam Ferguson, *An Essay on the History of Civil Society* (New Brunswick, Transaction Books, 1980).
[50] For discussion see Maurizio Viroli, *Republicanism* (New York, Hill and Wang 2002) 72.
[51] Kalyvas and Katnelson, above n 49, 35–36.
[52] See Benjamin Constant, 'De la Liberté des Anciens Comparée à celle des Modernes' in Benjamin Constant, *Ecrits Politiques* (Paris, Gallimard/Folio, 1997) 591–619.
[53] Ferguson, above n 49, 187.
[54] ibid 138.
[55] For discussion see Robert Goodin, 'Folie Républicaine' (2003) 6 *Annual Review of Political Science* 55; John Maynor, 'Without Regret: The Comprehensive Nature of Non-domination' (2002) 22 *The Review of Politics* 51. Kymlicka, for example, objects that republicanism 'privileges political participation over other spheres of human endeavour': Will Kymlicka, *Politics in the Vernacular: Nationalism, Multiculturalism, and Citizenship* (Oxford, Oxford University Press, 2001) 297 fn. This idea of neutrality has antecedents in early-modern political thought. Fergus, for example, 'advanced a vision of the modern state as a juridical institution to protect the liberties of persons rather than to buttress a specific moral code.': Kalyvas and Katnelseon, above n 49, 56.

contemporaries—republican and otherwise—were especially preoccupied by the apparently corrupting effect of commerce and wealth, and consequently the difficulty of sustaining civic virtue in commercial society. With the collapse or decline of the old aristocratic world, it was feared that a new set of passions—and particularly a spirit of accumulation—would rise.[56] Even Madison, a much more liberal and optimistic republican compared with Rousseau, told Congress that since farmers were 'the most truly independent and happy' of citizens, it followed that 'the greater the proportion of this class to the whole society, the more free, the more independent, and the more happy must be the society itself.'[57] And even Smith—not particularly republican, but a champion of commerce—acknowledged 'the tendency of market societies to promote the enervation and degeneration of the martial virtues.'[58] As Skinner notes, pre-Renaissance, medieval republicanism had held that 'the pursuit of private gain is inimical to public virtue',[59] identifying an intrinsic conflict between commercial life and republican ideals. Thus the rise of commercial society, especially in the period preceding the industrial revolution, posed acute challenges to republican thinking. Whereas the ancient model of civic virtue relied on the political economy of slavery—which allowed a restricted citizenry to pursue distinction and fulfilment in public life—the moderns could not achieve the same devotion to public affairs, as the transactional world of commerce would naturally orient them away from a concern for common goods and the public realm. The rising figure of the bourgeois, comfortable and insincere, haunted many republicans. What defines the bourgeois, in part, compared to the aristocrat or the peasant, is not only his frivolity and weakness—his 'love of convenient pleasures [that] inhibits his greatness'[60]—but also that he pursues distinction in the private world of commerce and wealth, with all its associated cultural trappings. In *Letter to d'Alembert*, Rousseau opined that in the modern city, man is 'only distinguished by his credit, and only esteemed for his wealth.'[61] Thus recognition and esteem would be focused on the private realm. As Spitz puts it:

> '[T]he Republic decisively recedes into the past as Western societies become more oriented towards commerce, finance and the production of wealth ... so that the political

---

[56] Janara notes: 'It is worth noting that various psychoanalytic thinkers have pointed to the restless modern human drive to accumulate, count, control and manipulate money and property as a compensation for something lost.': Laura Janara, 'Commercial Capitalism and the Democratic Psyche: The Threat to Tocquevillian Citizenship' (2001) 22 *History of Political Thought* 317, 326.

[57] James Madison, 'Republican Distribution of Citizens' cited in Andreas Kalyvas and Ira Katznelson, 'Republic of the Moderns: Paine's and Madison's Novel Liberalism' (2006) 338 *Polity* 447, 465.

[58] Ryan Hanley, 'Commerce and Corruption: Rousseau's Diagnosis and Adam Smith's Cure' (2008) 7 *European Journal of Political Theory* 137.

[59] Quentin Skinner, *The Foundations of Modern Political Thought* Vol 1 (Cambridge, Cambridge University Press, 1979) 42–45.

[60] Hanley, above n 58.

[61] Jean-Jacques Rousseau, *Lettre à d'Alembert* (1758). See Allan Bloom, Charles Butterworth and Christopher Kelly, *Rousseau: Letter to d'Alembert and Writings for the Theatre* (Lebanon NH, University Press of New England, 2004) 51.

community based on common political deliberation … gives way to a corrupted collective life constituted by egoism and competition.⁶²

In such circumstances, the challenge for any republican project of constitutional design will be to how it might be possible to foster the relevant dispositions and virtues, providing a stable form of participative and non-dominating republican government under transformed social conditions. However, the question of whether it is feasible to revive classic virtues is wholly separate from that of whether it is *desirable*.⁶³ A perennial dilemma of republican thought is whether or not, and how, it is possible to foster civic virtues to the requisite extent, and with a sufficient degree of stability, without engendering excessive burdens on individual freedom or engendering oppressive requirements of social conformity.⁶⁴

A. Republican Politics for the Moderns

Taking the tension between commercial life and civic virtue as a given, the choice for political thinkers of this period is either to seek to somehow reverse, stem or tame the emergent commercial society, or more plausibly, to abandon, severely downscale, or at least radically reformat the demands of civic virtue itself. However, not all eighteenth century thinkers accepted the fundamental antagonism between commerce and republican politics. Long before the eighteenth century, it has been suggested, by Frans Baron amongst others, that 'commercial republicanism', based on the pursuit of common goods *through* material wealth, partly defined the political thought of the Renaissance period.⁶⁵ Of course, a social structure based around commerce and trade has egalitarian implications contrary to the relatively fixed order of the medieval world.⁶⁶ More pertinently, a range of eighteenth century thinkers offered various theories as to how the apparently self-interested and often venal practices of commerce could be reconciled with public morality in general terms. Whereas commercial pursuits seemed to distance men from the pursuit of glory and distinction in the public realm, Pocock has

---

⁶² Fabien Spitz, 'The *défense républicaine*: Some Remarks about the Specificity of French Republicanism' in Samantha Besson and José-Luis Marti, *Legal Republicanism: National and International Perspectives* (Oxford, Oxford University Press, 2009) 292.
⁶³ For sceptical discussion, see Goodin, above n 55.
⁶⁴ See Goodin, ibid.
⁶⁵ Cary Nederman, 'Commercial Society and Republican Government in the Latin Middle Ages: The Economic Dimensions of Brunetto Latini's Republicanism' (2003) 31 *Political Theory* 644, 646.
⁶⁶ 'In *Democracy in America*, Tocqueville suggests that commerce and the energetic pursuit of industry feed on sensibilities innate to modern democracy' … 'With relations of noblesse oblige and fealty torn asunder, the inhabitants of democracy feel beholden to themselves alone. In the wake of legally entrenched, socially ossified, family-based class structure, it seems that the individual can and must make his or her own destiny, and love of the idea of equality creates among democracy's inhabitants a new kind of personal ambition.': Janara, above n 56, 321–22. See also Alexis de Tocqueville, *Democracy in America* (Isaac Kramnick ed, Gerald Bevan trans, London, Penguin, 2003).

argued that in eighteenth century thought, virtue was increasingly connected to the refinement of manners in commercial society rather than in the public political realm. Commerce was defended from criticism specifically on the grounds that virtue—unlike the ancients' version—was to be exercised not in the domain of political action but rather through 'relationships and interactions with other social beings'—with the commercially-oriented subject 'developing more and more aspects of his personality' in 'an increasingly transactional universe of commerce and the arts'.[67]

More generally, thinkers like Mandeville, and later (to a lesser extent) Smith, attempted to show how—counter-intuitively at the period—the ostensible vices of commercial life were in fact conducive to a kind of public morality, and so they offered moral defences of luxury and wealth.[68] In his essay on commerce, David Hume argued that the rise of industrial society would serve to enhance men's security and thus their sociability.[69] Smith shared Rousseau's concerns as to the corrupting effect of vanity and distinction in the pursuit of wealth, but unlike Rousseau, believed in the educability of commercial sentiment and the possibility of elevating the sentiments of commercial man, distinguishing between the 'love of praise', which was potentially corrupting, and a more evolved 'love of praiseworthiness'—the love of doing what is praiseworthy rather than merely praised—that the ascendant bourgeois could achieve.[70] Thus 'he shared with Rousseau a fundamental aim: an elevation of self-love capable of liberating individuals from dependence on the opinions of others'[71]—however, he believed this elevation could be achieved within, and not beyond, the market society. Thus 'in modern times, the market became an institutional equivalent of ancient public spaces within which citizens of the classical *polis*, through speech and deed, struggled for recognition.'[72] Similarly, for Ferguson, virtue and private interest were 'opposed

---

[67] JGA Pocock, 'Virtues, Rights, and Manners: A Model for Historians of Political Thought' (1981) 9 *Political Theory* 353, 365.

[68] See however Brandon Turner, 'Mandeville against Luxury' (2016) 44 *Political Theory* 26.

[69] David Hume, *Essays: Political and Moral* (Edinburgh, Fleming, 1777). Similarly, Smith argued that commerce would positively enhance virtue, suggesting 'it is commerce that introduces probity and punctuality' in the human character: Adam Smith, *Lectures on Jurisprudence* (Indianapolis, Liberty Press, 1982) 528.

[70] Adam Smith, *Theory of Moral Sentiments* (Edinburgh, Strathan, 1759). Hanley observes: 'Smith was particularly sympathetic to Rousseau's insistence that commercial society is fundamentally driven by a vanity that threatens to corrupt its participants.' He 'fully agrees with Rousseau that men in commercial society depend on others not only for material goods but also for the moral good of recognition, which itself is the source of potential corruption.' Thus, 'the task of political life is then neither to excise the love of praise (that is, to return us to the natural goodness of the savage) nor to inculcate a thoroughgoing enthusiasm for praiseworthiness (that is, to encourage the production of the sort of citizen found in Rousseau's political writings), but rather to restore the balance between the two loves [of praise and praiseworthiness] that had been established by nature but was threatened by the furious pursuit of esteem in commercial society.' Hanley, above n 58, 143–44.

[71] Hanley, ibid.

[72] Kalyvas and Katznelson, above n 49, 23. They note: 'Smith's grounded philosophical anthropology connects modern subjectivity to novel economic structures and newly emergent capitalism.': ibid 36. Similarly, 'Smith's comparison of the ancients to the moderns underscores how wealth had displaced public devotion to the city as the currency of greatness and recognition.': ibid 41. Thus, the

to one another but only by mistake',[73] and argued they could be realigned. Indeed this intellectual attempt at reconciling commerce and civic virtue had begun well before the eighteenth century: the transition from medieval to renaissance republicanism meant that

> it [became] possible for [civic] humanists to look at life … with the eyes of citizens proudly acknowledging work and self-acquired possessions as the foundation of morality and the greatness of their city.[74]

These contemporaries (or near contemporaries) of Rousseau are, like Montesquieu, all theorists, in one way or another, of *doux commerce*—the idea that 'the practices and benefits of trade would soften manners, ease tensions between states and factions, and otherwise encourage gentler habits among citizens of commercial societies.'[75] This was an image of 'responsible citizens, who freely contracted with each other for their mutual advantage and were moved … towards individual, social, material and moral improvement.'[76] Smith, in particular, admires—despite his Rousseauan sympathies—the commercial virtues of 'industry, honesty, thrift, temperance, and prudence.'[77] The seeds of this view were established much earlier in the Renaissance and even the medieval world, and particularly in a 'conception of the common good [which] includes centrally the creation and exchange of those material necessities required for physical welfare and comfort.'[78] But tellingly, as Bellamy observes, this optimistic liberal premise, ascendant in the eighteenth and early nineteenth centuries, was refuted not merely by the obvious dysfunction of self-regulating markets, but also by the 'possessive individualism'—as well as the class conflict—that came to define industrialised society in practice.[79]

B. The Morality of Commerce: Constitutional Translations, Republican Adaptations

James Madison, in particular, arguably adapted these optimistic philosophical insights, whether directly or indirectly, in the domain of political and

---

pursuit of wealth itself gives expression to the same need for recognition that animated the ancients' love of glory and public spiritedness. Thus despite his liberal adaptations, Smith 'accepted the underlying anthropological and philosophical presuppositions of republicanism, according to which the intentions and actions of the person … are constituted within intersubjective, public networks and moral relationships.': ibid 44. It was this very 'pursuit of moral approbation', that Rousseau called *amour-propre*, which 'created the modern ethic of rational acquisition.': ibid 46. Thus Smith, like other republican innovators, retained a 'republican nostalgia.': ibid 47.

[73] Ferguson, above n 49, 146.
[74] Hans Baron, *In Search of Florentine Civic Humanism* (Princeton NJ, Princeton University Press, 1988) 226, as cited in Nederman, above n 65, 645.
[75] Turner, above n 68, 27.
[76] Richard Bellamy, *Liberalism and Modern Society* (Philadelphia, Pennsylvania State University Press, 1992) 3.
[77] Hanley, above n 58, 141.
[78] Nederman, above n 65, 646.
[79] Bellamy, above n 76, 3–4.

constitutional thought, in an attempt to reformat classical republicanism for the commercially oriented moderns. Madison was arguably the first major thinker to have offered an influential attempt to reconcile ancient political ideas—like freedom as non-domination—with the social framework of modern societies. His challenge, as a theorist of constitutional design, was how republican government could be realised in a highly commercial and differentiated society that contrasted so markedly with the homogenous, austere life of the ancient polities. Like Paine, he believed the template of the ancient republics could not 'address social complexity, value plurality and individual autonomy.'[80] And he was to argue not only that commercial society was compatible with republican politics despite its tendencies towards factionalism and self-interest—but that these apparent threats or pathologies could even be harnessed in its cause.[81] Most distinctively, Madison argued that the best safeguard against domination by political or social factions—a perennial republican concern—lay not in the inculcation of austere virtue but rather through institutional mediation by competing factions, whose particular interests would be cancelled out, or at least checked, in a large and diverse state, using historically novel devices such as federalism, political representation and a tripartite separation of powers which, unlike the mixed regime of the classical republic, was functional rather than class-based.[82] Madison's conjecture, in short, was that within an appropriate institutional framework, it was possible to realise freedom as non-domination without the bracing, demanding virtues of the ancient republics.[83]

In the broader historical perspective, Madison's attempt at realising ancient republican goals in the seemingly unlikely context of a large, commercially oriented society, seems improbable or at least highly counterintuitive, given the extent to which historical republican politics depended on rather bracing forms of social cohesion of the kind associated with ancient societies. One plausible interpretation of Madison's seemingly anomalous approach is that, compared with other historical republicans, he simply adopted a more optimistic understanding of the interplay between public and private interest. Most republicans had viewed the pursuit of private interest as intrinsically a threat to civic virtue, and their constitutional strategies had focused on taming or suppressing the corrupting effect of private and commercial dispositions. Burtt argues that ancient republicans like Cicero emphasised the 'inculcation of duty' through moral discipline such that

---

[80] Kalyvas and Katznelson, above n 49, 105.
[81] Tocqueville can also be read as viewing private industry as conducive to democracy, but in his case, rather by constituting a bulwark—like civil society—against an otherwise overweening state. Thus 'Tocqueville sees democracy producing a psychology that urges industrialization and commerce.': Janara, above n 56, 322. He also views democratic culture, particularly its egalitarianism, as moderating the corrupting effects of commerce and industry. See Janara, ibid for discussion, especially 322–23.
[82] See Kalyvas and Katznelson, above n 49, Ch 2.
[83] Madison's aim is 'to invent a compound institutional configuration that could address the problem of neutrality without endangering popular sovereignty or eradicating the plurality of interests and passions.' Kalyvas and Katznelson, ibid 96.

citizens' 'personal desires find satisfaction only through public service'.[84] Rousseau himself equally sought to reorient citizens from private to public concerns, but rather by establishing incentive structures to ensure public activities would simply be more pleasurable than private pursuits.[85] However, a different, more liberal strand of republican thought—represented by thinkers like Harrington as well as Madison—did not expect individuals would set aside or conquer self-interest, or 'sacrifice personal advantage to a greater public good',[86] but rather that under appropriate conditions, self-interest 'can in itself produce politically virtuous behaviour.'[87] In other words—echoing or presaging the moral theorists of early capitalism—they assumed a greater degree of harmony between public and private interest, at least under certain conditions. In short, 'the pursuit of ... self-interest can produce civically virtuous actions in a properly structured political environment.'[88] This is reflected in many of the institutional devices of the Madisonian constitution, particularly federalism, representation and the separation of powers. The focus is not on preventing the pursuit of private interest as such but rather on sustaining a balance or equilibrium between 'factions', such that none dominate.[89]

Thus the Madisonian conjecture, in short, is that appropriate institutional devices can prevent political domination without an austere, homogenous social bedrock. Compared to Rousseau, the constitutional mechanisms Madison suggested would not aim to inculcate civic or publicly oriented behaviour as such, but simply ensure that the pursuit of factional interests in the political process is harmonised with citizens' common interest in enjoying freedom, roughly understood as security from arbitrary power.

This approach has obvious attractions, simply because it imposes fewer burdens on individuals and intuitively seems less threatening to individual freedoms. On the other hand, however, this more optimistic strategy seems empirically unfeasible and intrinsically unstable, simply because it assumes that appropriate institutional mechanisms, alone—without the burdens and demands historically imposed by republican citizenship—will ensure a sufficient priority for common goods in political life and successfully prevent domination especially in social and economic spheres. The more liberal solution seems more attractive abstractly speaking, but somewhat lacking from the point of view of feasibility and stability.

---

[84] Shelley Burtt, 'The Good Citizen's Psyche: on the Psychology of Civic Virtue' (1990) 23 *Polity* 10, 35.
[85] ibid.
[86] ibid 26.
[87] ibid.
[88] ibid 28.
[89] Holmes argues that similarly, Tocqueville identified a 'happy coexistence of public and private spheres' in the early American republic. Stephen Holmes, 'Tocqueville and Democracy' in David Copp, Jean Hampton and John Roemer, *The Idea of Democracy* (Cambridge, Cambridge University Press, 1993) 42.

C. Rousseau's Rejection of the Republican Compromise with Commerce

By contrast with Madison, what is striking about Rousseau's constitutional thought is the extent to which he rejects, wholesale, any idea that a genuine republican politics can be reconciled with the social and economic life of the moderns. Thus Rousseau can be read as offering a more uncompromising account of the social and economic foundations of a successful republican politics, and a more stridently sceptical stance as to the moral effects of commercial society.

It is worth digressing to note that modern liberal republics did not of course—and have not—abandoned the project of civic virtue entirely, but simply confined it to a modest domain. As I discuss in the next chapter, typical modern republics will, along with civic education through public schools, typically employ a piecemeal civic ritualism through limited devices like flags and other symbols, anthems, oaths, civic awards and feast days, albeit in ways that are quite far removed from the pervasive demands of ancient ritualism. Similarly, contemporary civic-republican philosophy will tend to support mechanisms aimed at promoting civic virtues, or at least sentiments of civic belonging, but in relatively modest, piecemeal ways, that eschew excessive burdens on individuals, especially in the context of the ethical and moral pluralism that defines liberal society.[90] And while Rousseau does place considerable emphasis on the constitutional importance of rituals and symbols—at least in *Poland* albeit to a lesser extent in in *Corsica*—one way of reading his commitment to autarky, as an economic and social project, is as a wholesale rejection of the idea that a republican state can foster the appropriate virtues and dispositions, with sufficient intensity and stability, solely by piecemeal symbolic and ritual interventions in societies that are otherwise dominated by the transactional life of commerce and its associated social structures. What his autarkical project suggests—not implausibly—is that such piecemeal attempts at inculcating civic dispositions are futile without attention to the formative influences of wider social and economic life. Additionally, the specificity of his constitutionalism—and its relationship to ideas of freedom—also lies partly in his wholesale rejection of any Madisonian idea that potentially destructive private interests can simply be contained, checked and filtered simply through appropriate institutional mechanisms. While Rousseau was not, of course, writing in response to Madison and so did not directly confront these ideas, his view is nonetheless implicitly sceptical as to the possibility of any spontaneous, or stable, equilibrium between competing interests. And indeed, this scepticism is arguably vindicated in the subsequent historical experience of the Madisonian republic, which has, in its general

---

[90] As Honohan notes, historical republics aimed to inculcate civic virtue by conferring honour and 'social approval' on virtuous behaviour. Iseult Honohan, *Civic Republicanism* (London, Routledge, 2007) 5.

trajectory, failed to check concentrations of power and wealth and the dominance of economic interest over political life.[91]

D. The Destructive Force of Commercial Society

The specificity of Rousseau's embrace of agrarian society should not be overstated. The virtues of rustic smallholders feature as a prominent theme in the wider republican history of thought: it has been argued that Madison and Paine—much more liberal figures than Rousseau—shared a 'similar appreciation … of the rural basis of civic virtue.'[92] What distinguishes Rousseau, then, is the degree to which he rejects the coexistence of virtuous agrarianism with a nascent commercial society. While Rousseau rejects any piecemeal devices for fostering civic virtue in liberal society, equally, of course, he rejects wholesale Hume's or Smith's idea that virtue might be sustained and rooted in the practices of commercial life itself. To understand the radicalism of his constitutional prescriptions for autarky, it is worth considering in greater depth the specific grounds of Rousseau's hostility to commerce. As a preliminary point, it is worth distinguishing his objection to economic inequality from his objection to wealth per se, although of course they are closely related. On the one hand, Rousseau uncontroversially argues that economic inequalities of the sort that emerge in commercial society may allow some citizens to dominate others at an interpersonal level. Thus he insists in the *Social Contract* that 'no citizen shall ever be wealthy enough to buy another.'[93] Similarly, he argues that an agrarian economy will protect Corsican smallholders from becoming dependent on any masters—domestic or foreign—so that, in a familiar republican trope, they will have to obey only the 'law itself'.[94] This, essentially, is why his constitutional prescriptions aim to protect agrarian smallholdings as the framework for freedom as non-domination. With echoes of Lycurgus' Sparta,[95] his Corsican Constitution will also facilitate redistribution of land. In vague terms, Rousseau suggests the government may distribute land from a substantial commons to those who labour upon it, and that the law of succession may return land to the commons.[96] While property law will protect private holdings, excessive accumulations may be requisitioned, under law:[97] the Constitution 'must operate towards equality, so that everyone has something and nobody too much.'[98]

---

[91] See generally Joseph Fishkin and William Forebath, 'Reclaiming Constitutional Political Economy: An Introduction to the Symposium on the Constitution and Economic Inequality' (2015–16) 94 *Texas Law Review* 1287.
[92] Kalyvas and Katznelson, above n 57, 466.
[93] *Social Contract*, above n 2, Bk II, Ch 2.
[94] *Corsica*, above n 4, 40.
[95] John McCormick, '"Keep the Public Rich, but the Citizens Poor": Economic and Political Inequality in Constitutions, Ancient and Modern' (2013) 34 *Cardozo Law Review* 879.
[96] *Corsica*, above n 4, 68.
[97] ibid 75.
[98] ibid 86.

This is somewhat puzzling, because in his third *Discourse* on political economy,[99] Rousseau ardently defends property not only as a social mechanism for guaranteeing individuals independence, but, in Hanley's terms, as a right 'antecedent to government'—and insists it should be minimally disrupted.[100] In any event, this link Rousseau draws between domination and economic inequality has obvious ancient-republican antecedents, particularly in the agrarian laws of ancient Rome,[101] and is also echoed in contemporary neo-republican theories of non-domination.[102]

Thus, like other republicans, Rousseau aims to substantially mitigate wealth inequality partly to prevent wealthier citizens from dominating poorer ones.[103] Fundamentally, however, Rousseau's main objection to economic inequality is not based on the domination that is entailed by the inter-personal power relationships associated with wealth disparities. Ultimately, his overriding concern as a constitutional designer is to sustain the kind of society—with the requisite virtues and dispositions—that can give effect to the 'general will' that he theorised more abstractly in the *Social Contract*. Or, put in a less theoretically specific way—and setting aside the philosophical debates about the philosophical nature of the general will—he aims to create a society whose politics gives priority to common goods and common interests above factional concerns or private interests. His emphatically negative attitude towards commerce and wealth must be seen in this light. In short, he assumes that commerce and economic inequality undermine the cohesion and solidarity that are needed for citizens to actually legislate the general will in this broad sense. The corrupting effects of wealth cannot, then, be understood in purely comparative or relative terms. In typically strident and provocative style, he asserts in *Corsica*: 'Commerce produces wealth, but agriculture,

---

[99] Jean-Jacques Rousseau, *Discourse on Political Economy* (1755) in Jean-Jaques Rousseau, *Discourse on Political Economy and On the Social Contract* (Christopher Betts trans, Oxford, Oxford University Press, 2009).

[100] Hanley does also note: 'Elsewhere—and especially in his works on Corsica and Poland—Rousseau will indeed advocate a "conservative, even reactionary" economic vision that may owe much to Sparta.': Ryan Hanley, 'The Political Economy of Freedom: Revisiting Rousseau's Third Discourse' in Eve Grace and Christopher Kelly, *The Challenge of Rousseau* (Cambridge, Cambridge University Press, 2013) citing Yoav Peled, 'Rousseau's Inhibited Radicalism: An Analysis of His Political Thought in Light of His Economic Ideas' (1980) 74 *American Political Science Review* 1034.

[101] McCormick, above n 95.

[102] Sitaraman notes: 'From the ancient Greeks onward, political philosophers were preoccupied with the problem of economic inequality and the structure of government.
Unless a society had a strong middle class, the wealthy elites would clash with everyone else—the rich oppressing the poor, the poor seeking to confiscate and redistribute the wealth of the rich. Economic inequality led inevitably to political inequality, and as a result, to instability, class warfare, and revolution. A vital task of constitutional theory was to design governments that would not fall prey to the tumults that accompanied economic inequality.': Sitaraman, above n 35, 1303.

[103] Hanley: 'A chief concern throughout his political writings is of course less the amelioration of poverty than the mitigation of inequality—a difference that would distinguish him conspicuously from Adam Smith, among others.': Hanley, above n 100, 12.

liberty. You could say it would be better to have both wealth and liberty; but they are incompatible.'[104]

On the one hand, perhaps his insistence on economic autarky gives some clues as to Rousseau's broader sense of how the general will—the will of the political community that grounds political liberty—is to be instantiated politically, socially and institutionally. More specifically, on the other, it helps to illustrate how it is not merely economic inequality, but rather wealth and commerce per se, that Rousseau understands as being inconsistent with republican goals. Rousseau's assumption, in effect, is that the dispositions and virtues needed for the general will to be realised cannot survive the destructive social effects wrought by commerce and private interest, nor can they be located within a suitably adjusted or tamed form of it. And this suggests, again, that a politics of the common good cannot be sustainably secured simply by attempting to regulate the interplay and equilibrium of private interests, whether through institutional structures or otherwise. Instead it requires a specific set of *public* virtues and dispositions, generalised across society rather than just a patrician elite—and not merely an institutionally mediated equilibrium between competing factional interests.

Thus to some extent, Rousseau's thesis, in effect, is that wealth and its pursuit is corrupting, and incompatible with the virtues of the general will, *independently* of the relational or comparative inequalities it tends to engender. One possible explanation is that commerce is incompatible with republican politics simply because it is too absorbing and time consuming and distracts citizens from the burdens of participation.[105] This was the essence of Benjamin Constant's rejection of ancient republican ideals applied to the early-modern world: whereas classical republican politics had relied on the political economy of slavery, modern citizens were too preoccupied with private interests.[106] Less stridently, Tocqueville, another nineteenth century critic of Rousseau, feared that the spirit of materialism might 'soften and imperceptibly loosen the springs of [political] action', sapping the dispositions of citizenship.[107]

However, this explanation seems unconvincing in Rousseau's work. Rousseau does not envisage citizens of autarkies as necessarily being involved in great depth with the minutiae of government, or as devoting their time and efforts to public affairs. The kind of virtue required of them does not require much spare time and is far removed from Constant's picture of civically inclined patrician citizens: in fact, he specifically decries 'idleness' as one of the negative effect of commerce and wealth.[108] He even implores the Poles to 'cultivate your fields ... and have

---

[104] *Corsica*, above n 4, 31.
[105] Expressing the opposite view, Holmes argues that for Tocqueville, 'commerce and democratic politics are mutually interdependent. Each solves problems produced by the other. And each encourages the formation of habits that, when carried into the other domain, have beneficial consequences.' Holmes, above n 89, 44.
[106] Constant, 'De la Liberté', above n 52.
[107] Tocqueville, above n 66, 534.
[108] *Corsica*, above n 4, 53.

no other care.'[109] Thus the modern political economy is not un-republican simply because it distracts citizens from politics, and the virtues to be promoted by autarky are not those of political deliberation and contestation, but rather of temperance and forbearance. Citizens do not need to be especially trained for political life, and there is little sense, in Rousseau, of Aristotelian civic humanism—of the idea that citizens will attain self-realisation through political activity.[110] Moreover, Rousseau's idealised republican politics is distant from any leisured, patrician vision because although his constitutional prescriptions are aimed at stemming any spirit of accumulation, they seek to valorise and exalt *work*: while 'idleness' is repeatedly emphasised as a social ill, industriousness—mostly in the fields—is repeatedly lauded as an essential virtue.

An alternative, more plausible explanation is that, for Rousseau, the pursuit of money and wealth, and the possession of excess or unnecessary wealth, simply diminishes the altruism and solidarity that are necessary for citizens to discern and prioritise the general will. In the second *Discourse*, he suggests that commercially oriented citizens 'find their account in the unhappiness of others',[111] alluding to the destructively competitive and parasitic nature of commerce.[112] Thus Hanley, for example, argues that for Rousseau, commerce 'stimulates in men a desire for esteem and consideration such that they can only live in the eyes and opinions of others'[113]—stemming from his wider view of *amour-propre* as a potentially destructive passion. In this view, agrarianism simply shuts off the conduits for a corrupted *amour-propre* that proliferates in commercial society.[114] And indeed in *Corsica*, Rousseau appeals to the natural egalitarianism of simple, rustic societies, citing Switzerland's insular, autarkic cantons—a 'union of men who had no masters'.[115] He claims that the introduction of commerce to the erstwhile Swiss autarkies induced a spirit of servitude and hierarchy at the expense of agrarian egalitarianism.[116] Agriculture, he claims, will sustain the 'egalitarian

---

[109] *Poland*, above n 3, Ch XI.

[110] This is supported by Cohen's view that Rousseau's 'strong assertions about the need for attention to public business' represent a 'device to prevent the dissolution the society of the general will: as conditions of the stability of the legitimate order, not as constitutive elements of the conception of legitimacy itself.': Joshua Cohen, *Rousseau: A Free Community of Equals* (Oxford, Oxford University Press, 2010) 57.

[111] '*Chacun trouve son compte dans le malheur d'autrui*': Jean-Jacques Rousseau, *Discours sur l'origine et les fondements de l'inégalité parmi les hommes* (Paris, Flammarion, 1755/2008) 41.

[112] Taking a more optimistic view, Tocqueville assumes that in the early United States, egalitarian and anti-aristocratic ideals, with a rejection of innate social hierarchies, will lead to a demand for 'material comfort' and 'moderate luxuries': Janara, above n 56, 323.

[113] Hanley, above n 58, 139.

[114] McLendon argues that since 'amour-propre is largely concerned with the problems surrounding identity construction in commercial, urban societies, [it] can be lessened to manageable levels in more rural societies, that is, agrarian provincial life.': Michael Locke McLendon, 'Rousseau and the Minimal Self: A Solution to the Problem of Amour-propre' (2014) 13 *European Journal of Political Theory* 341.

[115] *Corsica*, above n 4, 33.

[116] ibid 53. France discusses how Geneva, in particular, was a society conflicted between rustic autarky and Francophile modernisation. France, above n 6.

temperament' of the Corsican people:[117] just as autarky will prevent domination by external powers, by the same measure it stems the development of social hierarchy in Corsica.[118] Furthermore, in *Corsica*, he specifically links the accumulative dispositions of commerce with 'destructive vices', especially 'covetousness'.[119] Thus commerce is identified as an untamed, dangerous conduit for *amour-propre*, which the Constitution must re-orient towards benign forms. Stemming commerce will, by implication, re-orient the nexus of public distinction and prestige towards benign activities that are conducive to the common good. Thus, arguably Rousseau's recommendations on taxation, both in *Corsica* and the third *Discourse*, target 'surplus' wealth—especially luxuries—as much because of the corruption excess wealth causes, as they aim to mitigate economic inequality in relative or relational terms.[120]

There is a great deal of plausibility in the idea that Rousseau's objection to commerce lies largely in his view that commercial activity in itself represents a corrupted form of *amour-propre*—one which, in contrast to Smith's view, cannot be successfully remediated or tamed. However, this in itself provides an incomplete picture. Rousseau's aversion to commerce is, in some senses, simply an extension of his hostility towards what might be described, in broad terms, as social differentiation, fragmentation or specialisation—a theme that will run throughout this book. As I will develop in later chapters, Rousseau generally understands social *complexity*—whether cultural, symbolic or in this case economic—as an insidious but potent source of domination.[121] On the one hand, he advocates autarky simply because he understands that economic self-sufficiency will avoid the kinds of dependency that are entailed in complex systems of economic distribution. On the other hand, however, he associates economic complexity, and the associated division of labour, with the wider ills of social differentiation more generally. In *Corsica*, in particular, Rousseau consistently associates commerce with the emergence of liberal tastes and social practices that, in other works, he views as corrupting because they entail stratification along symbolic, ritual and cultural lines. Arguably, therefore he focuses less on the corrupting effects of commerce per se—which are quite real—and rather more on the associated social changes, not only urbanisation, but equally the growth of sophisticated culture and 'fine arts' that offer a fertile site for untamed but insidious—and ostensibly *innocent*—forms

---

[117] *Corsica*, above n 4, 30.

[118] Autarky, he notes, was ironically made possible only through Genoese repression, because its naval blockade enforced self-sufficiency. *Corsica*, above n 4, 35.

[119] '[A]s long as Corsicans use money, they will love it, and as long as they love it, the republic will be harbouring emissaries and traitors within it who will influence its deliberations and will pawn the State to masters;: *Corsica*, above n 4, 86.

[120] Hanley notes: 'One of the most striking elements of the third Discourse is a seemingly ubiquitous antipathy to the wealthy.': Hanley, above n 100, 13.

[121] Indeed in *Corsica* Rousseau frequently invokes the virtue of 'simplicity'—both in relation to agrarian occupations as well as the system of government itself.

of *amour-propre*.[122] He laments that the egalitarianism of Switzerland's erstwhile autarky was undermined by the influence of foreign 'tastes' which, he suggests, led to the emergence of new social hierarchies.[123] He is hostile to commerce in large part because he associates it with the emergence of bourgeois lifestyles—which, while associated (in a quite gendered way)[124] with 'inane vanity' or 'softness and debauchery',[125] are politically destructive essentially because, as well as obviously dulling the martial virtues, they involve competition for largely meaningless and arbitrary forms of social distinction.[126] Thus in summary, commerce is bound up with a broader, destructive bourgeois *habitus* that Rousseau understands as fundamentally inconsistent with republican goals.

Thus while I will discuss Rousseau's approach to culture and symbolic power in the next chapter, it is worth noting that his aversion to commerce is in some senses an extension of a broader aversion to societies that are structured by competition for *private* distinction—that is, where *amour-propre* is consummated in private forums (including through economic accumulation) and through highly specialised social pursuits (in the cultural and social life of commercial societies). As I will further develop in chapters three and four in particular, his redemptive ambition is that the sources of social distinction must be rendered public—and radically transparent. Only in such a society can the virtues of the general will be realised. While commercial life involves the kind of competitiveness that might be inconsistent with republican virtues, more importantly early-modern commerce thrives in the kind of divided, fractured societies where the sources of distinction become increasingly complex and specialised. Commerce begets, and arises in the context of, insidious social hierarchy, because Rousseau understands the convertibility of economic capital vis-à-vis other kinds of capital, such as social and cultural capital.[127] A society structured around competition for economic capital will, he conjectures, orient people towards competition for other, related forms of capital, to the point where the sources of esteem and approbation become highly esoteric and quasi-invisible. His idea is that citizens who compete for diffuse, esoteric sources of distinction cannot discern the general interest as they are distanced, figuratively speaking, from the austere peasants deliberating under the 'oak tree' in a holistic and transparent social order.

Commerce, then, is destructive not merely because of its proximate corrupting effects, but because of the deep ways in which it structures subjectivities

---

[122] See further ch 3.
[123] *Corsica*, above n 4, 45–46.
[124] While, like Montesqueiu, Rousseau was concerned that the 'commerce of luxury' would entail 'moral vice', unlike Montesquieu—who saw luxury as having a moderating effect—he believed that 'the moral decline of society brought on by the loss of female modesty is too high a price to pay for the increased liberty sought by Montesquieu.' See Mary L Bellhouse, 'Femininity and Commerce in the Eighteenth Century: Rousseau's Criticism of a Literary Ruse by Montesquieu' (1980) 13 *Polity* 285, 294.
[125] *Corsica*, above n 4, 40.
[126] See further ch 3.
[127] See further ch 3.

and subjecthood. An austere agrarianism—underpinned by constitutional mechanisms—serves as a framework for a society that is radically egalitarian in the sense of rejecting social differentiation or specialisation. Autarky not only prevents material inequalities, but also stems the emergence of new axes of distinction based on culture and taste.

Thus to an extent, the Constitution will promote an autarkical political economy so as to stem the emergence of broader, complex economy of social distinction that Rousseau sees as engendering hierarchy and alienation even in early-modern societies. Commercial society is unsuitable for republican politics because the sources of distinction are privatised. In turn, this underlines how Rousseau does not aim to promote an authentic way of life *for its own sake*—as part of a perfectionist or romantic commitment—but rather because he understands that commercial society engenders dangerous dynamics of social distinction that threaten republican political goals. Thus Rousseau's commitment to a simple, agrarian social order can be understood to a large extent as an effort to stem social complexity as part of his broader aim of 'making the community itself a source of the esteem sought by individuals.'[128]

It is worth emphasising the sheer breadth and scope of Rousseau's hostility to commerce, wealth and economic inequality relative to the wider republican history of thought. Ancient Greek and Roman republicans certainly sought to check economic inequality. However, typically they viewed disparate or excessive wealth as problematic only because of its capacity to engender power imbalances that threatened to constitute political domination—they did not understand wealth as such as being inconsistent with civic virtue.[129] They identified 'the threat posed to liberty by economic inequality', but without problematising wealth as such[130]— and their constitutional measures against excessive inequality were, correspondingly, a great deal more modest than what Rousseau proposes.[131] By contrast, Rousseau was not merely concerned that economic inequality would allow the rich to monopolise political power, but rather that wealth *as such* was inconsistent with republican virtue. His prescriptions for land redistribution in *Corsica* echo, for example, the Gracchis' agrarian laws in the late Roman republic, and we can surmise that they partly reflect a similar aim of preventing excessive concentrations of power:[132] yet they are part of a wider, more radical set of measures that problematise wealth at a much deeper level.

---

[128] Frederick Neuhouser, 'Freedom, Dependence and the General Will' (1993) 102 *Philosophical Review* 363, 390.
[129] McCormick, above n 95.
[130] ibid 880.
[131] However, McCormick points out that unlike Athens, which tolerated a degree of economic inequality, 'Aristocratic Sparta, by contrast, attempted to secure its own ideal of civic liberty by substituting economic equality for political equality.': ibid 881.
[132] McCormick: 'The Agrarian Laws, sponsored by Tiberius and Gaius Gracchus, limited the amount of public lands any citizen could hold, and redistributed to the plebeians public lands already held in custody by wealthy Romans. In the *Discorsi*, Machiavelli marks the reform efforts of these

Of course the contrast can be overdrawn, and Rousseau's distinctiveness exaggerated. Machiavelli—who sought a greater degree of socio-economic equality than had the ancient Romans—said, quite mysteriously, that 'well-ordered republics must keep the public rich and citizens poor.'[133] Yet on the whole, historical republicans tended to treat questions of economic distribution in view of a broader concern for maintaining balances or harmonies of political and social power. Even Machiavelli, who saw the Roman measures against inequality as insufficient, was concerned primarily with the question of how inequality engendered political domination.[134] On the one hand, I have argued that commerce, for Rousseau, undermines republican virtue simply because economic inequality begets other, more insidious axes of hierarchy, based in particular on culture and taste. As I will argue later in the book, Rousseau, more than Marx, understands the extent to which cultural capital and symbolic power represent semi-autonomous determinants of social power. On the other hand, however, commercial life itself is understood as intrinsically corrupting given its promotion of runaway, untamed *amour-propre*. Thus, again, a convincing interpretation of his autarkical politics is that it aims to tame *amour-propre* so as to ensure it is consummated and channelled in benign forms—a theme built upon in later chapters.[135]

I have said relatively little about the specific demands or components of civic virtue, and rather more about the sources and nature of corruption. And perhaps indeed, Rousseau largely views virtue in negative terms, as an absence of corruption rather than as a complex process of moral elevation—as the 'simple goodness [that is] natural to [citizens] in their uncorrupted, self-sufficient state.'[136] Indeed Douglass, in particular, argues that Rousseau never abandons 'nature', and its 'inalienable gifts', as a regulative standard for political society.[137] As I discuss further in chapter four, the virtues of the general will are not understood as deliberative virtues of public reason, to be acquired as a specific set of intellectual or cognitive

---

ill-fated brothers as a decisive moment in the history of the Republic.': ibid 885. Montesquieu, noted: 'The indefinite permission to make testaments, granted among the Romans, gradually ruined the political provision on the sharing of lands; more than anything else it introduced the ominous difference between wealth and poverty; ... some citizens had too much, an infinity of others had nothing. Thus, the people, continually deprived of their share, constantly asked for a new distribution of lands.' Charles-Louis Montesquieu, *Spirit of the Laws* (Cambridge, Cambridge University Press, 1748/1989) 523. And like Machiavelli, James Harrington—who was influential amongst the American founders—argued that Roman republicanism declined through 'negligence committed in their agrarian laws.': James Harrington, *The Commonwealth of Oceana* (Pocock ed, 1992) 43; cited in Sitaraman, above n 35, 1316.

[133] McCormick, above n 95, 885.
[134] ibid.
[135] Thus, 'by giving its citizens a reciprocally granted equal status, the society of the social contract tames amour-propre.': Robert Jubb, 'Rawls and Rousseau: *Amour-propre* and the Strains of Commitment' (2011) 17 *Res Publica* 245, 250.
[136] Hanley, above n 58, 139.
[137] Robin Douglass, *Rousseau and Hobbes: Nature, Free Will and the Passions* (Oxford, Oxford University Press) 10–12.

skills. Rather, they are understood, in largely a-rational terms, as emerging spontaneously within appropriate social frameworks. Civic virtue flourishes more or less spontaneously in the absence of the kinds of corruption wrought by modern, fragmented social orders. Civic virtue is not, then, the product of any specific acculturation or socialisation; rather, it flourishes in a peculiar kind of social life and political economy. Indeed, Rousseau conceives of civic virtue largely in relation to ostensibly apolitical practices. Mysteriously, he says 'the best vehicle of government is the love of the polity, and this love can be cultivated in the fields.'[138] Thus what is required, for the general will to be perceived, is not any specific deliberative skill but rather the kinds of affect and solidarity that flourish in a holistic, and austere social order. In an illuminating passage in *The Social Contract*, he refers to the general will being discernible 'only through good sense'—by 'peasants gathered under an oak'.[139] Citizens, then, do not need to be specifically trained or educated for political engagement. The irony is perhaps that in other contexts, radically austere ways of life—such as practised, for example, by religious communities—are often interpreted as a threat to republican and democratic politics, because they seem to entail complete disengagement from politics and the state.[140] Indeed ostensibly, austerity is *dour* and introspective, and rejects the expressivity and openness associated with democratic sociability.

At one level, Rousseau seems to express nostalgia for a cohesive and holistic social order, railing against the (then embryonic) fragmented world of liberal individualism. Indeed, many of his Enlightenment contemporaries expressed fascination with the remnants of 'primitivism' in a modernising Europe.[141] In vaunting pastoral life and the family, he uses the metaphor of the *patrie* as a human body, contracting vice like 'disease'[142]—in a way that seems to locate and value the individual as part of an organic social order rather than as an abstract moral agent. However, what is ostensibly a nostalgic utopia—a virtuous autarky—is actually an expression of bracing realism as to how a politics of civic virtue can be realised. Again, Rousseau is sceptical as to how common goods can prevail over factional interests in highly fragmented and differentiated societies, and so offers an uncompromising account of what is necessary in order for an authentic republican politics to take life. Liberal thinkers like Rawls imagine citizens reasoning from a standpoint of abstract, hypothetical symmetry (the 'original position'), in which they set aside their particular interests and identities.[143] In turn, he is remarkably optimistic as to how the principles decided in this original position

---

[138] *Corsica*, above n 4, 82.
[139] *Social Contract*, above n 2, Bk IV, Ch I.
[140] For example, in United States constitutional law the quintessentially austere Amish way of life was pitted against the state's interest in citizens receiving a minimal degree of formal education. *Wisconsin v Yoder* 406 US 205 (1972).
[141] France, above n 6.
[142] *Corsica*, above n 4, 67.
[143] John Rawls, *Political Liberalism* (Cambridge MA, Harvard University Press, 1996).

are sustainably endorsed and instantiated in a society that is highly fragmented, diverse and a-symmetrical. In a sense then, the conjecture underlying Rousseau's constitutionalism is that the virtues of public reason can be realised only in a context of substantive social equality. In short, underlying Rousseau's directive constitutionalism is a highly demanding interpretation of what is required in order for a politics of public reason to take life. His socially directive constitutionalism is not predicated on the desirability of an authentic, austere way of life for its own sake, but is best understood as a response to the socio-economic grounds of servitude and domination.

IV. Rousseau's Concept of Constitutionalism

Compared with contemporary constitutional thought—for which arguably—'liberal constitutionalism simply *is* constitutionalism'[144]—Rousseau's constitutional project is distinctive partly because it assumes an avowedly interventionist role in shaping the dispositions and virtues of citizens. It is distinctive, on the one hand, because it is a socially-directive constitutionalism, which in itself sets it apart from a liberal constitutionalism—or its Anglo-American variant at least—that traditionally is focused only on political structures and negative individual liberties. But more pertinently, it is distinct from our contemporary constitutionalism because it aims directly to mould and shape citizens' characters, in a way that is ostensibly reminiscent of ancient concepts.[145]

In this light, the contrast between Rousseau's constitutionalism and our contemporary version is both a contrast concerning what aims and purposes a good constitution should have, but also one concerning the basic concept of a constitution. How can we relate Rousseau's ostensibly alien understanding both of the concept and purpose of a constitution to our contemporary thought? Of course, Rousseau wrote (just) before the period, following the American and French revolutions, that gave birth to our now dominant understanding of a constitution as a master-law or even as a consciously created political code—or, in Paine's understanding, as a 'conscious formulation by a people of its fundamental law.'[146] It has been argued that 'what we understand as the political constitution in modernity has become unduly narrowed to the institutional coordination of governance and the recognition of private rights'.[147] And in this light, Rousseau's project not

---

[144] Mark Tushnet, 'Varieties of Constitutionalism' (Editorial) (2016) 14 *International Journal of Constitutional Law* 1, 2.

[145] Russell Hardin, 'Why a Constitution?' in Dennis Galligan and Milla Versteeg (eds), *Social and Political Foundations of Constitutions* (Cambridge, Cambridge University Press, 2013).

[146] Charles McIlwain, *Constitutionalism Ancient and Modern* (Indianapolis, Liberty Press, 2010, first published 1940) 2.

[147] Alun Howard Gibbs, 'The Horizons of the Constitution: *Politeia*, the Political Regime and the Good' (2016) 27 *Law and Critique* 83, 86.

only assumes a different, wider set of objects and goals, but reflects a wider, and ostensibly classical concept of constitutionalism itself. This concept of a Constitution corresponds to what Strauss describes in classical thought as 'the regime' or *politeia*—which is 'the order, the form, which gives society its character ... a specific manner of life ... the form of life living together, the manner of living of society.'[148] Rousseau's constitutionalism, while relating the structure of the state to the sovereign people, is contiguous with this kind of social vision—with a concept of *politeia* that embraces the state's 'whole economic and social texture as well as matters governmental in our narrow modern sense.'[149] And this points to something of a puzzle, because whereas Rousseau seemingly follows an 'older tradition of linking *politeia* to "the good"',[150] it was the shift away from the question of the good towards that of power which allowed the centrality of popular sovereignty—which Rousseau embraces—as displacing an older, different 'sense of collectiveness as the basis for political community.'[151]

Thus Rousseau's constitutionalism, in terms of concept and perhaps form, is ambiguously poised between ancient (or archaicising) and modern. While like the ancients, he understands the Constitution holistically, as incorporating not only 'the whole life of the state'[152] but also as 'embod[ying] a scheme of life',[153] equally, nonetheless, he sees it not as a purely organic, evolutionary order but as a self-conscious and highly contingent political act—not, perhaps, 'enacted', legislatively, in the sense of constituent power, but contrived by great men amidst fraught circumstances and fortuitous contexts.

As for the *purpose* as distinct from the concept of Rousseau's constitutionalism—that is, its purpose in promoting virtue—it is worth pointing out that any constitutional system will, of course, impact citizens' dispositions and subjectivities at least indirectly. But Rousseau is explicit in *embracing* such a role. In *Poland*, for example, he asserts that the institutional devices he recommends will 'shape the genius, character, tastes and manners of [the] people.'[154] More stridently, he suggests that an autarkic constitution will rid Corsica of 'vices contracted during its servitude'.[155] And what is striking in particular is that his constitutional prescriptions are squarely and directly aimed at fostering favoured dispositions not just in the narrow domain of the political—as per the familiar republican account—but across all social domains. In turn, this reflects his understanding, as outlined in chapter one—that domination is deeply rooted in ostensibly mundane social practice. Based on this very concern, Rousseau unreservedly commits to a kind of

---

[148] As cited in Gibbs, ibid 86.
[149] McIlwain, above n 146, 22.
[150] Gibbs, above n 147, 100.
[151] ibid.
[152] McIlwain, above n 146, 22.
[153] William Newman, *The Politics of Aristotle* (Oxford, Oxford University Press, 1902) 210.
[154] *Poland*, above n 3, Ch III.
[155] *Corsica*, above n 4, 49.

social determinism in his constitutional thought, seeking to shape preferred dispositions across all of social life and not merely in the political domain. In *Corsica*, we might recall, he aims 'to determine [Corsicans] pleasures, desires, tastes ... to guide and set limits to their ambitions.'[156] And he sees culture, in anti-essentialist terms, as pliable and capable of manipulation; he says of the Corsicans, for example, that 'every people has or should have a national character, and *if it lacks this, we must start by giving it one*.'[157] Ardour and 'industriousness' are not given features of a people, but rather, can be fostered and maintained by appropriate institutional mechanisms (at least given certain fortuitous circumstances).[158]

One of the definitive premises of liberal democratic constitutional thought is that it cannot be a function of the state, or of the Constitution, to promote a favoured conception of the good or a particular ethical theory. This draws upon liberal philosophers like Dworkin but especially Rawls, who influentially argued that in a context of ethical and moral pluralism, the 'public conception of justice' could not rest on any 'comprehensive doctrine', whether religious or philosophical.[159] The liberal state must disavow any aim to elevate the character of its citizens at least according to a specific philosophical or religious understanding. And the constitutional cultures of liberal polities like the United States have, in general, wholeheartedly embraced this view. If anything, the constitutional machinery will aim to *check* or resist any attempt at inculcating particular, specific 'comprehensive doctrines'—for example, in clauses guaranteeing religious liberty or prohibiting establishment of religions, and so on.

Many contemporary thinkers, especially republicans and communitarians, have convincingly challenged the liberal idea that the state can, or indeed should, somehow remain neutral with respect to competing conceptions of the good, or citizens' characters and dispositions.[160] As Bellamy convincingly argues, it is in any event impossible to coordinate or reconcile competing rights-claims without reference to some substantive account of human flourishing.[161] And to an extent, divorcing questions of the good from the realm of constitutionalism is not merely a philosophical question concerning the legitimate ends of state power: equally it has been argued that from Machiavelli onwards, the very concept of the Constitution or the regime came to be characterised, in a context of assumed social conflict, by a focus on *power* rather than on the good.[162] To an extent, then, the eschewal of the good in constitutional thinking simply reflected the growing autonomy of politics in the post-medieval world.[163]

---

[156] ibid 51.
[157] ibid 43, emphasis added.
[158] ibid 82.
[159] Rawls, above n 143.
[160] See, eg, Michael Sandel, *Liberalism and the Limits of Justice* (Cambridge, Cambridge University Press, 1998).
[161] Bellamy, above n 76.
[162] Gibbs, above n 147, 87–88.
[163] ibid 89.

On the one hand, it is of course unrealistic in the first instance to believe that liberal institutions, which *claim* neutrality as to citizens' characters or life plans, in fact have no formative role or influence with respect to identity and subjectivity.[164] More specifically, contemporary republicans in particular have argued that it is unfeasible to promote non-domination as a social and economic project while observing strict 'neutrality' in the liberal sense. Maynor, for example, argues that since republicanism 'affects the whole of an individual's life',[165] it has a transformative and structuring effect across all social relations, and therefore must reject liberal ideas of neutrality. And others question whether any republican project can confine itself to promoting virtues in a narrow, public domain. Weithman, for example, questions whether republican virtues can be confined to the 'political' domain, disconnected from broader understandings of human excellence. He points out that for ancient republicans, 'private' moral virtues such as 'temperance' were indissociable from 'civic' or political virtues in the narrower sense, and that these are needed to give life to republican aims.[166,167] This is probably why many historical republican thinkers rejected any sharp distinction between civic virtue and moral virtue as such. John Adams, for example, insisted 'public virtue cannot exist … without private.'[168]

Moreover, contemporary 'real-world' republican discourse offers plenty of examples of states committing to more expansive, transformative notions of civic virtue, rejecting Rawlsian strictures. Laborde notes that the French-republican tradition, in particular, has aimed not simply to promote narrowly political virtues but also 'the more demanding virtues of mutual empathy and even altruistic devotion to the community of citizens'—this being needed to provide the requisite 'motivational anchorage'[169] for republican citizenship.

In one sense then, the liberal claim of neutrality is historically anomalous. Eisgruber notes the 'long and venerable tradition to the idea that constitutions shape the character of citizens living under them.'[170] And it has been argued that while 'in the classical understanding of *politeia* there is a significant connection

---

[164] For a related discussion see John Maynor, 'Without Regret: the Comprehensive Nature of Non-domination' (2002) 22 *Politics* 51; Paul Weithman, 'Political Republicanism and Perfectionist Republicanism' (2004) 66 *The Review of Politics* 294.

[165] Maynor, ibid 51.

[166] Weithman, above n 164, 300.

[167] Honohan argues that citizens in contemporary states must be educated towards an awareness of their 'shared common predicament and common fate': they must have an awareness that their own private good—and the good of their families and localities—is intimately connected with that common good. They must understand how their own interests are so profoundly bound up in the interests of their fellow citizens. Iseult Honohan, 'Educating Citizens' in Iseult Honohan and Jeremy Jennings (eds), *Republicanism in Theory and Practice* (London, Routledge, 2015) 199.

[168] Adrienne Kock and William Peden, *The Selected Writings of John and John Quincy Adams* (New York, Knopf, 1946) 52.

[169] Cecile Laborde, 'On Republican Toleration' (2002) 9 *Constellations* 167, 176.

[170] Christopher Eisgruber, 'Civic Virtue and the Limits of Constitutionalism' (2001) 69 *Fordham Law Review* 2131, 2133.

between the question of the "good" and the constitution', this 'has become occluded or obscured by modern constitutional thought.'[171] In this light, Rousseau's thought appears, ostensibly at least, to belong within a tradition of anti-liberal, perfectionist constitutionalism that eschews neutrality and aims to promote specific concepts of virtue. However I will argue that while Rousseau rejects any piecemeal project of civic virtue in a narrowly defined public or political realm, its radicalism and breadth should not be confused with any commitment to philosophical perfectionism as such. The social determinism and the radical social scope of Rousseau's constitutional project should not be confused with its *philosophical* scope. It is true that Rousseau has a certain sense of the good life—based on authenticity and virtue—in agrarian, holistic societies, and particularly in the 'Golden Age' that he speculatively imagines between the state of nature and the onset of agriculture and social complexity.[172] However, in an idea that will be further developed throughout this book I will argue that austerity, in Rousseau's autarkies, is not aimed at promoting a particular vision of human flourishing as such. Rather, it stems, ultimately, from a desire to combat insidious forms of social domination that he associates with more complex, differentiated societies that began to emerge in the early-modern period. Thus its classical focus on the 'good' can be overstated, and its thoroughly *modern* orientation obscured.

V. Autarky between Realism and Utopia

In one sense, the link Rousseau identifies between constitutionalism and economic structure is entirely familiar, both in ancient and early modern thought.[173] It seems anomalous only by reference to very recent historical norms: indeed 'throughout history, economic division—the division between the rich and poor—was a central preoccupation of constitutional theory and design.'[174] Nonetheless to the contemporary mind, and perhaps even by eighteenth century standards, Rousseau's specific autarkical prescriptions seems outlandish and implausible.[175] In short, the societies he depicts in *Corsica* and *Poland* seem highly utopian, particularly in the

---

[171] Gibbs, above n 147, 83.
[172] Douglass, above n 137, Chs 1–2.
[173] Sitaraman notes: 'For most of the history of political thought, one of the central problems of constitutional design was the relationship between the distribution of wealth in society and the structure of government." Sitaraman, above n 35, 1301.
[174] Sitaraman distinguishes between 'class-warfare' constitutions, aimed at mitigating class conflict by incorporating different classes into government, and 'middle-class' constitutions, such as the United States constitution, that relied upon and presupposed a broad-based and numerous middle class possessing the temperate virtues necessary for republican government. ibid 1305.
[175] Putterman considers whether or not they are serious recommendations as distinct from social polemic. Ethan Putterman, 'Realism and Reform in Rousseau's Constitutional Projects for Corsica and Poland' (2001) 49 *Political Studies* 481.

degree of harmony and social cohesion he envisages. This is not, emphatically the (relative) harmony of the Machiavellian or even the Aristotelian republics, which are all premised, to some extent, on a balance, equilibrium of creative tension between classes and interests—in a context of assumed *conflict* and indeed of difference. Yet the very point of Rousseau's autarkic republics—in particular, *Corsica*—is, arguably, that they are effectively classless, or at least with minimal class differentiation, and free of the associated tensions and conflicts. He even uses the metaphor of the body, rid of 'vices contracted during servitude', to describe the harmony and strength of Corsica following freedom from Genoese rule.[176] Again, this is something of a puzzle because this orientation towards the 'good', towards seeing a Constitution as contiguous with a given way of life, seems historically anomalous with the post-Machiavellian shift to questions of conflict and power.

Of course, we must always consider the moral costs of political utopias. On the surface, Rousseau's autarky seems to demand the kind of strict social cohesion that undermines individual autonomy and the plurality, ethical and cultural, of public life. It seems individuals must forsake prosperity and its benefits for the sake of freedom.[177] Agrarian austerity seems perversely severe and demanding as a political project. At some points, at least, it seems to entail 'the recreation of Sparta within modernity—replete with abnegation of all self-interest and the extreme and austere politics which has subversion of self-interest as its primary end.'[178] On the other hand, I will argue in chapter three that Rousseau does not, in fact, understand austerity in terms of dour self-sacrifice; rather it is pleasurable and joyful. Indeed if the prosperity and even the pluralism offered by commercial society simply engender and express a corrupted *amour-propre*, they are no great loss, after all. In this view, Rousseau does not seek the sacrifice of private interest, but only the recovery of *authentic* private interest that is naturally harmonious and consistent with the general will.[179] Since this is a utopia, these are not moral costs—at least if we take his project on its own terms.

Some have argued that Rousseau's suggestions are not *serious* reform plans—that they are intended as provocation and social polemic in the changing world of mid-eighteenth century Europe.[180] Yet while it is impossible to deny that Rousseau's autarky has at least certain airs of utopia, counter-intuitively it also expresses an avowed realism as to the possibility of republican politics under specific, historically contingent social circumstances. As I have already argued, the radicalism of

---

[176] *Corsica*, above n 4, 49.
[177] For Downing and Thigpen, *prosperity* may be considered part of the common good, as it will enable the pursuit of diverse ways of lives; austerity, however, only facilitates 'ascetic' life plans. Lyle Downing and Robert Thigpen, 'Virtue and the Common Good in Liberal Theory' (1993) 55 *Journal of Politics* 1046, 1052.
[178] Hanley, above n 100, 20.
[179] For discussion see Steven Affeldt, 'The Force of Freedom: Rousseau on Forcing to be Free' (1999) 27 *Political Theory* 299.
[180] For discussion and rebuttal, see Putterman, above n 175.

his constitutional prescriptions stems from his understanding of the difficulties of realising a politics of the common good in a transactional, atomised world defined by commerce and the pursuit of private interest. Again, this suggests that far from being a romantic utopia, Rousseau's autarky expresses a bracing realism as to the social and economic preconditions of republican politics.

In one sense, then, Rousseau's austerity reflects a peculiar, and realist, understanding of *stability*—that is to say, a theory as to how an abstract political philosophy, whether of freedom and justice, can be realised and sustained under real social conditions. According to one view, the republic Rousseau imagines, whether abstractly in the *Social Contract* or concretely in Poland and Corsica, is intended as fatalistic social polemic rather than as a project that can feasibly be realised in real, contemporaneous European societies—or at best, as part of a distant political horizon rather than a plausible political project. However, what his autarkical politics indicates is, in fact, a concern for questions of feasibility, and specifically, as to how radical republican ideas around freedom and self-government could be realised, in specific historical societies, by harnessing fortuitous circumstances—such as Corsican rusticity and isolation—so as to engineer and sustain the kind of social circumstances in which a republican politics might succeed. Rousseau's flexibility in his prescriptions for Corsica and Poland demonstrates an understanding that in order to realise abstract political ideals, constitutional mechanisms must adapt to and harness contingent historical, cultural and even geographical features. One of the challenges of constitutional design, in effect, is to exploit contingent local particularisms so as to promote and sustain the social conditions of republican politics. Corsican isolation and rusticity suggest autarkical mechanisms, but other societies, with different resources, might require alternative devices and forms.[181] Indeed Rousseau echoes Montesquieu in suggesting: 'there is in the nature and soil of every country certain qualities which render a certain form of government more apt than others, and every form of government will tend to influence its peoples towards particular types of occupations'.[182] 'Good legislation', he says, will 'cultivate and exploit their own strengths.'[183]

By contrast, liberalism offers implausibly optimistic accounts of how principles of justice can be realised under intractable conditions of scarcity and conflict: Rawls, for examples, envisages an 'overlapping consensus' in which people with conflicting 'conceptions of the good' endorse a 'public conception of justice' based on their common faculties of reason.[184] But for Rousseau, like other anti-liberals, the central problem of politics is not our disagreement as to the 'good life', or question of ultimate truth. Rather, the challenge of political co-existence, in conditions

---

[181] In *Poland*, Rousseau affirmed "each country has advantages peculiar to itself which should be extended and fostered by its constitution." *Poland*, above n 3, Ch XIII.

[182] *Corse*, above n 4, 32.

[183] ibid 29. Yet conversely, in *Poland*, he affirmed: 'it is national institutions which shape the genius, character, tastes and manners of a people.' *Poland*, above n 3, Ch III.

[184] Rawls, above n 143.

of scarcity and conflict, is defined in large part by affect and sentiment, which in turn are dependent on social and economic life. The sources of stability (in this sense) lie in social and economic structure, rather than in the intellectual consensus Rawls envisages.[185]

Rousseau's radical autarky of course imposes burdens of the kind that contemporary neo-republicans will reject. In particular, as I have said, his scheme seems to sacrifice pluralism and diversity for the sake of republican social cohesion. The romantic autarky Rousseau sketches—with its isolationist monoculture—seems to engender a stifling social conformism, and at worst, brute assimilation. Crucially, on the one hand, Rousseau downplays the role of direct coercion in suppressing dispositions and vices thought of as undermining republican aims. Rather, civic virtues will flow more or less spontaneously from an autarkic and agrarian political economy. On the other hand, however, Rousseau's radical response to the problem of stability raises the perennial question as to how—if at all—the rather demanding requirements of republican citizenship can be reconciled with the highly individuated and fragmented nature of liberal social orders. It raises the challenge as to how the more optimistic, liberal version of republicanism associated especially with Philip Pettit—sometimes labelled Atlanticist or Italian-Atlantic, and which firmly repudiates Rousseau—can reconcile its goals of non-domination with the political economy of capitalism and its inherent instability. The radicalism of Rousseau's social framework for republican politics reveals, in particular, how pessimistic—or perhaps realistic—he is, compared to the neo-republicans, concerning the intractable and insidious nature of domination in economic and social life. The emphasis in his constitutional writings on the elusive nature of republican virtue, and the challenge of sustaining it to the requisite extent, reinforces the view that for Rousseau, 'a free republic ... is not something natural but ... a very unusual and fragile human construct.'[186]

Thus Rousseau's diagnosis of the sources and constitution of inequality and domination, within a liberal society fashioned by the spirit of commerce, highlights important weaknesses in neo-republican theory and its mechanisms of actualisation in diverse, fragmented societies. While it is true that Rousseau's austere antidote to a deeply insidious social and economic domination might itself engender a countervailing form of statist domination, conversely more liberal, optimistic versions of republicanism—which are more complacent as to the social framework of republican virtue—seem 'bereft of mechanisms for realising their vision'.[187] Even Rousseau's own liberal (near) contemporaries—while optimistic—understood the immense challenge of stability, and particularly the problem of

---

[185] Jubb, above n 135.
[186] Margaret Canovan, 'Arendt, Rousseau, and Human Plurality in Politics' (1983) 45 *Journal of Politics* 286, 289.
[187] Goodin, above n 55, 56.

maintaining free political institutions in the face of atomisation and inequality. From Ferguson to Constant, they understood that 'private autonomy generates huge inequalities and shapes new patterns of subordination that undermine the moral and institutional conditions of a free political community.'[188] Such insights are arguably underappreciated by contemporary 'neo-republican' thinkers.

While Rousseau's focus on political economy—and particularly economic equality—seems archaic and out of kilter with contemporary constitutional thought, in some ways it speaks to nascent contemporary concerns as to the inefficacy of our constitutional structures and forms in stemming ascendant threats to political freedom—and especially the spectre of oligarchic domination. On the one hand, the framers of the United States Constitution understood (relative) economic equality amongst citizens—largely rural freeholders—as a prerequisite of political stability and freedom.[189] And 'from the beginning of the Republic through roughly the New Deal, Americans vividly understood that the guarantees of the Constitution are intertwined with the structure of our economic life',[190] while favouring policies that precluded excessive concentration of land ownership in particular.[191] Today, this tradition of constitutional political economy is 'dormant', but there are signs of renewed interest in view of the apparent inefficacy of liberal institutions and forms against oligarchic drift[192]—even if such anti-oligarchic or egalitarian imperatives are difficult to express within the court-centric culture of contemporary constitutionalism.[193]

In more general terms, perhaps Rousseau's enduring insight, again, is that the affective and dispositional resources of republican self-government are deeply

---

[188] Kalyvas and Katznelson, above n 49, 58.

[189] Sitaraman, above n 35.

[190] Fishkin and Forbath note: 'Throughout the nineteenth and early twentieth centuries, reformers of widely different stripes [argued] that we cannot keep our constitutional democracy—our "republican form of government"—without certain essentials: constitutional restraints against oligarchy and a political economy that sustains a robust, wide-open middle class, broad enough to accommodate everyone ... arguments about constitutional political economy begin from the premises that economics and politics are inextricable and that our constitutional order rests on and presupposes a political-economic order.': Fishkin and Forbath, above n 91, 1289.

[191] Sitaraman, above n 35.

[192] 'With few notable exceptions, constitutional theorists rarely discuss the distribution of wealth in society in ways that implicate the basic structure of the Constitution.': ibid 1303.

[193] Fishkin and Forbath note: 'The conventions of our contemporary constitutional discourse hold—to oversimplify slightly—that the only real constitutional claims are ones enforceable, at least in principle, by courts. These conventions suggest that constitutional claims are political conversation stoppers that set boundaries on the scope of democratic policy making. Part of [our] project is to help readers see beyond these current conventions and to recover a different way of thinking about American constitutionalism ... For the proponents of the democracy of opportunity tradition, arguments about constitutional political economy were not outside constraints on democratic politics. They were the substance of a democratic constitutional politics. Far from being conversation stoppers, they were at the heart of one side of a series of great national debates over how to understand the relationship between our Constitution and our economic and political life ... Today, there is only one group that consistently makes arguments about constitutional political economy: the libertarian right. Libertarians have a substantive vision of a political and economic order they believe the Constitution requires. They have long translated that vision into rights claims that can be enforced in court.': Fishkin and Forbath, above n 91, 1290.

dependent on social and economic structures. Thus his eccentric autarkical project helps to illustrate a concept of constitutionalism that aims not only to coordinate and to constrain state power, in the liberal-democratic mould, but that has a *directive* function: that of fostering dispositions and social conditions that will facilitate a certain kind of politics. What this shows, amongst other things, is that the contemporary debate concerning the social horizons of constitutionalism has important antecedents in Rousseau's thought. The directive nature of Rousseau's constitutionalism can be mistaken for a perfectionist or a romantic commitment: that is to say, that his constitutional devices are aimed at encouraging certain patterns of life because they correspond to a particular notion of what a good life is—that is, to a particular understanding of human flourishing. For Hanley, for example, Rousseau understands early-modern liberalism as heralding an 'assault on human excellence', which he laments with reference to the 'nobler virtues' of the ancients.[194] And indeed, ostensibly this is the horizon and premise of directive and anti-liberal constitutionalisms which—as Walker puts it—are aimed at 'channel[ing] the energies of individuals toward favored patterns of life.'[195] However, I argue that his directive constitutionalism is not premised on fostering a particular vision of human flourishing or excellence as such, but is, rather, aimed at promoting freedom—albeit understood in a particular way. And specifically, austerity is promoted not as a vision of the good life, but simply as means of combating various insidious kinds of domination that Rousseau sees as being embedded in liberal social orders. Thus I have argued that Rousseau's socially directive constitutionalism reflects a wholly different understanding concerning the nature and source of servitude in social relations, which ultimately stems from the anthropology and historical genealogy of unfreedom outlined in the second *Discourse*.

VI. Conclusion

The overall argument of this book is that Rousseau's constitutionalism aims to promote austerity, broadly speaking, as a social framework within which the abstract republican ideals of the *Social Contract* can sustainably be realised. In this chapter I have explored the economic dimensions of this austerian constitutionalism. And Rousseau's prescription of autarky, as a foil against social and economic domination, reveals a great deal concerning his understanding the sources and structure of inequality and domination in emergent, liberal social orders. The autarkical turn of Rousseau's constitutional thought is clearly implausible in our contemporary politics. However, the enduring question is how constitutional structures relate to the economic and social dimensions of republican freedom.

---

[194] Hanley, above n 58, 137.
[195] Graham Walker, 'The Constitutional Good: Constitutionalism's Equivocal Moral Imperative' (1993) 26 *Polity* 91, 95.

3

The Constitution of Symbol and Ritual

> By having their minds constantly employed on the arts of luxury, [men] grow effeminate and dastardly.[1]

I. Introduction

While Rousseau's constitutional projects for Corsica and Poland focus a great deal on socio-economic issues and specifically on the goal of fostering a virtuous autarky, they also place very strong emphasis on symbols, rituals and ceremonies as an integral aspect of the constitutional order and as an instrument of republican stability in general. While such matters occupy quite a peripheral role in our contemporary, written Constitutions and attract relatively little attention in constitutional scholarship, Rousseau's symbolic and ritual focus is, nonetheless, arguably quite recognisable in our contemporary constitutional cultures and practices. In fact, it has been argued that Rousseau's constitutional prescriptions for pageantry, festivals, feasts and so forth, presage and resemble in many ways the mild ceremonial practices of our contemporary states, and their function in integrating citizens in a common identity. In turn, Rousseau might be thought of as a progenitor of the civic ritualism found in modern constitutional cultures. However, I will argue that despite the apparent parallels, symbols and rituals occupy a wholly different, more radical function in Rousseau's constitutionalism compared to ostensible later equivalents. In particular, his rituals and symbols aim not to supplement, but to supplant entirely the private ritual and symbolic practices of liberal society, which he views as fundamentally threatening to the republican order and its virtues.

Thus while Rousseau's arguments as to the corrupting effects of cultural practices are well known, I will argue that he offers a critique, pre-emptively perhaps, as to the inefficacy, futility and indeed the hypocrisy of piecemeal

---

[1] Adam Smith, *Lectures on Jurisprudence* (Indianapolis, Liberty Press, 1982) 540.

ritual and symbolic practices in liberal states whose social orders are marked by complex hierarchies rooted in distributions of cultural and symbolic capital. His civic ritualism can only be understood in light of his critique of liberal culture as an instrument of distinction and social hierarchy. Through the lens of Rousseau's wholly more radical understanding, I will consider the tensions, limits and contradictions of civic ritualism, in the broad sense, as it exists in contemporary constitutional culture. Echoing the book's wider theme, I will argue that Rousseau's focus on the ritual and symbolic dimensions of constitutional design helps to illustrate a liberal blindspot in contemporary constitutional thought concerning the source and constitution of domination itself—and particularly its presence in ostensibly innocent and mundane social forms. However, I will also consider how Rousseau's focus on political affect and emotion speaks to a peculiar object of constitutional design—the cultivation and control of the 'passions'—that is incongruously absent in contemporary constitutional thought, yet which persists, albeit obliquely, in our wider constitutional culture.

I will begin by considering why, and indeed how, contemporary Constitutions address the symbolic and the ritual and relatedly, why this question has been neglected in constitutional thought. I will then compare this with Rousseau's treatment of symbolic and ritual questions in his constitutional projects, and argue against any meaningful similarity. Finally, I will show how Rousseau's implicit rejection of piecemeal civic ritualism, coupled with his critique of privatised ritual and symbolic practices, help to illustrate a blindspot in liberal democratic constitutional thought concerning both the nature and sources of domination in liberal societies, and the function of Constitutions in fostering and channelling the political passions.

II. Symbolism and Ritualism in Contemporary Constitutional Thought

Currently, questions of ritual and symbol lie at the margins of constitutional respectability. Fundamentally, the idea that Constitutions might prescribe, enshrine or even gently cultivate the ritual and symbolic life of the state sits uneasily with the standard liberal-democratic way of understanding the proper purpose and ends of constitutionalism. According to the standard view, Constitutions properly have an allocative or coordinating function that demarcates governmental powers, usually (although not always) a 'negative' function in limiting the reach of state power through rights, and in some cases—though not traditionally in the Anglophone world—a socially-directive function, social or economic, which orients state power towards particular substantive policies or goals. While such taxonomies are of course rough and ready and contestable, the problem, in any event, is that constitutional provisions that prescribe say, flags or festivals, ceremonies and anthems, cannot easily be located within any such plausible, standard account of the functions and ends of liberal-democratic constitutionalism. Constitutions properly define the state, its functions and its relation to the people, but—it is assumed—are, or should be indifferent as to the emotional and spiritual life of both.

Perhaps this lack of enthusiasm is explained, in part, by a prevailing belief that such constitutional devices serve aims that are illicit or at least highly suspect. In practice, specific symbols and rituals may simply represent constitutional expressions of cultural or ethno-nationalist politics, placing them beyond the pale of respectable liberal aims.[2] If anything, contemporary Constitutions—far from prescribing symbols and rituals—will tend to *constrain* and regulate their deployment by public authorities (particularly, but not exclusively where they have a religious character). Some of the celebrated landmarks of liberal jurisprudence have involved courts invoking constitutional principles to protect citizens from mandatory participation in symbolic or civic rites[3]—even where such participation takes the abstract form of tax contributions.[4] For example, in *West Virginia State Board of Education v Barnette*, a majority of the United States Supreme Court concluded that while compulsory flag-saluting in public schools served a legitimate aim of fostering civic sentiment, patriotism or 'good citizenship', this could not trump individual dissent. The majority of the justices emphasised the virtues of voluntarist, organic patriotism over legally prescribed ritual exercises. Justice Jackson suggested that '[t]o believe that patriotism will not flourish if patriotic ceremonies are voluntary and spontaneous instead of a compulsory routine is to make an unflattering estimate of the appeal of our institutions to free minds.'[5]

Liberal scruples aside, any vestigial symbolic and ritual aspects of constitutional content might not be considered sinister and dangerous, but simply as trivial and unworthy of much attention. Constitutional provisions dealing with flags, anthems and other such innocent baubles might simply be viewed as embarrassing, but usually harmless anachronisms—as products of historical accident but neither as serving any useful constitutional purpose, nor, however as necessarily undermining the premise and aims of liberal-democratic constitutionalism.

At best, then, liberal thought assumes that ritual and symbolic matters are peripheral to the enterprise of constitutional design. At worst, it will be actively

---

[2] See generally Karen A Cerulo, *Identity Designs: The Sights and Sounds of a Nation* (New Brunswick NJ, Rutgers University Press, 1995).

[3] *West Virginia State Board of Education v Barnette* 319 US 624 (1943). For Justice Frankfurter, dissenting (at 662), the judgment effectively denied the state 'the power to employ educational symbols.' Eric A Posner, 'Symbols, Signals, and Social Norms in Politics and Law' (1998) 27 *Journal of Legal Studies* 765.

[4] See, eg, *Everson v Board of Education* 330 US 1 (1947); *Engel v Vitale* 370 US 421 (1962); *Committee for Public Education v Nyquist* 413 US 756 (1973); *Grand; Rapids School Dist v Ball* 473 US 373 (1985); *Larkin v Grendel's Den* 459 US 116 (1982).

[5] Above n 3, 643. He also states: 'Love of country must spring from willing hearts and free mind (at 641).'

apprehensive towards constitutional content that assumes an identity-affirming function that it considers illicit. And of course, 'constitutional' theory—the theory that is concerned with the functions and purposes of constitutions—will be informed, directly or indirectly, by such substantive political theory concerning, say, the legitimate purposes and ends of state power more generally.

In any event, it is anomalous that while symbolic and ritual provisions persist even in quintessentially liberal Constitutions and constitutional cultures, their existence is mostly ignored or unaccounted for by constitutional theory. Normative qualms aside, it is hardly clear why this should be the case. The fact remains: a great deal of our *constitutional politics*—both historically and in the contemporary world—involve questions of symbol and ritual, reflecting, perhaps, a broader identity-affirming function of Constitutions, especially in a context of relatively resilient nationalism. Constitutions themselves are sometimes sources of ritual and symbol.[6] Symbols and symbolic conflicts are, on the one hand, both prescribed and regulated by constitutional provisions or norms, but more generally, they form part of constitutional culture in its broad sense. The most obvious examples arise in contexts of ethnic or cultural conflict or as part of post-conflict constitutional settlements—in societies like Northern Ireland, with its persistent conflicts over flags and other symbols.[7] Yet symbolic controversies of this kind are not confined to obviously divided or conflict-ridden societies: in 2015, New Zealand, for example, held a referendum to replace its colonially inflected national flag.[8] And as we will see, the ambivalent constitutional function of symbol and ritual can be related to a wider, controversial question: the legitimate role, if any, of Constitutions in fostering civic passions and affect.

III. Rituals and Symbols in Corsica and Poland

While in the *Social Contract* Rousseau elaborates the idea of the general will in philosophical and institutional terms, his constitutional projects for Corsica and Poland address the affective dimensions of civic virtue and public reason.[9] Whereas it is famously mysterious how citizens are to discern the general will in

---

[6] For Grey, the United States Constitution 'has been, virtually from the moment of its ratification, a sacred symbol, the most potent emblem (along with the flag) of the nation.': Thomas Grey, 'The Constitution as Scripture' (1984) 37 *Stanford Law Review* 1, 3. See also Dieter Grimm, 'Integration by Constitution' (2005) 3 *International Journal of Constitutional Law* 193.

[7] See, eg, Flags and Emblems (Display) Act (Northern Ireland) 1954. See also Neil Jarman, 'Pride and Possession, Display and destruction' and Dominic Bryan, 'Between the National and the Civic' in Thomas Hylland Eriksen and Richard Jenkins, *Flag, Nation and Symbolism in Europe and America* (London, Routledge, 2007).

[8] Eleanor Roy, 'New Zealand votes to keep its flag after 56.6% vote to keep the status quo' *The Guardian* (24 March 2016).

[9] Jean-Jacques Rousseau, *Du Contrat Social* (Paris, ENAG, 1988/1762) (hereinafter *Social Contract*).

cognitive or deliberative terms,[10] it is clear they must 'love' the polity and its laws, both in order to discern the common good and to respect its institutional and legal expressions. Therefore, a crucial function of Rousseau's Constitutions will be to foster the affective basis of republican citizenship. While this will be achieved partly through the familiar republican devices of public education and civil religion, what is striking in his works in both *Corsica* and *Poland* is the extent to which he emphasises seemly eccentric constitutional devices—both symbolic and ritual—that will assure the stability and cohesion of republican state and society.

In *Poland*, Rousseau associates symbols and rituals with the genius of ancient legislators or lawgivers, and suggests their purpose was to found a sense of citizenship and political community. He notes that Numa, the early Roman king, created citizens

> less by means of laws, which they had yet little need of in their rustic poverty, than by means of attractive institutions which attached them to one another and to their common soil; he did this by sacralising their city with those rites—ostensibly frivolous and superstitious—the force and effect of which is so rarely appreciated.[11]

Thus he celebrates the ancient legislators for their understanding of the symbolic and ritual dimensions of statecraft. They:

> [S]ought bonds that could attach citizens to the *patrie* and to each other; and found these in peculiar practices: in religious ceremonies which were always national and exclusive; in games which kept citizens frequently assembled; in exercises which enhanced their pride and self-esteem along with their vigour and strength; in spectacles which … touched their hearts, inflamed them with a lively spirit of emulation, and attached them strongly to [the] *patrie*.[12]

Since civic 'rites' are ostensibly 'frivolous', they need not necessarily develop organically or spontaneously, and can be contrived anew as part of the art of statecraft. Their content, then, is somewhat arbitrary and open-ended. Like Numa, Moses, in particular, bestowed 'peculiar rites and ceremonies' on the Hebrews.[13] In this spirit, Rousseau in *Corsica* and *Poland* prescribes a number of peculiar, often eccentric ritual and ceremonial practices as part of the constitutional structure. In particular, he gives extensive attention to feast days, commemorations and public games. While these are somewhat arbitrary and contrived, he does insist that ritual and symbolic practices should emphasise national specificities: for example, he

---

[10] Dobel argues: 'Rousseau's project resembles less the attempt of someone like Haber-mas to create the perfect preconditions of rational communication than it does the cases Clifford Geertz examines, in which society struggles to develop a coherent symbolic universe.': J Patrick Dobel, 'The Role of Language in Rousseau's Political Thought' (1986) 18 *Polity* 638, 640.

[11] Jean-Jacques Rousseau, *Considérations sur le Gouvernement de Pologne et sur sa réforme projetée* in *Collection complète des oeuvres* (Genève, 1780–89) vol 1 Ch IV; for a translation see 'Considerations on the Government of Poland' in Frederick Watkins, *Jean-Jacques Rousseau: Political Writings* (New York, Thomas Yelsen, 1953) Ch 2 (hereinafter *Poland*).

[12] *Poland*, ibid Ch 2.

[13] ibid, Ch 1.

asserts: 'let neither the [Polish] king nor the senators nor any public figure wear anything but the national costume. ... you must invent games, festivals and rituals peculiar to this particular court'.[14] In a similarly nationalist spirit, he prescribes periodic public commemorations of Polish liberation:[15] in Corsica, the 'most worthy' of foreigners will be granted honorary citizenship every 50 years and this will be marked by a 'general celebration across the island.'[16]

He also identifies a peculiar importance in oath swearing, and composes a collective oath by which the Corsican Constitution will be promulgated:[17] it must be sworn on the same day across the island as a condition for acquiring citizenship. He also specifies an oath men must swear in order to graduate to full citizenship[18] once certain conditions are met.[19]

However, verbal communication such as oath swearing occupies a relatively modest role. Dobel notes that since citizens must not only be rationally 'convinced' of the authority of the social compact but also 'persuaded', a-rationally, Rousseau's constitutionalism aims at 'establishing a community of shared meanings'.[20] This underlies the need for public ceremonies and rituals to deploy various forms of 'non-verbal communication ... symbols, sound, sight, ritual.'[21] Thus his prescriptions extend, as we will see, beyond formal ceremonials such as oath-swearing to embrace a diverse scheme of pageantry—festivals and parades, games and celebrations—deploying 'the intoxicating power of ... rich sensual delights.'[22]

IV. The Political Function of Symbols and Rituals

Rousseau's emphasis on pageantry and festivity, using civic rituals and symbols, partly reflects his emphasis on experiential and non-verbal forms of political

---

[14] ibid, Ch 3.
[15] ibid, Ch 3.
[16] Jean-Jacques Rousseau, *Projet de Constitution pour la Corse* (Paris, Nautilus, 2000) (hereinafter *Corsica*) 82.
[17] ibid 51.
[18] 'In the name of Almighty God and the gospels, by a sacred and irrevocable oath, I unite myself, my person and goods, in my will and in all my power with the Corsican nation, to belong to it in all my property, I and all that depends on me. I swear to live and die for the nation, to observe all its laws and obey its legitimate leaders and magistrates, where required by law. Thus may God help me in this life and have mercy on my soul. Long live liberty, justice and the Corsican Republic. Amen.' ibid 85.
[19] These conditions are that they are married, have at least two children, and have enough land for subsistence: ibid 51.
[20] Dobel, above n 10, 639.
[21] ibid.
[22] In Putterman's description, 'the intoxicating power of ... rich sensual delights.': Ethan Putterman, 'Realism and Reform in Rousseau's Constitutional Projects for Corsica and Poland' (2001) 49 *Political Studies* 481, 487.

education. Historically, signs and symbols—especially flags and statues[23]—played a strong role in political communication simply by virtue of limited literacy and education levels and have, to an extent, simply been overtaken by other kinds of political communication. In this spirit, Diderot observed: 'appeals to the heart by means of the senses [are] more within reach of the common man. The People make better use of their sight than of their understanding.'[24] For example, political statues served as an important pedagogical tool in provincial France during the initial fragile phase of the Third Republic, offering 'an immediate and apparently unmediated way of communicating political values to a people who might be wavering in political loyalties … [making] it possible for [them] to imagine common membership in this [republican] community.'[25]

However, ritual and pageantry is not simply an alternative *medium* for communicating republican ideas and concepts. Rather, it speaks to the nature of political cognition and political reason, and ultimately of citizenship and political community itself. Fundamentally, Rousseau's emphasis on rituals and symbols reflects a broader scepticism towards any vision of abstract political reasoning that is unsupported by passion and emotion.[26] Rousseau mysteriously insisted that citizens must not only be 'convinced' but also 'persuaded' by the social contract: it is noteworthy, then, that the role of devising specific rituals falls to the *legislator*—the mysterious, vaguely paternal figure who endows the republic with its institutions and deploys subtle forms of persuasion to set these in motion. The legislator can use neither force nor political reason as such, but must rely instead on a form of beguilery or enchantment that is achieved primarily through ceremony and ritual. The historic legislators used rituals to generate national and civic passions—Rousseau notes how Moses, for example, used 'peculiar rites and ceremonies' to mould a 'free people' out of a 'wandering and servile hoard'.[27] Thus as Strong argues, Rousseau's insistence that ideas must penetrate 'heart' as well as 'brain' cannot be dismissed as 'mushy romanticism'; otherwise, such ideas remain 'unincarnate'.[28] Indeed he refers to patriotism as an 'intoxicating' sentiment, without which 'liberty is but an empty word, and laws but a chimera'.[29] And as we will see in chapter four, Rousseau's concern is that purely abstract political discourse, unsupported by affect, is not only ineffective: it also threatens to constitute an insidious tool of domination in the liberal social order.

---

[23] William Cohen, 'Symbols of Power: Statutes in Nineteenth-Century Provincial France' (1989) 31 *Comparative Studies in History and Society* 491.
[24] As quoted in Cohen, ibid 492.
[25] ibid 492.
[26] The Constitution, he says, must 'elevate souls'. *Poland*, above n 11, Ch 3. Equally, in the *Social Contract* he says: 'the State's genuine constitution' is 'graven not in marble or in bronze, but in the heart of the citizens.' *Social Contract*, above n 9, Bk II, Ch 9. Similarly in *Poland*, he affirms: 'There will never be a good and solid constitution unless the law reigns over the hearts of the citizens.' *Poland*, above n 11, Ch 1.
[27] *Poland*, ibid Ch 2.
[28] Tracy Strong, *Rousseau: the Politics of the Ordinary* (London, Sage, 1994) 9.
[29] *Poland*, above n 11, Ch 12.

Indeed, while Rousseau's insight is that symbolic and ritual exchanges partly 'determine the quality of our cognition' in politics,[30] this equally reflects his understanding of the limits of language. Conventional language enables abstract thought and reasoning, and thus is essential to political authority and citizenship. However, he conjectures that we are unlikely to internalise abstract political concepts without non-verbal and experiential stimuli.[31] Legal and political concepts are expressed in abstract language yet 'possess no emotional power';[32] and worse, in their abstract form they risk becoming simply a plaything, an intellectual parlour game.[33] Rousseau understands that political morality is internalised—and political stability realised—through emotional and aesthetic processes. Thus symbols provide the 'emotional power and persuasiveness' that give life to abstract political language.[34] For Dobel, the Rousseauan political imagination will 'crystallise around concrete images'[35]—'strong but appropriate public symbols'[36]—we can think, for example, of the simple but potent symbolism of a tricolour flag, or the austere and virtuous political heroes immortalised as statues.[37] Public rituals give 'concrete meanings'—practical, experiential and visual—to concepts of liberty and justice.[38] Symbols 'form clear pictures which give concrete content to words'[39]—they ensure 'public meanings' are 'engraved' in citizens' minds.[40] And while symbols have an important educative function that supplements and supports abstract political thought in visual form, rituals perform the same function experientially, ensuring citizens do not passively absorb symbolic meanings. Therefore political education is experiential and participative: Rousseau affirms it must 'substitute the actions of men and citizens for the sophists' sterile babbling.'[41] It is worth noting that emotional and aesthetic processes are valuable not only in assisting the *comprehension* of political concepts: they also facilitate *action*, of the kind that Rousseau lauds in the first *Discourse*, and which he juxtaposes with the aridity of abstract philosophising. His insight, then, is that 'gestures, signs, and ritual … can undergird morality and politics because they can invoke emotions which influence action.'[42]

---

[30] See generally Shawn Rosenberg, 'Rethinking Democratic Deliberation: The Limits and Potential of Citizen Participation' (2007) 39 *Polity* 335.
[31] See generally Dobel, above n 10.
[32] ibid 646.
[33] Jean-Jacques Rousseau, *Discours sur les sciences et les arts* (Paris, Livres de Poche, 2012/1751).
[34] Dobel, above n 10, 648.
[35] ibid 652.
[36] ibid.
[37] Cohen, above n 23.
[38] Dobel, above n 10, 650.
[39] ibid.
[40] ibid.
[41] Jean-Jacques Rousseau, *Discourse on Political Economy* (1755) in Jean-Jacques Rousseau, *Discourse on Political Economy and On the Social Contract* (Christopher Betts trans, (Oxford, Oxford University Press, 2009) 31.
[42] Dobel, above n 10, 644. See also, generally, Michael Walzer, *Politics and Passion: Towards a more Egalitarian Liberalism* (New Haven CT, Yale University Press, 2006).

The specific symbols and rituals Rousseau prescribes offer a kind of visual metaphor of republican values; their simplicity is juxtaposed with the ostentatiousness both of monarchical or despotic spectacle, on the one hand, and the frivolity of private luxuries or amusements, on the other: for example, he suggests that athletic festivals will 'divert people from dangerous idleness, effeminate pleasures, and frivolous wit',[43] and that military commemorations should have 'a pomp not brilliant and frivolous, but simple, proud and republican'.[44] Thus he tells the Poles to 'avoid the luxurious trappings used in the courts of kings.'[45] In imagining spectacles that are appropriate to a republic, he must strike a balance between an aesthetic that is grave and authoritative, yet which eschews any spirit of domination or subordination. Although they must be 'simple', republican spectacles should also be 'noble and imposing', as the 'heart of the people follows its eyes'.[46] Thus 'the festivals of a free people should always breathe an air of gravity and decorum',[47] distinguished from pompous extravagance. In proceedings of the Polish Diet there must be 'not only rule and order, but also ceremony and majesty'.[48] Appropriate spectacles will help dissociate state authority from the 'caprice of arbitrary power.'[49] Whereas ostentatious 'baubles' express authoritarian caprice, republican symbols will convey the regularity and justice of political authority.[50] In this spirit, Rousseau prescribes essentially austere symbols: in *Poland*, he admires 'the two woolsacks placed ... in the British House of Lords'—'a touching and sublime decoration.' Thus he proposes 'two sheaves of wheat similarly placed in the Polish Senate.'[51]

Rousseau's understanding of political cognition mirrors his general theory of education. In *Emile*, he emphasises the experiential focus of early education and the 'authority of example' juxtaposed with the sterility of abstract schooling:[52] effectively he extends this to an account of how political philosophy is internalised and comes to life. Just as teachers should use non-verbal communication 'to animate the force of reason', political leaders must deploy a similar educative strategy through rituals, in which the regularity and justice of republican power is visually performed.[53] This helps to explain what Rousseau means by insisting that citizens must be 'persuaded' as well as 'convinced'. The social contract cannot be presented simply as a 'rational solution' to the problem of social co-operation; republican laws 'must not only be intellectually comprehended but must hold

---

[43] *Poland*, above n 11, Ch 3.
[44] ibid.
[45] ibid.
[46] ibid.
[47] ibid.
[48] ibid, Ch 7.
[49] ibid, Ch 3.
[50] Similarly, wearing badges and symbols will help officials to internalise their civic duties, ibid.
[51] *Poland*, ibid, Ch 3.
[52] Jean-Jacques Rousseau, *Emile or On Education* (A Bloom trans, New York, Basic Books, 1979).
[53] Dobel, above n 10, 649.

prescriptive power that motivates us to act correctly.'[54] To a great extent, accordingly, Rousseau's programme is focused not so much on the rational communication or doctrinal inculcation of republican ideas, but rather on the exaltation of approved behaviours and dispositions through mechanisms of honour and recognition—for example—through public prizes and awards, though which 'the patriotic virtues should be glorified.'[55] This evokes, and seeks to instrumentalise, what Pierre Bourdieu later referred to as 'all the hierarchies and classifications inscribed in objects ... in institutions or ... in language',[56] harnessed as a means of ensuring the stability of republican forms and dispositions. And while Rousseau's programme is partly predicated on the promise of symbolic, emotional and a-rational kinds of political communication, it is also a response to the potential for domination that is latent within political deliberation and discourse. As discussed further in the following chapter, this scepticism is shared by various strands of contemporary political theory. Rosenberg, for example, argues:

> It seems unrealistic to assume that a commitment to fairly consider another's concerns can be based simply on the recognition that another person, as a thinking, sentient personality, is formally equivalent to oneself and therefore equally deserving of attention and consideration. Similarly it seems unrealistic to assume that a commitment to a common good will emerge solely on the basis of reflections on what is ethical and reasonable.[57]

Again, this can be read as echoing Rousseau's bracing sense of realism as to the fate of abstract liberal ideas in the highly unstable, fragmented social order of the moderns. Rawls has more optimistically argued that modern citizens who hold diverse comprehensive doctrines and worldviews may, by forming an 'overlapping consensus',[58] internalise and act from a shared concept of justice. Similarly, Habermas' account of the deliberative public realm seems to downplay the affective or non-rational dimensions of citizenship.[59] But for other political theorists, such theories are premised on far too optimistic an understanding of moral psychology. It is insufficient that we recognise the 'integrity' of other citizens to engage in political deliberation; we must be 'emotionally connected' with them as well— through experiential stimuli which 'make that other person's pains and pleasures one's own.'[60] Liberalism, then, ignores the symbolic dimensions of the social and political universe, and the integrative function of political and social symbols.

Effectively, a similar concern underlies Rousseau's pervasive emphasis on symbolic and ritual forms of political communication. His concern is that purely

---

[54] ibid 648.
[55] *Poland*, above n 11, Ch 3.
[56] Pierre Bourdieu, *Distinction: a Social Critique of the Judgement of Taste* (Richard Nice trans, Cambridge MA, Harvard University Press, 1987) 471, emphasis added (Nice's translation).
[57] Rosenberg, above n 30, 348.
[58] John Rawls, *Political Liberalism* (Cambridge, Harvard University Press, 1996).
[59] Jurgen Habermas, *Between Facts and Norms: Contributions to a Discourse Theory of Law and Democracy* (Cambridge, MIT Press, 1996); *The Theory of Communicative Action: Volumes 1 and 2* (Boston, Beacon, 1984/1987); for discussion see Rosenberg, above n 30.
[60] Rosenberg, ibid 348.

abstract public reason is not only insufficient to internalise political morality, but may also—as discussed further below—represent a subtle but potent form of domination or symbolic violence. In contrast to Rawlsian liberalism, the fundamental problem of political order, for Rousseau, is not a *propositional* one at all, concerning disagreement as to the 'good', or agreement on the 'right'. Rather, it concerns the possibility of political communication itself, and more specifically the problem of establishing a form of communication that is not intrinsically or insidiously dominating (a question revisited in chapter four).

In sum, Rousseau's emphasis on emotions and passions reflects a broader concern for *stability*—that is, the concern, already explored in chapter two, as to how abstract political principles can feasibly be internalised, endorsed and reproduced by citizens. What his constitutional prescriptions suggest, again, is a deep scepticism as to the motivational force of such principles when presented as such, or when communicated and inculcated in purely rational forms. In our contemporary world, Nussbaum, for example, argues that liberal principles of justice require 'appeals to the emotions, using symbols, memories, poetry, narrative or music, which lead the mind toward the principles and in which the principles themselves are at times embedded.'[61] Yet the challenge, of course, is how the liberal state can orchestrate and galvanise political emotion without fostering particularistic and exclusionary sentiments that negate the substance of the very principles that are to be celebrated. The challenge is to 'conceive a strong set of perceptions, memories and symbols that have deep root in the personality and in people's sense of their own history', but without enshrining doctrines of cultural or linguistic privilege.[62]

V. The Radical Scope of Rousseau's Civic Ritualism

Despite the eccentric emphasis Rousseau places on symbols and rituals, such concerns do not, on the face of things, seem all that far removed from the practices of real republics, both historical and contemporary. Arguably, Rousseau's civic ritualism presages, and is reflected in, the rites and symbols adopted by nationalists and republicans in the late eighteenth and nineteenth centuries and which persist in contemporary democracies.[63] The Rousseauan political aesthetic is echoed, for example, in the *Marseillaise* and the 'jaunty yet simple tricolour'.[64] Seemingly, the function of ceremony and ritual is to foster sentiments of civic belonging—in relatively non-oppressive, even undemanding ways—and accordingly, to motivate

---

[61] Martha Nussbaum, *Political Emotions* (Cambridge MA, Harvard University Press, 2013) 10. She also notes: 'part of justifying a normative political project is showing that is can be reasonably stable': ibid 16.
[62] ibid 16.
[63] Dobel, above n 10, 654.
[64] ibid 658.

political action and political participation, thereby animating and stabilising republican politics and helping citizens internalise political principles in the manner discussed.[65] In this vein, Dobel, for example, argues that Rousseau 'reminds us that there may be plausible relations between singing the national anthem, celebrating Independence Day, and establishing public memorials, on the one hand, and the quality of debate and action within a state on the other.'[66] Putterman, alternatively, argues that the main purpose of Rousseau's ritualism is to secure acceptance of law, given the limits of coercive enforcement.[67] It is 'designed to bring [opinion and mores] into conformity with the laws to ensure that the two never (or only ever rarely) clash.'[68] And similarly for Mason, the role of Rousseau's austerity generally is to reconcile citizens to (just) laws, so that they 'look on, and feel about, positive laws in the same way that we regard natural laws [this being] the mark of a good political order ... accept[ing] the limits [positive laws] impose on us without resentment or frustration.'[69]

Thus, perhaps the dominant view of Rousseau's austerity generally—including his civic ritualism—is that it aims, first, to motivate civic sentiment and political action, and second, to reconcile private identities and interests to the requirements of the general will or to the demands of the republican order generally. The latter aim, in particular, is apparently familiar in the civic symbols and rituals of contemporary republics—in images of an imposing but just order, in the sword and scales, solemn military parades and so on. As for the former, Putterman, for example, argues that Rousseau's ceremonials presage and parallel spectacles that are relatively commonplace in contemporary liberal democracies—for example the 'pyrotechnical extravaganza of London's millennium-day celebration [or] the patriot missile led Desert Storm parade up ... Wall Street in 1991.'[70] Although more ambitious in technological scale than anything Rousseau contemplated, he argues 'their purpose is analogous' because they 'foster powerful subconscious identifications with the *patrie*',[71] invoking 'subconscious reminders of all of the good that the mother country conveys.'[72]

However, I argue this dominant interpretation, which makes Rousseau's ritualism seem so familiar—and so prescient—offers too narrow an account of its political function in his thought. Like our contemporary civic rituals and symbols, Rousseau's prescriptions aim to offer a kind of civic stimulus, to foster

---

[65] However, Honohan notes 'celebrations, commemorations and public holidays may create a general feeling of belonging without making people any more open to engage with their fellow citizens.': Iseult Honohan, *Civic Republicanism* (Abingdon, Taylor and Francis, 2002) 242.
[66] Dobel, above n 10, 658.
[67] Putterman, above n 22.
[68] ibid 485.
[69] John Hope Mason, 'Forced to be Free' in Robert Wokler (ed), *Rousseau and Liberty* (Manchester, Manchester University Press, 1995) 135.
[70] Putterman, above n 22, 490.
[71] ibid.
[72] ibid.

sentiments of fraternalism and political community. Yet in the contemporary world, civic ritualism occupies a piecemeal and compartmentalised role at best: crucially, it coexists with and supplements, at most, a complex and diverse world of private symbols and rituals, which affords citizens various outlets for cultural and aesthetic self-expression. However, for Rousseau, civic ritualism cannot simply supplement, or even rival private ritualism and cultural expression without being rendered deeply hypocritical and ineffectual.

When his constitutional project is read in light of his wider social and cultural critique, it seems clear that the purpose of his civic ritualism is not to supplement, but to supplant entirely the complex ritualisms of the liberal world, largely because he understands the cultural activities of early liberal society not only as deeply inauthentic, but also as a subtle, yet insidious form of corruption that is inimical to republican aims. Thus, while recognising that cultural practice is inevitably a conduit for *amour-propre*, the radical aim of his constitutional prescriptions is to ensure that citizens' need both for cultural expression and aesthetic *distinction* is exercised in a transparent public realm. Thus in summary, Rousseau's civic ritualism is radically distinctive because its aim is not solely to foster civic sentiment and political action, but rather to reorient and restructure the source and substance of cultural and aesthetic experience in wider society.

VI. Culture and Domination in the Early-modern World

Put differently, Rousseau's project is far removed from today's milder projects of civic ritualism partly because it embraces a radical aim of supplanting symbolic and social hierarchies in wider society, rather than stimulating civic sentiment in a narrowly defined political domain. Thus, his constitutional prescriptions must be understood in light of his deep ambivalence towards the cultural and social life of early-modern liberal societies, and particularly his apprehension towards social hierarchies based on cultural products and taste. Fundamentally, Rousseau understands culture and art, in the early-modern context, as sources of social *distinction*—as activities through which people exercise a corrupted *amour-propre*—and therefore, in turn, as a form of social inequality and domination that is inimical to the republican project.

On the one hand, Rousseau's constitutional prescriptions further illustrate the insight emerging from both the first and second *Discourses*: that social power, and thus domination, resides in symbolic and affective as well as material forms. In the philosophical anthropology of his second *Discourse*, Rousseau describes how, following the development of *amour-propre*, social hierarchy assumed symbolic forms; the 'great and rich' distinguish themselves and cement their status by creating 'a different symbolic universe' and 'trapping the rest into believing.'[73] And the sceptical view of arts and culture that he first articulated in the first *Discourse* is neatly summarised in *Preface to Narcisse* where he affirms: 'the taste for arts and letters originates in … *the desire for distinction*.'[74]

On the other hand, as an observer and critic of early-modern, and increasingly commercial societies, Rousseau is sensitive to the insidious hierarchies that are embedded and encoded in ostensibly mundane social practices—in everyday manners, tastes and dispositions. As already touched upon in chapter two, he understands that in commercially oriented societies, people increasingly obtain distinction and self-worth not only through material wealth, but through access to what sociologists might now call social and cultural capital ('the frivolous tastes created by opulence').[75] Rousseau understood that in such societies, increasing social differentiation and a nascent liberal cosmopolitanism gave rise to practices and tastes which were not only hopelessly inauthentic,[76] but which offered increasingly complex—and more insidious—axes of symbolic distinction. In *Poland*, Rousseau complains that Europeans increasingly 'all have the same tastes, passions, manners',[77] lamenting the loss of national cultural specificity amidst 'the general European tendency to imitate French tastes.'[78] Music, art and discourse all constitute sites of social power, and engender peculiar, insidious kinds of social domination. Thus in *Corsica*, Rousseau complains: 'the arbiters of opinion and taste in a people become the arbiters of its actions.'[79] Luxury goods and fine arts, he laments, are the product of 'vanity' rather than 'pride'; the latter applies to things intrinsically beautiful; the former to those cherished for the social prestige they confer. Luxuries represent 'ostentation' and 'pretentious pleasure'.[80] Essentially, he understands that in early-modern liberal society, social and cultural practices—through which individuals achieve both recognition and distinction—give expression to a corrupted *amour-propre*, the self-love that is consummated by the esteem of others. Thus in the second *Discourse* Rousseau described propertied society as a 'frenzy for distinction'.[81] *Amour-propre*, in early-modern liberal society, is given

---

[73] Dobel, above n 10, 651.

[74] Jean-Jacques Rousseau, *Preface to 'Narcisse: or Lover of Himself'* (1752), see translation and introduction in Benjamin Barber and Janice Forman, 'Jean-Jacques Rousseau's "Preface to *Narcisse*"' (1978) 6 *Political Theory* 537, 547, emphasis added.

[75] *Poland*, above n 11, Ch 11.

[76] Insofar our tastes and practices are determined by competition for status and recognition, we are beholden to external, alien forces for our sense of identity; we are alienated from ourselves. To perform encoded social rituals is, in Reisert's words 'to condemn oneself to being nothing but a hollow man or a phony, the hapless product of impersonal social forces.': Joseph Reisert, 'Authenticity, Justice and Virtue in Taylor and Rousseau' (2000) 33 *Polity* 305, 306.

[77] *Poland*, above n 11, Ch 3.

[78] ibid.

[79] *Corsica*, above n 16, 77.

[80] ibid.

[81] Jean-Jacques Rousseau, *Discours sur l'origine et les fondements de l'inégalité parmi les hommes* (Paris, Flammarion, 1755/2008) 142.

expression, in particular, through cultural consumption, as 'leisured cosmopolitans' seek to 'please and win recognition from others.'[82] And he complains that whereas distinction in classical societies is won through virtue, it is supplanted by 'decorum' in the highly practised, refined manners that define the early-modern, commercial society.[83]

Accordingly, this explains why Rousseau's austerity is to be realised not only through the autarkic economic project outlined in chapter two, but also through a pervasive public ritualism that fully supplants private symbolic and ritual practices. Civic ritualism, then, is a component of Rousseau's broader response to the corrupt social world of early liberalism. And the purpose of Rousseau's public ceremonies—games, awards and so on—is to ensure that recognition and esteem are focused on public objects, such that *amour-propre* is consummated in a transparent, public realm. We may recall that Rousseau's central concern is how it may be possible to establish a non-dominating form of government despite the apparently pervasive need of human beings to distinguish themselves and acquire recognition from their peers. Acknowledging that we can never recover the perfect independence—psychological or material—of the state of nature, the purpose of his constitutional plans is largely to construct a society in which *amour-propre* in consummated in benign, or at least less threatening, forms. His focus on public symbols and rituals is, accordingly, merely one component of a broader programme of austerity whose purpose is to stem those forms of domination and social hierarchy that are latent in the social practices of liberal society, and which he views as inconsistent with republican liberty. Just as his autarkical projects aim to prevent *amour-propre* being consummated, untamed, in the private commercial domain, the purpose of his public ritualism is to provide a public, transparent and *common* forum in which we can realise a non-dominating, inclusive and more innocent form of cultural expression. Rousseau's ritualism pursues the same aim, in the cultural and expressive domain, as his autarkic economic project—that is, to tame *amour-propre* and ensure it is consummated in benign forms.

Rousseau's understanding of culture and taste as instruments of social distinction is prescient in sociological terms. On the one hand, he understands that social power and domination are rooted in our need for, and our dependency upon, recognition. In liberal society, dependency of this kind entails an insidious kind of domination partly because, as Gauthier observes, 'dependence on another person is [for Rousseau] ... not simply dependence on his power; most deeply, it is *dependence on his recognition*.'[84] And in this context, he understands that domination is intractably embedded in the production and exchange of symbolic, cultural

---

[82] Charles Ellison, 'Rousseau and the Modern City: The Politics of Speech and Dress' (1985) 13 *Political Theory* 497, 498.

[83] Above n 74, 551.

[84] David Gauthier, *Rousseau: the Sentiment of Existence* (Cambridge, Cambridge University Press, 2006) emphasis added.

and social capital. It is exercised and experienced through 'positional goods'[85]—through the unequal distribution of the competences that are needed to acquire and exercise social recognition.

Moreover, Rousseau not only anticipates the Marxist understanding of culture and social practice as expressions of social and economic power relations, but presages post-Marxist sociologists—particularly Pierre Bourdieu—who understand social and cultural practices not merely as expressions of antecedent, material power structures, but rather as significant sources of social power in their own right. For Bourdieu, social practices operate as a function of social power structures, but are not crudely determined by a materialist class structure. The *habitus*, for Bourdieu, is the set of durable dispositions, tastes and preferences—learned but unconscious—which orients our actions and practices towards the objective social structures and socio-cultural contexts within which we operate.[86] Correspondingly, taste and culture operate as instruments of distinction in competitive social 'fields' that generate and reproduce specific kinds of social and cultural capital. Our subjectivity—encompassing our tastes and dispositions—is formed partly in response to the requirements of negotiating these fields. Our tastes and dispositions serve partly to distance us from lower groups,[87] yet are 'naturalised' as intrinsically meritorious. Thus we experience a sort of false consciousness ('misrecognition' or *doxa*) by understanding our social practices—or indeed those of higher-status groups—as neutral and innocent. And for Bourdieu, it is largely social *symbols*—symbols of value, legitimacy and prestige—that embody 'relations of power'[88] and underlie unconscious forms of hierarchy and domination. *Symbolic power* is the power to determine legitimacy in categories of taste, preference and competence and thereby to impose hierarchies of value and prestige. *Symbolic violence* refers to the insidious or invisible character of that power. *Symbolic domination* refers to the power of certain groups to maintain and reproduce social hierarchies by imposing their evaluative schemas—and thus, forms of unconscious, invisible discipline—within the dispositions and assumptions of dominated agents.

Similarly, on the one hand, Rousseau's disdain for the theatricality of liberal urban life—with its phony mannerisms and affectations—presages Bourdieu's account of social power relations as being embedded in the mundane and the everyday, and particularly 'in the most automatic gestures or the apparently most insignificant techniques of the body.'[89] On the other hand, Rousseau understands that while social and cultural practices serve to procure and confer individual distinction and to this extent are both arbitrary and inauthentic, by the same

---

[85] ibid 19.

[86] Jen Webb, Tony Shirato and Geoff Danaher, *Understanding Bourdieu* (London, Sage, 2002) 14.

[87] See generally Bourdieu, above n 56.

[88] Jane Fulcher, 'Symbolic Domination and Contestation in French Music: Shifting the Paradigm from Adorno to Bourdieu' in Victoria Johnson, Jane Fulcher and Thomas Ertman, *Opera and Society in Italy and France from Monteverdi to Bourdieu* (Cambridge, Cambridge University Press, 2007) 314.

[89] Bourdieu, above n 56 69.

measure he understands that what seem to be ostensibly innocuous practices—such as art, music, and discourse—are important sites of power and domination. In particular, he believes practices like theatre and music 'cannot be understood except in terms of the moral and political.'[90] In the first *Discourse*, for example, he decried the 'inequality introduced among men by distinctions of talent'.[91] His analysis of eighteenth century social rituals presaged Bourdieu's claim that 'art and cultural consumption are predisposed, consciously or deliberately or not, to fulfil a social function of legitimating social differences.'[92]

Thus while Roy argues that for Rousseau, 'art ... only serves as the handmaiden of existing institutions'[93] what this overlooks is that he understands cultural practices like art as sources—and not simply as expressions or derivatives—of social power and class structure. Indeed in the early-modern context, Rousseau's concern was that in increasingly complex and differentiated societies, symbolic domination would acquire newly potent, but also peculiarly *insidious* forms. In his second *Discourse*, he notes 'the devouring ambition ... the desire to place oneself above others, inspiring ... a surreptitious envy *which is all the more dangerous for the fact that it is often masked as benevolent*.'[94] Indeed this echoes Bourdieu's claim that symbolic social classifications are efficacious because 'they function below the level of consciousness and language, beyond the reach of introspective scrutiny.'[95] In tandem with increasing social differentiation, cultural and intellectual practices assume complex, specialised and exclusivist forms. Correspondingly, categories of value and merit become deeply encoded and require elaborate, but essentially arbitrary, forms of learning. For example he complains, in Dobel's terms, that music has been 'taken away from the community and made into a ponderous academic discipline'.[96] Indeed Rousseau extends this analysis to intellectual life itself: he says the 'taste for letters ... arises from the desire to distinguish oneself.'[97] As I will consider in chapter four, language itself is not a neutral medium of communication but rather an instrument of domination and power.

Thus, the cultural practices of liberal society help to obscure hierarchy and domination. Bourdieu claims that 'dominated agents ... tend to attribute to themselves what the distribution [of value and status] attributes to them, reproducing in their verdict on themselves the verdict [pronounced] on them.'[98] Rousseau's concern is, similarly, that we identify natural authority in refined manners and authorised dispositions, and that contingent and arbitrary social constructs are then mistaken as natural and innocent.

---

[90] Tracy Strong, 'Theatricality, Public Space and Music in Rousseau' (1996) 25 *SubStance* 110, 112.
[91] Rousseau, above n 41, 69.
[92] Bourdieu, above n 56, xxx.
[93] Jean Roy, 'Rousseau's "Letter to D'Alembert on the Theatre' and Revolutionary Aesthetics' in *Jean-Jaques Rousseau et la Révolution* (North American Association for the Study of Jean-Jaques Rousseau, 1991), page 201.
[94] Rousseau, above n 41, 69, emphasis added
[95] Bourdieu, above n 56, 466.
[96] Dobel, above n 10, 651.
[97] Rousseau, above n 74.
[98] Bourdieu, above n 56, 452.

VII. Culture and Aesthetics under Austerity

Rousseau's ambivalence towards liberal cultural practices as sources of social domination underscores the radicalism of his all-embracing public ritualism—and of its distinctiveness compared to the modest, piecemeal civic ritualism of later, liberal republics. The purpose of austere spectacles—parades, games and so on—is not only to convey the substance of republican political values, but also to facilitate cultural and aesthetic expression in an inclusive, transparent and non-dominating form. Rousseau recognises that in liberal society aesthetic and cultural experience is appropriated to inaccessible, specialised fora which require specialised techniques and competences to successfully navigate. Thus 'music migrates to the concert hall [and] ritual public action … to the theatre … Citizens no longer meet in open courtyards surrounded by symbols to deliberate.'[99]

The republican spectacle, open and accessible, will provide an alternative to the specialised cultural pursuits of differentiated liberal societies—but more pertinently it will foil their *encoded complexity*, because unlike, say, opera or even many sports, taking part in such activities requires no specialised competences or techniques. Rousseau's politics of austerity does not aim to remove or ignore the need for aesthetic experience, cultural consumption or even symbolic distinction. Rather, he aims to supplant the symbolic hierarchies encoded in private cultural consumption with aesthetic experiences and symbolic distinctions that are compatible with (and even supportive of) republican politics. Thus a pervasive republican symbolism and ritualism can stem the domination wrought by the cultural complexities of liberal societies. Crucially, in turn, this means republican 'spectacles' cannot be confined to a compartmentalised 'public' or political domain, but must pervade social life generally. Thus, Rousseau's republican spectacles are not valued *primarily* for the civic stimulus these offer, but rather, their capacity to recover a form of cultural and aesthetic expression that is authentic and non-dominating.

Indeed the pervasive, all-embracing scope and purpose of Rousseau's republican rituals is illustrated by their highly localised, almost spontaneous character. On the one hand, *Poland*—and to a lesser extent, his project for Corsica—envisage large-scale, state-orchestrated ceremonials: imposing, set-piece events such as official feast days or athletic festivals. And in general, a great deal of republican spectacle is to be officially orchestrated in the guise of formal ceremonies or assemblies. However, in *Letter to d'Alembert* in particular, we can see a gentler, subtler aspect of republican ritualism—which appears more as an organic outgrowth of republican social forms than as a top-down, officially imposed practice. In particular, in the course of his extended critique of theatre, Rousseau celebrates Geneva's tradition of simple, inclusive festivities. These republican

---

[99] Dobel, above n 10, 651.

'spectacles' are not constitutionally prescribed as such—they are not officially orchestrated, top-down ceremonials: rather, they are embedded in the fabric of social life. Republican festivities, he says, might simply amount to a joyful and spontaneous gathering around 'a crown of flowers in the square.'[100] And crucially, they do not occupy a discrete 'political' domain but are integrated within social life generally and occur in the context of a cohesive, austere society.

Thus far from the stereotype of dour conformity that we might associate with state spectacles, Rousseau—in *Letter to d'Alembert*, at least—rejects any vision of sterile set-pieces, or didactic state ceremonials in which citizens are passive observers. Instead he celebrates a vision of republican festivity which springs spontaneously from the cohesion and solidarity of a republican society. Crucially, republican 'spectacle' of this kind simply could not occur in complex, differentiated and commercially oriented societies, and could not be constitutionally prescribed. This explains why it is mistaken to identify parallels to Rousseau's ritualism in contemporary social and political practices, in the mild and sporadic ceremonials—the national festivals, anthems and state funerals—of today's liberal republics. While these might prompt sporadic patriotic sentiment, this is alien to Rousseau's sense of civic ritualism. He warns the Corsicans that their liberty cannot be sustained by ephemeral, transient 'passions' experienced in the aftermath of liberation— instead, he says, it is sustained by their '*way of being*'.[101]

Ceremonials, then, cannot foster the appropriate dispositions unless there is already sufficient solidarity and simplicity of mores in the relevant society; otherwise we risk hypocrisy—and a mere simulacrum of patriotic sentiment. And this is precisely why republican ritualism begins to seem futile in liberal society— because as set-piece spectacles, they are dissociated from the everyday and the mundane. Rearick, for example, notes that while the Third French Republic deployed diverse spectacles, particularly republican festivals, to secure stability against reactionary forces, 'the conditions for successful community celebration were rapidly disappearing in fin-de-siècle France'—in a context of industrialisation, urbanisation and class stratification.[102] The success of republican spectacle depended on a kind of social cohesion that was disappearing—upon an 'old folkloric culture [that] was dying'—the culture of the 'village fetes' whereas 'in the cities anomie and social conflict were hallmarks of the age'. Thus in an industrialising and liberalising society, the republican spectacle had limited reach, as republican elites 'retreated to a comfortable "classical" tradition of mechanically invoking official dogma in overworked allegory, speechifying, and self-glorifying pageantry'.[103] Crucially, these historical processes meant that the republican

---

[100] *Lettre à d'Alembert* (1758). For an English translation see Allan Bloom, Charles Butterworth and Christopher Kelly, *Rousseau: Letter to d'Alembert and Writings for the Theatre* (Lebanon NH, University Press of New England, 2004) 6863 (author's translation).

[101] Above n 16, 88, emphasis added.

[102] Charles Rearick, 'Festivals in Modern France: The Experience of the Third Republic' (1977) 12 *The Journal of Contemporary History* 435, 455.

[103] ibid 455.

spectacle retreated to a limited domain that citizens, for the most part, would merely spectate upon.

This interpretation can be supported by analogy with Rousseau's critique of the theatre. In *Letter to d'Alembert*, he extends the critique of the first *Discourse* by arguing against the prevailing Enlightenment view that theatre promotes moral virtue. Rather, he argues, it merely plays on or manipulates the dispositions and attitudes already present in the audience as a society or micro-society.[104] By analogy, republican theatrics will be effective only within an austere and egalitarian society. We cannot affirm our patriotism and solidarity as a sporadic, ritual genuflection to citizenship—say, on formal feast days—and then return to an atomised existence. Republican ritualism cannot be compartmentalised as theatre is to life; it must be integrated across all of social life. Arguably, the citizen-spectator of contemporary civic rituals—the fair-weather citizen—resembles the hypocritical theatre-goers that Rousseau depicts. We feel virtuous at the moral reflection supposedly drawn from the experience, but like theatre it 'demands nothing of us'.[105] The 'transient, vain emotions'[106] he ascribes to the theatre-goer are perhaps equally salient in compartmentalised civic rituals like flag-saluting and anthem-singing. Indeed Kohn argues that Rousseau's critique of theatre presciently anticipates a modern phenomenon of passive spectatorship of spectacles in commercial and capitalist society, which undermines the possibility of intersubjectivity in public space.[107]

In part, Rousseau's critique of passive spectatorship reflects his preference for experiential forms of moral education: even if theatre can teach us what is right in the abstract, it cannot teach us the practice of virtue as it requires nothing of the spectator.[108] Rousseau's critique is not only of theatre, but of spectatorship in general.[109] Republican spectacles must, then, be participative, experiential and embedded in social life—not sporadic, didactic and passive. 'Make the spectators the spectacle', he affirms—'*make spectators the actors*'.[110]

---

[104] Above n 100, 9.

[105] ibid 12 (author's translation).

[106] ibid (author's translation).

[107] Kohn states: 'The exhibition, amusement park and shopping arcade reflect the proliferation and expansion of the dynamics that Rousseau identified in their nascent form in the theater. The mass is constituted through a collective experience of isolation that incites desire for an object while isolating one from another.': Margaret Kohn, 'Homo Spectator: Public Space in the Age of the Spectacle' (2008) 34 *Philosophy and Social Criticism* 467, 476–77. Indeed Ozouf notes that for critics, theatre compounded the faults of 'traditional' and pre-revolutionary festivals—particularly in its exaltation of social hierarchy: 'treatises on architecture had for decades denounced the theatre as a place in which social hierarchy and an intoxicating display of social stratification had reached their apogee. The theatre was a "dark little place" that Diderot judged incapable of "holding the attention of an entire nation", … giving the theatre the fractional, unsharable character of private entertainment.' By contrast, the 'utopian festival … placed everyone on the same level'. Mona Ozouf, *Festivals and the French Revolution* (Alan Sheridan trans, Cambridge MA, Harvard University Press, 1988) 3, 8.

[108] He opines 'the ancients spoke of humanity in less polished language, but knew better how to exercise it'. *Letter to d'Alembert*, above n 100, 16 (author's translation).

[109] Kohn, above n 107.

[110] *Letter to d'Alembert*, above n 100, 62, emphasis added ('donnez les spectateurs en spectacle').

In turn, this supports the idea that Rousseau envisages republican ritual not only as fostering participative civic dispositions, but rather as supplanting and substituting private social and cultural practices wholesale, as a facet of everyday social life. Putterman muses that it is difficult to see how ritualism and ceremonials can be a 'rampart for justice in any state' simply because it is difficult to envisage how they may elicit 'universal support for the laws',[111] how the 'ephemeral surges of pride' they procure can 'satisfy the [social] compact's need for universal obedience.'[112] But this is explained by the fact that, as I have argued, the purpose of such rituals is much broader than the need to secure civic obedience or respect for authority—or even to promote participation. The purpose of civic ceremonials in liberal-democratic states is fundamentally different because they aim to supplement rather than supplant the aesthetic and cultural pursuits of liberal society. They are integrated within and do not challenge the complex cultural diversity of liberal society, which Rousseau identifies as being itself a source of hierarchy and domination.

On the surface, Rousseau's republican ritualism seems—like his project of austerity more generally—to risk undermining cultural pluralism and expressive individuality. A commonplace view of Rousseau, indeed, is that he seeks to impose homogeneity for the sake of cohesion and stability, thus sacrificing individuality and diversity. Moreover, his aesthetic project is not concerned solely with exemplifying or celebrating virtue, but rather with distributing approbation and blame. These public rituals are to have a deeply moralising, judgmental character: Rousseau complains that in the moderns' public festivities, 'public blame and approbation are inconsequential.'[113] The aim of such exercises is 'not only to make [young people] robust and agile and to acculturate them early on in equality and fraternity', but also '*to live in the eyes of their fellow citizens and to desire public approbation* ... to this end, the prizes will not be distributed by masters, but by the judgment and acclamation of the spectators.'[114] While Rousseau's aim is to liberate citizens from dependency on the recognition of others, in doing so he seems to make us dependent on what is simply an alternative, state-orchestrated nexus of recognition.

Again, however, what Rousseau seeks is not to sacrifice festivity and self-expression, but rather to rescue it from the competitive and esoteric forms that it assumes in the fragmented social order of early liberal societies. He is not concerned with the sacrifice of private interest to the common good, but rather, as Affeldt claims, with the recovery of *genuine* private interest,[115] which is congruent with the common good. Ostensibly, the austerity of Rousseau's ritualism implies

---

[111] Putterman, above n 22, 486.
[112] ibid.
[113] *Poland*, above n 11, Ch 2.
[114] *Poland*, above n 11, Ch 4, emphasis added.
[115] Steven Affeldt, 'The Force of Freedom: Rousseau on Forcing to be Free' (1999) 27 *Political Theory* 299, 309.

severe discipline and forbearance—and a fetter on individual self-expression. However, based on his description of Genevan festivities—'lively' dancing and 'all heads spinning with a drunkenness sweeter than wine'[116]—Strong notes his commitment to a sort of 'Bacchanalia of the political.'[117] Far from dour conformity, his vision of austerity is, counter-intuitively, quite convivial and exuberant.[118] Puzzlingly, in *Letter to d'Alembert* Rousseau describes public assemblies as fostering 'gentle bonds of pleasure and joy' amongst the people,[119] who must 'surrender themselves to the sweet sentiment of happiness'.[120] Their festivities, he says, must be 'free and generous'[121]—hardly fitting our usual sense of austerity. Rousseau's rituals are not austere, then, because they deny or reject pleasure, but rather because they eschew the exclusivity and the perverse, contrived complexity he identifies in more complex social rituals, that render them accessible only to those with the requisite competences and know-how. He pleads: 'let us not adopt *those exclusive spectacles which enclose the few in dark lairs*, holding them fearfully in silence and inaction and offering them ... nothing but the images of servitude and inequality.'[122] Where he says republicanism's 'innocent spectacles' must take place 'in the open air ... illuminated by the sun',[123] this affirms their conviviality, but also serves as a metaphor for their accessible, egalitarian simplicity. In republican festivities, 'the many societies become one, and everything becomes common to all.'[124]

Thus the point of austerity is not dour sacrifice, but rather radical transparency across our social practices. When Rousseau insists that athletic prizes will be distributed by 'the judgment and acclamation of the spectators',[125] this can be taken as a metaphor for his broader ideal of transparency: that merit and competence must not be encoded in specialised rituals. This enthusiasm for public scrutiny—for a radical transparency—is not some quasi-Orwellian ambition to extend public control over private life. Rather, it aims to foil the potent force of private symbolic distinction by promoting transparency in our social practices—a

---

[116] Strong's translation. Strong, above n 28, 490.

[117] Strong, above n 90, 123.

[118] Concerning the bacchanalia, and thus potentially the licentiousness and immorality of festivals, Ozouf notes: 'Paradoxically, they were a guarantee of acceptable behaviour, for the excesses they authorized served as a safety valve: they prevented intemperance from spreading to daily life and throughout the social body as a whole.': Ozouf, above n 107, 4.

[119] *Letter to d'Alembert*, above n 100, 62 (author's translation).

[120] ibid.

[121] ibid 63.

[122] ibid 62, emphasis added.

[123] ibid.

[124] ibid 63. Ozouf notes: 'Once, long ago, there had been another sort of festival. In the remote past, the festival had been something like the contract in [Rousseau's] *Essai sur l'Origine des Langues*, with no binding clauses, "a happy age when nothing marked the hours." ... a festival without division a nd almost without spectacle. Far back in the mists of time, a festive assembly had been held in which the participatns found their satisfaction simply in the fact of being together. There had been a primitive, a primordial festival ... but it seemed to have been lost.': Ozouf, above n 107, 4.

[125] *Poland*, above n 11, Ch 4.

transparency which, for Starobinski, is achieved through 'the festival' as well as the general will itself.[126] Cognisant of the struggle for symbolic recognition in differentiated social 'fields', Rousseau aims to re-orient this within an alternative 'field' in which the primary form of symbolic capital is itself *political*, public and transparent. While we will still, in Rousseau's vision, be *dependent on recognition*— a recognition that is orchestrated by the republic itself—the difference is that, in contrast with the corrupted, fragmented liberal society, the source of recognition is radically decoded, public and transparent. This is similar, in effect, to his view of dependency on the general will. We cannot recover freedom as perfect independence; social interdependence as such is inevitable. But we can be *politically* free where we are mutually dependent on a (general) will that we can accept as our own—and similarly, we can escape symbolic domination where we are dependent on an aesthetic or symbolic code, but one which is radically inclusive, transparent and common. This is another dimension in which Rousseau aims at 'making the community itself a source of the esteem sought by individuals as a consequence of their *amour-propre*'.[127] And consequently, *amour-propre* is not merely tamed or neutralised, but positively harnessed in exalting virtuous behaviours and dispositions—and providing outlets for the passion which do not rely on the denigration or subordination of others.[128]

Thus Rousseau's ideal republican ritualism is a 'festival without invidiousness',[129] free of insidious complexity and exclusion. Whereas Strong claims that for Rousseau, music, through its *unity*, simultaneously realises and represents citizenship— the 'pure form of humanness'[130]—this can be extended to public rituals. The intoxicating togetherness of civic revelry erases our need for symbolic distinction. For Strong, 'the effect of the gaiety is to lose all sense of self-consciousness in the revelry of one's public identity'; thus the revellers 'are not looking at themselves or others in the potentially dominating way noted [in the first *Discourse*].'[131] Only in this de-coded, holistic revelry can one 'simply be what one is, naturally.'[132] This casts a different light on Rousseau's seemingly severe assertion that 'the only pure

---

[126] For this argument see Jean Starobinksi, *Jean-Jacques Rousseau: Transparency and Obstruction* (Chicago, University of Chicago Press, 1988). For a countervailing view see Jonathan Marks, 'Jean-Jacques Rousseau, Michael Sandel and the Politics of Transparency' (2001) 4 *Polity* 619.

[127] Frederick Neuhouser, 'Freedom, Dependence and the General Will' (1993) 102 *The Philosophical Review* 363, 390.

[128] Neuhouser notes: 'the distinctive resources *amour-propre* offers for ameliorating human existence reside in precisely the "relative" features that distinguish it from *amour de soi*, namely, that it encourages us to accord weight to the normative judgments of others subjects and that it leads us to seek to achieve (a primitive version of) the comparative status—that of equal moral standing—on which the only possible solution to evil depends.' This counters 'the prevailing view among readers of Rousseau ... that *amour-propre* is a wholly negative phenomenon, always and only a source of havoc in human society.': Frederick Neuhouser, *Rousseau's Theodicy of Self-Love: Evil, Rationality and the Drive for Recognition* (Oxford, Oxford University Press, 2010) 15.

[129] Strong, above n 90, 123.
[130] ibid.
[131] ibid.
[132] ibid 124.

joy is public'.[133] Whereas differentiated private rituals involve the self-performing arbitrary cultural codes for the approval of the other, republican rituals—to borrow Gauthier's phrase—see 'self and other united in a single whole.'[134]

This also confirms that the ritualistic aspects of Rousseau's constitutional strategy are dependent on his broader politics of austerity: the state cannot lay down appropriate ceremonial and symbolic practices in the absence of the appropriate social and economic forms which, in turn, foster the dispositions and virtues that represent the pre-conditions for an authentic republican ritualism. Again this underscores how far removed his prescriptions are from the mild ritualism of contemporary liberal democracies. While 'establishing a community of shared meanings … is essential to [Rousseau's] project',[135] it is clear, given his sense of the symbolic hierarchies in broader society, that these 'shared meanings' cannot be confined to politics in its narrow sense.

VIII. Civic Ritualism and Constitutional Design: Contemporary Problems

I have considered, on the one hand, why symbolic and ceremonial matters seem to attract negligible attention in contemporary constitutional thought. I have equally argued, on the other, that contemporary symbolic and ritual practices are far removed, in scope and purpose, from Rousseau's more radical project, which is intrinsically linked to a broader critique of liberal culture. However, while Rousseau's project is concerned with creating a very specific and demanding kind of republican society, nonetheless I will argue that his symbolic and ritual project speaks to a broader question: the affective grounds of political community. And while his aim of manipulating and reorienting *amour-propre* seems quite remote from contemporary preoccupations, I will argue that it speaks to a broader preoccupation that has been overlooked, in liberal thought, as an object of constitutional design: that of fostering and channelling political passions.

I have argued that Rousseau's aim is not simply to inculcate *virtue* in the narrow sense of duty or self-sacrifice, but rather to cultivate pleasures and *passion* in a manner that is conducive to republican aims. And in this sense, Rousseau is, counter-intuitively, a surprisingly *modern* figure: eschewing the ancient aristocratic ideal of duty and honour, he emphasises the more egalitarian force of passion. Or as Burtt argues, for Rousseau the psychological basis of civic virtue itself lies not in the 'compulsion to duty' but rather the 'education of passions.'[136]

---

[133] *Letter to d'Alembert*, above n 100, 68 (author's translation).
[134] Gauthier, above n 84, 65.
[135] Dobel, above n 10, 629.
[136] Shelley Burtt, 'The Good Citizen's Psyche: on the Psychology of Civic Virtue' (1990) 23 *Polity* 23, 24.

And as I have argued, Rousseau's aim is not that citizens sacrifice private pleasure, but rather that their need for pleasure, festivity and ultimately for mutual recognition, is consummated in an accessible, transparent and public realm.

Indeed, most historical accounts of civic virtue seem unrealistic, in modernity, because they demand the sacrifice of private interest and private pleasure for the sake of an elusively defined common good—and fail to acknowledge the potency of private interest and individual fulfilment. On the other hand, a republican settlement based purely on the mediation or coordination of private interest is, as discussed in chapter two, intrinsically unstable. Ostensibly, then, appeals to passion and emotion seem more tenable under modern and egalitarian conditions, and more promising than a purely interest-based politics. Yet most liberal thinkers have been wary of the political force of passion.[137] As Nussbaum observes, 'liberal political philosophers sensed that prescribing any particular type of emotional cultivation might easily involve limits on free speech and other steps incompatible with liberal ideas of freedom and autonomy.'[138]

Yet while it may seem embarrassing or even *sinister*, in our age, to speak of the state fostering or manipulating passions, an enduring concern is how it is possible to foster a sufficient affective basis for political community—under the political economy of capitalism—while somehow accommodating human diversity and independence. Put differently, it is a dilemma as to how citizens can be affectively integrated without entailing unacceptable or oppressive costs.

While a Rousseauan civic ritualism might have authoritarian shades,[139] alternatively it might be understood as a strategy for the republican state 'to maintain its legitimacy without incessant resort to manipulation or violence.'[140] Nussbaum, for example, argues that political emotions—or what I will call the passions—are a legitimate concern in 'liberal democracies'.[141] 'All societies', Nussbaum argues, 'need to think about the stability of their political culture over time.'[142] Such societies might, for example, aim at 'limiting envy and disgust in favour of inclusive sympathy', and to 'guard against division and hierarchy by cultivating appropriate sentiments of sympathy and love.'[143] She argues that political emotions have two basic purposes: positive and negative. They will 'engender and sustain strong commitments to worthy projects that require effort and sacrifice', thus extending sympathies from the local and familial to the national and global; equally, they will keep in check the destructive tendencies of 'denigration' and 'subordination', of

---

[137] See Walzer, above n 42.
[138] Nussbaum, above n 61, 4.
[139] ibid 2: 'sometimes people suppose that only fascist or aggressive societies are intensely emotional and that only such societies need to focus on the cultivation of emotions'. See also Rebecca Kingston, *Public Passion. Rethinking the Grounds for Political Justice* (Montreal and Kingston, McGill-Queen's University Press, 2011).
[140] Dobel, above n 10, 642.
[141] Nussbaum, above n 61, 2–11.
[142] ibid 2.
[143] ibid.

'disgust' and 'envy'.[144] Thus we might view such concerns as a legitimate part of the enterprise of constitutional design. We might recognise that 'symbols may acquire a motivational power that bare abstractions could not possess'.[145] The 'terrain of emotion', she argues, should not be ceded to 'illiberal forces'.[146]

Insofar as the purpose of Rousseau's symbols and rituals is to educate and tame *amour-propre*—and to channel it towards benign forms—this seems far removed from any bona fide purposes of contemporary liberal constitutionalism. However, despite the longstanding reticence of liberal thinkers towards the role of passion in politics,[147] many contemporary political theorists have defended the idea that the liberal state might assume a wider, related purpose of promoting or incentivising certain sentiments and passions that support the aims of the liberal state, albeit in rather modest and limited ways. There is little sense, however, of this being legitimately an aim or function of liberal-democratic constitutions.

Whereas Rousseau's concern is that the cultural domain becomes a site of unhinged and egotistic competition, this can be related to wider contemporary concerns. As a social theorist he presciently identifies a socialisation process that is partly dependent on symbolic classifications and distinctions. Effectively, he seeks to use constitutional mechanisms to harness this as a means of stabilising republican forms and dispositions. He calls to mind Bourdieu's observation that, 'through all the judgements, verdicts, gradings and warnings imposed by the institutions specially designed for this purpose … the social order is progressively inscribed in people's minds.'[148] Rousseau understands, on the one hand, that the success or otherwise of a republican project depends on complex dispositions and motivational resources, encompassing citizens' affect, sociability and sensibility. And like Bourdieu, he equally understands that while the public socialisation process is irreducible to official mechanisms, it can be deeply affected and channelled by such institutional devices. Thus in contrast with the mainstream of contemporary constitutional thought, he recognises that the constitutional structure can fruitfully shape and influence the public socialisation process in ways that support republican ideals of liberty and justice.

Thus while Putterman and others are mistaken in drawing parallels between Rousseauan civic ritualism and the spectacles of the modern, liberal republics—the independence days, civic awards, military commemorations and so on—these

---

[144] ibid 4.
[145] ibid 16.
[146] ibid.
[147] For Walzer, liberal writers see the politics of *interest* as more rational and less dangerous. Political passion is juxtaposed with the tranquil commercial bourgeois of the eighteenth century—with the society of *doux commerce*. A displacement of 'conviction' is displaced by 'interest'. Walzer, above n 42, 122. The aim, he says, is to blur the line, to 'rationalise (some of) the passions and impassion reason' … 'our feelings are implicated in the practical understanding as well as in the political defense of the good and even of the right'. In politics, we must 'choose comrades'. But 'no one will believe that rational agreement or calculations of interest exhaust the idea of political commitment'. ibid 126, 128.
[148] Bourdieu, above n 56, 471 (Nice's translation).

do speak to a broader, underappreciated function of constitutionalism in undergirding and influencing the mechanisms of civic socialisation.

Of course, such contemporary projects are inevitably circumscribed by many of the same features of liberal society that Rousseau lamented. In the modern setting, the experience of the Third French Republic (1875–1940) is noteworthy. In the early phase, republican governments deployed ritual and symbolic strategies—particularly festivals and state funerals—to ensure the stability of the new dispensation against Catholic and monarchist reaction. In the early years of the republic, this project enjoyed some measure of success as it became the subject of popular enthusiasm. Initially republicans—in the spirit of austerity—were eager to juxtapose the 'seriousness' of the Republic with the 'frivolous fetes' of the fallen empire. Accordingly, the consolidating elites began to promote new festivals—for example, commemorating Voltaire and Rousseau, and later, Bastille day itself—which were popularly embraced. Thus official orchestration was sustained by a critical popular support: Bastille Day in 1880 was celebrated 'with extraordinary gaiety and grass-roots inventiveness across France.'[149] As Rearick describes:

> [I]n even the smallest republican villages, celebrators decorated dwellings and public buildings with flags and engaged in public rites such as dedicating a republican statue or bust or even a liberty tree, gathering for a 'democratic' banquet or punch, singing the Marseillaise together, and toasting the Republic parades, receptions, concerts, and popular games followed. Local leaders often devised elaborate programmes of such traditional favourites as 'grimace' contests, sack races, and climbing the greased pole … Drinking and dancing, *feux de joie* [fireworks], and—in the larger or more prosperous towns—fireworks continued long into the night.[150]

Ritualism and festivity, in short, became part of the nascent republican constitution. As Ben-Amos argues using the example of republican funerals, this new ritualism aimed to 'sacralise' the new regime and to impose itself upon public space (much like the Catholic processions it often sought to replace):

> The French Third Republic [made] skilful symbolic use of sacred space … To convey its unifying historical vision in terms of space, the … Republic had to occupy the sacred center of the realm and to integrate its own imagery into it.[151]

However, over the lifetime of the Third Republic, the force of republican ceremonials waned, creating tensions that became progressively more marked across the twentieth century. Rearick notes:

> The dream of spontaneity and fraternal joy had become a repetitive reality of prescribed set pieces, usually interesting only limited parts of the population. … as time went on

---

[149] Rearick, above n 102, 442.
[150] ibid 442–43.
[151] Avner Ben-Amos, 'The Sacred Centre of Power: Paris and Republican State funerals' (1991) 22 *The Journal of Interdisciplinary History* 27, 30. Ozouf notes: 'The festival was an indispensable complement to the legislative system, for although the legislator makes the laws for the people, festivals make the people for the laws.': Ozouf, above n 107, 9.

that memory [of the revolution] was less and less identified with the existing Republic and its celebrations. The Republic that so often tried to celebrate triumph amid scandal and crisis increasingly suffered from a failure of the festive imagination and spirit … the new elite directed its efforts not to the celebration of exciting ideals of liberty and equality, but to the glorification of an established regime. … republican leadership in its 'triumph' was too insecure to allow the full play of imagination in festival planning and in the boisterous zany play of celebrating crowds.[152]

Critically, Rearick suggests that the decline of republican festivity was linked to the broader social trajectory of liberalism and industrialisation: 'the French, especially Parisians, found private alternatives to public rites: by the 'nineties those who were able fled to the country or the seaside on holidays, leaving the city festivities to lower social and economic groups.'[153] Indeed, in a more sceptical and ironic age, it is difficult to imagine, for instance, Monet's depiction of the 1878 *Fete de la Federation*, with its 'brilliant profusion of tricolours'.[154] As Hazareesingh puts the French case, the republican festival—'crumbling since the sixties'—'seems defunct as pleasures are privatised.'[155]

This experience highlights, on the one hand, the practical difficulties involved in orchestrating civic ritualism in the face of increasingly sophisticated private spectacles and leisure pursuits.[156] Given problems of scale, relatedly, it is difficult to envisage how civic ritualism can be meaningfully participative rather than passively spectatorial—mirroring the wider challenge of scale that modernity poses to the classical republican concepts and devices.[157] More fundamentally, however, it points to the difficulty of transposing Rousseau's understanding—conceived of in a highly unitary and cohesive state—to a highly differentiated, class-structured society. As Lukes argues, neo-Durkheimian interpretations of civic

---

[152] Rearick, above n 102, 455.
[153] ibid 445.
[154] ibid 457.
[155] Sudhir Hazareesingh, Preface to Rémi Dalisson, *Célébrer la nation. Les fêtes nationales en France de 1789 à nos jours* (Paris, Nouveau monde éditions, 2009) 9. Dalisson observes that following the revolution of 1789, 'a consensus developed, on the part of rulers, as to the legitimizing functions of festivals, and on the part of the people, as to their civic and pedagogical function.' Yet after two centuries, what had long seemed 'the most natural thing in the world' increasingly came to be questioned in a context of 'globalization and communalism (*communautarisme*)'. ibid 12–13 (author's translation).
[156] According to some accounts, approximately half of Parisians attended the 'Festival of Law' of 3 June 1792. Wendy C Nielsen, 'Staging Rousseau's Republic: French Revolutionary Festivals and Olympe de Gouges' (2002) 43 *The Eighteenth Century* 268, 277. Ozouf notes that in the eighteenth and nineteenth centuries, French festivals were often the subject of criticism largely because they were too numerous: 'Behind this demand was a concern for greater economic efficiency. This above all was what condemned the endless succession of festivals: palace festivities, celebrations in the schools, academic processions, and craftsmen's and tradesmen's parades, all deriving from our "love of idleness". It was this that inspired the … calculation of lost national revenue that so preoccupied Montesquieu.' Moreover, 'the festivals were occasions of confusion, indecency, the improper mingling of the sexes, the blurring of social roles, the reign of night and of wine—in short, all that was contained in the Pandora's box named "abuses"'. Thus clergy, enlightened intellectuals and commerce were united against the culture of 'traditional' festivals. Ozouf, above n 107, 1–2.
[157] Kohn, above n 107.

rituals in capitalist democracies—understood as mechanisms of integration—tend to overstate the degree of value consensus that exists in such societies, and understate the 'conflictual' social context of such exercises.[158] Contemporary civic ritualism cannot, then, assume the social harmony underlying Rousseau's vision.

On the one hand, rituals and spectacles are historically used to shore up and legitimate the status quo and to procure consent; they may offer a means of integrating subordinate groups in the values and norms of dominant groups.[159] Indeed Bagehot observed, in the context of nineteenth century England, that the 'theatrical elements' of government 'inspire the most easy reverence',[160] and that their essential function is to procure obeisance from lower orders that are unable to rationally comprehend the functional or 'useful' elements of the Constitution. Thus Bagehot positively affirmed the capacity of ritual and spectacle to generate a kind of false consciousness.[161] He seeks to use 'imposing spectacles ... to impress an uneducated populace with the authority of the state.'[162] And while the spectacles and festivals that followed the French revolution aimed at giving dramatic representation to the principles of the new regime, Marx disputed their authenticity and claimed their appeal to an aesthetic of Roman stoicism served primarily to obscure the self-interest of the ascendant bourgeoisie.[163]

In contrast, any tenable, egalitarian vision of civic ritualism in diverse, differentiated societies must give some account of how it can aim towards a large degree of popular embrace but without representing a subtle form of symbolic domination. Relatedly, a further tension arises in that, as soon as public festivity is genuinely popular and spontaneous, it risks becoming a site of dissent and subversion that the state will seek to orchestrate and constrain—such that the substance or meaning of the exercise becomes destabilised.[164] As Rousseau demonstrates himself in the contrast between *Poland* and *Letter to d'Alembert*, the civic and the popular aspects of republican festivity are inherently in tension. This tension exists largely

---

[158] Steven Lukes, 'Political Ritual and Social Integration' (1975) 9 *Sociology* 289.
[159] ibid.
[160] Walter Bagehot, *The English Constitution* (London, HS King, 1873) 46.
[161] 'The most useful parts of the structure of government should by no means be those which excite the most reverence. The elements which excite the most easy reverence will be the theatrical elements—those which appeal to the senses, which claim to be embodiments of the greatest human ideas ... That which is mystic ... that which is brilliant to the eye; that which is seen vividly for a moment, and then is seen no more; that which is hidden and unhidden; that which is specious, and yet interesting, palpable in its seeming, and yet professing to be more than palpable in its results ... the characteristic merit of the English Constitution is that its dignified parts are very complicated and somewhat imposing, very old and rather venerable ... Its essence is strong with the strength of modern simplicity; its exterior is august with the Gothic grandeur of a more imposing age.' Bagehot, ibid.
[162] William Kuhn, 'Ceremony and Politics: the British Monarchy 1871–1872' (1987) 26 *Journal of British Studies* 133, 133.
[163] Karl Marx, *The Eighteenth Brumaire of Louis Napoleon* (1852), cited in Nielsen, above n 155, 275.
[164] Conversely, Ozouf notes that May 1968 has been interpreted as 'a reprisal for our ceremonial impoverishment.' The festival is potentially a 'reconstruction ... of a social bond that has come undone.': Ozouf, above n 107, 10.

because spectacle and festivity is inherently ambiguous—it has no fixed *propositional* content and so is subject to infinite adaptation and appropriation. But it is precisely this creative interplay between the official and popular (or subaltern) dimensions of rituals and festivals that makes them a site of political energy and creativity; indeed, it is the very fact of participation in such epistemological ambiguity that partly captures their republican idealism. Thus ritual can provide 'a source of creativity and improvisation, a counter-cultural and anti-structural force.'[165] While political speech can be monopolised or colonised by the legitimate interlocutors of a discursive bourgeois public sphere and exclude those who are not equipped with the requisite idioms, ritual and theatrics provides an alternative medium of political communication and contestation. Nielsen, for example, argues that while the French revolutionary festivals of the 1790s were largely considered failures, they offered an 'alternative public space in which women could and did perform'—in particular, they 'gave women access to the public stage'.[166] Thus public ritualism offers expanded interpretations of, and alternatives to, the discursive public sphere and its associated hierarchies.[167]

The instability and ambiguity of rituals—and the associated political creativity—is mirrored by political symbols. Olson, for example, illustrates how the revolutionary French-tricolour cockade was adapted in the colonial Caribbean setting—by colonialists as well as slaves—in a manner that was irreducible to the metropolitan understanding of revolutionary-republican ideals. Given its 'lack of propositionally specific claims' it acquired a versatility that rendered it 'a domain of possibilities and a screen of projection', that 'functioned as a kind of mirror to the elite understanding of the ideals of the new French republic.'[168] While Olson argues that the tricolour's 'indeterminate character gave it a distinctive political power', this is precisely the democratic promise of civic ritualism and symbolism—the fact that, as a means of political communication, it is irreducible to sterile didacticism.

IX. Conclusion

As I have argued, the paradox of Rousseau's civic ritualism is that while it embraces a radical, romantic aim that is unrecognisable in the contemporary context, his strategy for civic integration anticipates, in a sense, the challenge of realising republicanism in the modern world—because, eschewing appeals to aristocratic

---

[165] Lukes, above n 158, 302.
[166] Nielsen, above n 156, 269.
[167] On the other hand, republican festivals sometimes project the violent excess of the Revolution itself, and 'make a crime of isolation'. Ozouf, above n 107, 12.
[168] Kevin Olson, 'Epistemologies of Rebellion: the Tricolor Cockade and the Problem of Subaltern Speech' (2015) 43 *Political Theory* 730.

Conclusion

duty, it acknowledges and even aims to harness the considerable force of *pleasure* and self-expression.

Thus despite the radicalism of his ritual project, Rousseau demonstrates a certain realism in acknowledging that the republic, rather than appealing to self-sacrifice, must appeal to and harness our need of both recognition and pleasure. A range of constitutional incentives, such as public honours and approbations, will channel *amour-propre* towards less corrupting forms that are consistent with and supportive of republican politics. In a well-ordered republican state, our need for approval and esteem will harmonise and coincide with the requirements of the common good. Supporting the common good is simply made more *pleasurable* though a manipulative incentive structure which transforms the object and dynamic of public recognition. For Putterman, the 'incentive structure' of the Rousseauan state ensures that 'private interests will be more *pleasurable* when they mirror the common good';[169] similarly, Burtt notes that Rousseau aims to shape dispositions in such a manner that makes its pursuit 'immensely rewarding in emotional terms.'[170] Our pervasive need to win status and approval relative to others—the disposition which Rousseau believes lies at the root of political domination—can be reconfigured so as to support the dispositions of republican citizenship. Republican symbolism aims not only to reconcile, but to conjoin *amour-propre* and civic virtue.[171] Rousseau's recommendation of spectacle and ceremony has often been taken as proof of the unrealism of his constitutional writings, revealing him as a social critic or utopian polemicist rather than as a serious political theorist.[172] However, his concern for a robust and socially pervasive project of symbolic constitutionalism reflects his appreciation of the scale of the challenge in motivationally and affectively anchoring principles of political right in citizens' dispositions. And again, this aim is not unrecognisable or straightforwardly unacceptable in contemporary polities, given their aims of securing integration and affiliation.

Liberal constitutionalism, by contrast, will protect citizens against oppressive state ritualism or any hegemonic, intolerant symbolism. But it is silent against the unfreedom and domination latent in the cultural and social world of liberalism: it offers nothing against the alienation and hierarchy embedded in the symbolic and cultural universe of liberal society.

---

[169] Putterman, above n 22, 489.

[170] Burtt, above n 136, 25.

[171] 'signs, symbols, words, images, and stories … can capture imagination and *amour-propre* into the orbit of virtue and justice.': Dobel, above n 10, 652.

[172] Putterman, above n 22, see generally Judith Shklar, *Men and Citizens: a Study of Rousseau's Social Theory* (Cambridge, Cambridge University Press, 1969).

4

The Constitution of Deliberation

I. Introduction

Constitutions are concerned not only with the allocation and distribution of powers and competences between different organs, but also with the quality and character of political discourse and public deliberation. On the one hand, the enactment or ratification of Constitutions—whether by mass participation or elite micro-publics—is sometimes seen as an exemplary instance of deliberative democracy.[1] But Constitutions, in turn, will create and sustain various sites of official deliberation, protect (or contain) unofficial or non-state deliberative forums, and dictate or influence—at least indirectly—the character or scope of deliberation that takes place: its breadth and scope, its degree of inclusivity or specialisation, and so on. James Madison's appeal, in the *Federalist Papers*, for the elite filtering and mediation of mass popular opinion is perhaps the most celebrated of constitutional projects aimed at structuring and disciplining public deliberation.[2] Equally, Rousseau's constitutional projects are concerned not only with the grounds, but also the form and process of legislation and other public acts. Yet unlike Madison and other republicans, Rousseau is not concerned to contain the tyrannous passions of the masses, but rather the manipulative effects of elite speech. Notoriously, Rousseau—in contrast with other classical and modern republicans—is markedly sceptical as to the virtues and the emancipatory potential of political deliberation. Whereas most republicans (and indeed liberals) view deliberation (or proxy concepts) as intrinsic to meaningful political liberty or as a benchmark for legitimate political power, Rousseau seems to view it as an insidious source of symbolic and social domination. This explains, in part, his preference for ritual and experiential, over linguistic and deliberative or discursive forms of political communication. Alternatively, he simply recognises the potentially dominating character of deliberation in liberal, differentiated societies, and seeks to tame and constrain these effects within the same kind of austere social universe that is described in earlier chapters.

---

[1] Bruce Ackerman, *We the People 1: Foundations* (Cambridge MA, Harvard University Press, 1991); *We the People 1: Tranformations* (Cambridge MA, Harvard University Press, 1998).
[2] James Madison, Alexander Hamilton and John Jay, *The Federalist Papers* (I Kramnik ed, (London, Penguin, 1987).

In this chapter, I will explain how Rousseau's constitutional recommendations are aimed at foiling the political domination constituted by the field of political deliberation itself—and how this is linked to his wider project of austerity. I will argue that while Rousseau's constitutional project aims at sustaining a social universe where the sources of cultural and symbolic distinction are public and transparent, it also seeks to maintain transparency in the domain of political communication itself. Equally, I will show how his apprehension of deliberation as an emancipatory mechanism illustrates certain blindspots in the contemporary neo-republican account of freedom as non-domination—and consider how this insight might inform contemporary constitutional and political thought.

II. Rousseau on Deliberation, Dissensus, Dissent

One of the most striking aspects of Rousseau's political thought is his deep apprehension towards deliberation—or even political speech generally—as a potentially destructive social practice. Famously, he saw dissensus and political debate as harbingers of factionalism, corruption and civic decay. Far from illuminating the common interest, he claimed that political debate and discussion would actually prevent citizens from discerning the general will. Rousseau's scepticism towards deliberation arises chiefly in the context of the plenary assembly where the entire people, assembled, exercises sovereignty through legislation. In typically strident style, he insists: 'it is essential, for the general will to express itself ... that each citizen think only his own thoughts.'[3] Mysteriously, he speculates that the general will would prevail if fully informed citizens 'had no communication with each another'.[4] He argues in Book II of the *Social Contract*:

> If, when the sufficiently informed people deliberates, [and] *the citizens were to have no communication with one another* ... from the great many small differences the general will always results, and the decision would always be good.[5]

This viewpoint is linked to Rousseau's broader apprehension of 'factions' as disruptive sources of private or particular interest. He continues:

> It is therefore essential, if the general will is to be able to express itself, that there should be no partial society within the State, and that each citizen should think only his own thoughts ... But if there are partial societies, it is best to have as many as possible and to prevent them from being unequal ... These precautions alone can ensure the general will shall be always enlightened, and that the people shall in no way deceive itself.[6]

---

[3] Jean-Jacques Rousseau, *Du Contrat Social* (Paris, ENAG, 1988/1762), (hereinafter *Social Contract*), Bk II, Ch 3.
[4] ibid.
[5] ibid, emphasis added.
[6] ibid Bk IV, Ch 2.

He elaborates further on this link between deliberation and factionalism in Book IV:

> The more concert reins in the assemblies, that is, the more opinion approaches unanimity, the more the general will is dominant; but long debates, dissensions and tumult herald the rise of particular interests and the decline of the State. ... Even in the most tumultuous times, the *plebiscita* of the people, when the Senate did not interfere with them, always passed quietly and by large majorities. The citizens having but one interest, the people had but a single will.[7]

He continues:

> When in the popular assembly a law is proposed, what the people is asked is not exactly whether it approves or rejects the proposal, but whether it is in conformity with the general will, which is their will. Everyone, in giving his vote, states his opinion on this point; and the general will is found by counting votes (*calcul des voix*).[8]

Moreover, Rousseau does not explicate how the general will is discovered, if not through something akin to deliberation. In frustratingly hyperbolic terms, he suggests the general will is discernible 'only through good sense'—figuratively, by 'peasants gathered under an oak'.[9]

Rousseau does say, however, that when the general will prevails, 'there are no embroilments or conflicts of interests; the common good is everywhere clearly apparent, and only good sense is needed to perceive it.'[10] What is clear, then, is that the successful discernment of the general will is linked to the wider social context—that of austerity. He continues:

> Honest [*droit*] and simple men are difficult to deceive because of their simplicity; illusions [*leurres*] and refined pretences [*prétextes*] fail to impose upon them, and they are not even subtle enough to be dupes. When, among the happiest people in the world, bands of peasants are seen regulating affairs of State under an oak, and always acting wisely, can we help scorning the ingenious methods of other nations, which make themselves illustrious and wretched with so much art and mystery?[11]

He proceeds:

> A State so governed needs very few laws ... The first man to propose them merely says what all have already felt, and there is no question of ploys [*brigues*] or eloquence in order to secure the passage into law of what every one has already decided to do, as soon as he is sure that the rest will act with him.[12]

He also insists dissent is a symptom of civic decay:

> The general will becomes mute: all men, guided by secret motives, no more give their views as citizens than if the State had never been; and iniquitous decrees directed solely to private interest are passed under the name of law.[13]

---

[7] ibid.
[8] ibid.
[9] ibid, Bk IV, Ch 1.
[10] ibid.
[11] ibid.
[12] ibid.
[13] ibid.

Crucially, then, Rousseau goes against the whole grain of deliberative-democratic theory in prizing the act of voting itself above that of deliberation or discussion. Far from the act of voting being constrained or disciplined through a responsibility to deliberate, he portrays voting as being in need of protection from the corruption engendered by complex discourse. He illustrates this with reference to the classical world:

> As for the method of taking the vote, it was among the ancient Romans as simple as their mores, although not so simple as at Sparta. Everyone declared his vote aloud, and a clerk duly wrote it down; the majority in each tribe determined the vote of the tribe, the majority of the tribes that of the people, and so with *curiæ* and centuries. This custom was good as long as honesty prevailed among the citizens, and each man was ashamed to vote publicly in favour of an unjust proposal or an unworthy subject; but, when the people grew corrupt and votes were bought, it was fitting that voting should be secret in order that purchasers might be restrained by distrust, giving rogues the means of not being traitors.[14]

III. Deliberation and Non-domination

Rousseau's apprehension towards political deliberation as itself a potentially dominating practice can be understood, in one sense, as anomalous in light of the wider republican history of thought, both classical and modern.

Certainly, ancient and modern thinkers understood the potentially subversive uses of the different modes of political discourse—not only of 'deliberation' as it is now called, but especially of oratory, rhetoric and so on.[15] In general terms, however, the practice of deliberation—characterised by an exchange of reasons and a sincere, cooperative disposition aimed at rational persuasion—is widely understood by republican thinkers as potentially emancipatory or potentially as a foil to political domination broadly understood. Although republicans have not generally adopted the terminologies of deliberative-democracy theorists, deliberation, or some variant, is often presented as an integral aspect of republican citizenship. In some strands of the republican tradition, deliberation—or political speech more generally—is understood as a form of virtuous political action. For Arendt, political speech is a form of political action through which citizens insert themselves in the public sphere and so it represents an exercise and a realisation of political freedom. Thus the deliberative public sphere offers a site for the intersubjective formation of political identity, aimed at the recognition as much as the

---

[14] ibid, Bk IV, Ch 4.
[15] Gary Remer, 'Political Oratory and Conversation: Cicero versus Deliberative Democracy' (1999) 27 *Political Theory* 39.

conciliation of competing interests and identities.[16] Deliberation, in this lens, is humanising, fulfilling and emancipating.[17]

By contrast, republicans such as Philip Pettit, closer to the Roman tradition, tend to eschew any understanding, Arendtian or otherwise, of political speech generally—or deliberation specifically—as being intrinsically valuable as a means of self-realisation or recognition. Instead, deliberation can be valued as a type of political reasoning that is aimed at discerning and articulating common interests or common goods. In this vision of politics, deliberation enables citizens to make collective decisions based on common interests and values rather than deciding based on 'brute preference or bargained compromise.'[18] The public sphere is not, then, simply a mechanism for reconciling individual interests, but rather a forum for defining common goods and shared identities. And while the role of deliberation is to discern and articulate common goods, these are not understood as antecedent or pre-given, but rather as being determined through the practice of deliberation itself. Thus the dispositions and skills of 'deliberative engagement' are commonly juxtaposed with alternative understandings of cultural solidarity or cohesion as the basis of political community.[19]

Since republicans like Pettit understand freedom negatively—as an absence of domination—the role of deliberation is to render public power non-arbitrary and thus non-dominating. Public power is non-dominating, Pettit argues, where it is subject to an equally shared system of 'popular control'—where it is exercised 'on the people's terms'.[20] And deliberation, or some proxy, then becomes relevant, because if the people are to exercise democratic 'control', public power must be exercised on the basis of common interests—which must be defined deliberately rather than as pre-given ends. In short, then, the deliberative public sphere is necessary as a foil to political domination—as a mechanism that ensures state power tracks interests its subjects share.[21] Whereas 'political power is non-arbitrary … to the extent that it is forced to track the common avowable interests of members of the society',[22] the role of deliberation is to formulate and define such interests, to ensure they are genuinely 'common' rather than the product of some brute aggregation of preferences. As for how deliberation actually crystallises shared interests,

---

[16] Hannah Arendt, *Between Past and Future* (Harmondsworth, Penguin, 1977).
[17] For discussion see Keith Topper, 'Arendt and Bourdieu between Word and Deed' (2011) 39 *Political Theory* 352.
[18] Philip Pettit, 'Deliberative Democracy, the Discursive Dilemma and Republican Theory' in James Fishkin and Peter Laslett (eds), *Philosophy, Politics and Society* Vol 7 (New York, Cambridge University Press, 2003) 138–62, 140.
[19] See generally Iseult Honohan, 'Educating Citizens: Nation-building and its Republican Limits' in Iseult Honohan and Jeremy Jennings (eds), *Republicanism in Theory and Practice* (London, Routledge, 2005).
[20] ibid 153.
[21] Philip Pettit, *Republicanism: A Theory of Freedom and Government* (Oxford, Clarendon Press, 1997) Ch 2.
[22] Pettit, ibid, 154.

Pettit suggests that by engaging in shared practices of democratic contestation, citizens form common projects and concerns based on which government power is to be controlled. They form common interests and concerns—which are to impose directive influence on government—as a 'by-product' of their interactions in the various sites of democratic contestation.[23]

Pettit's neo-republican account, which frames deliberation as a mechanism for defining shared interests, is premised on certain optimistic assumptions that overlap, in large part, with the controversial premises of deliberative-democratic theory generally—which often understands deliberation as an antidote to domination, or at least as neutralising or mitigating social power disparities.[24] Pettit's stance assumes, on the one hand, a society with widespread practices of deliberation, such that could make democratic control meaningfully 'equal'. This runs against an increasing focus in deliberative-democratic theory on deliberation in specialised sites such as assemblies, and an apprehension towards the possibilities of deliberation in mass democracy.[25] Pettit's position also depends on certain assumptions concerning the quality of deliberation itself. Particularly, it assumes the possibility of a substantive equality amongst participants, of the sort and to the degree that would make deliberation a meaningfully shared exercise.[26] This reflects certain assumptions, on the one hand, concerning the nature of the society in which deliberation is conducted—as sustaining the kind of substantive equality that can host deliberation. On the other, it makes assumptions concerning the nature of deliberation itself as a social activity—as being at least potentially a benign and sincere, as distinct from a manipulative and deceptive, practice. It envisages reciprocity, reasonableness and a spirit of cooperative endeavour rather than crude adversarialism.[27] In effect, it optimistically assumes that Habermas' idealised account of the eighteenth century bourgeois public sphere—a spontaneous and organic, but

---

[23] Philip Pettit, *On the People's Terms: a Republican Theory and Model of Democracy* (Cambridge, Cambridge University Press, 2013) Ch 5. Pettit distinguishes his republican theory of deliberation from deliberative democratic theories on the basis that deliberation in relation to particular decisions or policies is not intrinsically valuable; rather, deliberation defines the norms which set boundaries on decision-making and regulate acceptable outcomes. ibid 264.

[24] For Bagg, 'Deliberative democrats view high-quality deliberation not merely as a symptom of a healthy democracy—a by-product of deeper structural changes—but as a distinct agent of change and a strategic political priority; not only as the theoretical, idealised end of the fight against concentrated power, but also as a primary means of waging that war': Samuel Bagg, 'Can Deliberation Neutralize Power?' (2015) *European Journal of Political Theory*, published online before print, 20 October 2015, http://ept.sagepub.com/content/early/2015/10/19/1474885115610542.abstract.

[25] See, eg, Simon Niemeyer, 'The Emancipatory Effect of Deliberation: Empirical Lessons from Mini-Publics' (2011) 39 *Politics and Society* 103.

[26] Pettit essentially relies on a version of public reason, arguing that deliberating citizens must use reasons which their fellow citizens have no good reason to reject. For Lamore, this 'turns out … to constitute the deepest stratum in Pettit's republican theory, *[guiding] the determination of the interests which just laws ought to promote.*': Charles Larmore, 'A Critique of Philip Pettit's Republicanism' (2001) 11 *Philosophical Issues* 229, 240, 241, emphasis added.

[27] See, eg, Simone Chambers, 'Deliberative Democratic Theory' (2003) 6 *Annual Review of Political Science* 307.

nonetheless a relatively discrete or even elite discursive realm[28]—can feasibly be extended to and realised across a vastly more heterogeneous and divided liberal society, notwithstanding the considerable epistemic as well as practical challenges this poses.[29] It imagines that a mode of conversation that, in the ancient world, was understood as feasible only among social intimates can be replicated democratically across a differentiated, mass society.[30]

IV. Deliberation as Domination

In stark contrast with more optimistic and liberal republicans, Rousseau apparently does not understand deliberation as a safeguard against, but rather as being itself an important *source* of political domination. This apparent view of deliberation as a source of domination must be contextualised by his wider social thought. In chapter three in particular, I argued that Rousseau's constitutional preoccupations are explained largely by his understanding of domination and servitude as being embedded in innocuous, ostensibly innocent forms of social and cultural practice—and that his austerity is best understood as a response to these dimensions of unfreedom. By extension and by analogy, here I argue that his apprehensive attitude towards political deliberation can be understood as a response to domination of a similar kind—that which is found in the mundane, and the everyday—in tastes, manners and dispositions.

---

[28] For Habermas, 'rational-critical public debate' was 'not a feature of premodern societies'. Remer, above n 15, 40.

[29] For Dryzek: 'The key constraint here is one of economy. Robert Dahl and many others have pointed out that meaningful participation in collective decision by anything more than a tiny minority is inconceivable in contemporary nation-states ... The time demands on participants are simply impossible in anything beyond a very small-scale political unit. As Michael Walzer puts it, "Deliberation is not an activity for the demos...".'. John Dryzek, 'Legitimacy and Economy in Deliberative Democracy' (2001) 29 *Political Theory* 651, internal citation omitted,.

[30] Remer contrasts *sermo* or 'conversation' with *contention*—encompassing public modes of oratory in Cicero's thought: 'Unlike common oratory, which a single active speaker delivers to a passive audience, a dialogue is a conversation between two or more interlocutors, reflecting, ideally, the give-and-take of their discussion. Although the dialogue is a type of conversation, it is set apart from other varieties of conversation in that it is an inquiry into problems of some importance, in which different positions are explored.' Equally, 'whereas contentio, that is, speech to the masses, is marked by "extreme energy and passion", and a 'vigorous style', sermo, which is speech among the select, is serene and restrained ... Both Socrates and Cicero use the dialogic method toward the same end of finding the truth. For them, the search for philosophical truth is better enhanced by the interlocutors' common bonds than by their antagonistic posturings.' Thus Remer equally argues that *contentio* 'foreshadows deliberative democracy': Remer, above n 15, 43–45. Chambers suggests: 'The size and unruliness of the mass public dictate that, unlike mini- publics where deliberation is symmetrical, face-to-face, and equal, deliberation here will often be asymmetrical, highly mediated, and distorted by the structural inequalities in society ... That the poor and marginalized do not have the same access to communicative power as the rich and established is a huge problem for deliberative democratic legitimacy.': Simone Chambers, 'Rhetoric and the Public Sphere: Has Deliberative Democracy Abandoned Mass Democracy?' (2009) 37 *Political Theory* 323, 339.

As discussed in chapter three, Rousseau largely understands social power relations as being structured around the possession and distribution of non-economic forms of capital—social, cultural and symbolic. Thus in the second *Discourse*, he hypothesises that when the first societies formed, 'a value came to be attached to public esteem ... [to] whoever sang or danced best, [or] *was the most eloquent* ... and this was the first step towards inequality'.[31] Man's 'rank and condition' came to depend not only on his 'property and power', but also his 'wit, beauty and talent'—including, as we have seen, his 'eloquence'—attributes which it became necessary to 'possess or affect'.[32]

Thus the genesis of social domination lay not solely in brute coercion or even material inequality, but rather in the emergent need for recognition—as humans begin to 'live in the opinion of others'.[33] In this competitive and hierarchical social world, our cultural, ritual and leisure practices are an expression of *amour-propre*, the self-love that is consummated via external recognition. In turn, Rousseau understands that *amour-propre* engenders a certain kind of social performativity, and like Pierre Bourdieu he recognises that the techniques and competences—the 'spurious passions'[34]—needed to navigate this social field—have an essentially arbitrary value when considered apart from the status they confer within such fields.

In the same vein, Rousseau views political deliberation as engendering a form of domination because, like other social and cultural practices, it serves on the one hand to confer distinction or social capital based on differential competences.[35] It is conducted—much like various other cultural practices—based on quite arbitrary forms of know-how. To participate in deliberation—to be taken seriously, indeed to be *heard*—requires participants to master certain arbitrary competences, relating in part to the embodied character of speech, the *habitus* through which speakers are recognised as legitimate and authoritative, including factors such as demeanour, poise, accent and idiom. This helps to explain Rousseau's disparaging reference to the 'refined flourishes' of political speech.[36] Thus Rousseau

---

[31] Jean-Jacques Rousseau, *Discours sur l'origine et les fondements de l'inégalité parmi les hommes* (Paris, Flammarion, 1755/2008) (hereinafter *Second Discourse*), 141 emphasis added.

[32] ibid.

[33] ibid.

[34] ibid 142.

[35] For Adam Smith, by comparison, 'there remained a close but unheeded connection between rhetoric and the drive for moral approbation and praise. The struggle for social recognition and the effort to be publicly esteemed continued to take place within rhetorical strategies of persuasion, through which a shift in venue: oration, over time, had moved for the sphere of politics to the realm of ethical theory, more particularly to the zone of sympathy ... the modern subject must captivate attention, invoke affection, and provoke a willingness to empathize. By carrying out this project, rhetorical discourse emerges as the natural language of recognition. Agents ... adopt strategies of ... persuasion ... Subjects make use of rhetorical means to present themselves as worthy of recognition.': Andreas Kalyvas and Ira Katznelson, *Liberal Beginnings: Making a Republic for the Moderns* (Cambridge, Cambridge University Press, 2008) 37.

[36] *Second Discourse*, above n 31, 142.

views political discourse itself much in the same light as other specialised social practices that confer distinction based on arbitrary forms of know-how.[37] This is essentially what he means where he alludes in the *Social Contract* to those 'political subtleties'—that is, sophisticated forms of discourse—that he understands as undermining political equality.[38] Rousseau's concern is that, much like various cultural and artistic practices, political speech, in liberal society, becomes a highly specialised, even esoteric pursuit that acquires its own internal logic. Of course, ancient as well as modern political thinkers have reflected on the abuse of political speech—the reality that speakers 'can intentionally or unintentionally misuse language'[39] to persuade an audience. Rousseau, however, is sensitive not only to linguistic manipulation in this more obvious sense, but also the socially performative character of deliberation more broadly speaking.

Rousseau recognises, then, that as cultural and social practices assume increasingly complex forms, classifications of merit and value become deeply obscure and encoded, leading to invisible or insidious kinds of domination. And this seems to undermine the idea that deliberation might ever meaningfully be a shared or equal practice. However, his apprehension towards deliberation, specifically, also stems from his particular view of language itself. Much like later critical theorists, Rousseau understands language not as a neutral tool of communication, but as an instrument of social power which unconsciously and invisibly imposes arbitrary classifications of legitimacy and value.[40] If discourses are understood as 'shared ways of comprehending the world embedded in language',[41] then language itself incorporates and reflects, rather than merely communicating, the relevant worldviews. Language, then, constrains and shapes, as well as innocently conveying our sentiments and ideas.[42] And essentially, Rousseau extends a similar analysis not only to language but also to intellectual life itself. In liberal society, intellectual life assumes the form of a specialised micro-society whose participants—those endowed with the requisite competences and an authoritative *habitus*—glibly manipulate ideas not necessarily (or only) to obscure and perpetuate an unjust status quo, but also to win mutual recognition within the internal logic of the discursive 'game' itself. Ideas, and their modes of articulation, provide forms of positional capital.[43] Thus both propositionally as well as linguistically, deliberation is

---

[37] For Adam Smith, '[rhetorical] persuasion ... in modern times ... is utilized by market actors who, through their economic activity, struggle to win the approval and esteem of their own distinctively configured historical communities.' Thus 'life in a market society ... is an ongoing exercise in rhetoric.': Kalyvas and Katznelson, above n 35, 40.

[38] *Social Contract*, above n 3, Bk IV, Ch 1.

[39] William Bosworth, 'An Interpretation of Political Argument' (2016) *European Journal of Political Theory*, published online before print, 7 September 2016.

[40] See generally Pierre Bourdieu, *Language and Symbolic Power* (J Thompson ed, Cambridge MA, Harvard University Press, 1999).

[41] Dryzek, above n 29, 658.

[42] John Boswell, 'How and why Narrative Matters in Deliberative Systems' (2013) 61 *Political Studies* 620.

[43] Jean-Jacques Rousseau, *Discours sur les sciences et les arts* (Paris, Livres de Poche, 2012/1751).

a competitive social practice—all the while presenting itself as sincere, meaningful and benign.

A. Rousseau as Critical Discourse Theorist

Rousseau's understanding of deliberation—both of its inefficacy and its own insidiously dominating character—is highly prescient in many senses. It presages later critical scepticism concerning the supposedly emancipatory potential of political speech, or of political voice in the broad sense. On the one hand, Rousseau's sense of the inefficacy of deliberation, in its propositional and rational senses, presages the affective turn in contemporary political theory, with its focus on the necessity of a-rational and emotive forms of civic solidarity.[44] Rosenberg, for example, argues that deliberative theories fail to acknowledge the cognitive limits of our deliberative capacities, and so understate the role of emotional ties in political communication. Echoing Rousseau's scepticism, he suggests

> it seems unrealistic to assume that a commitment to fairly consider another's concerns can be based simply on the recognition that another person, as a thinking, sentient personality ... equally deserving of attention and consideration [or] to assume that a commitment to a common good will emerge solely on the basis of reflections on what is ethical and reasonable.[45]

In a similar vein, and echoing Rousseau's ritualism, he argues we need to be emotionally connected to our co-deliberators in a manner which can 'make that other person's pains and pleasures one's own.'[46]

On the other hand, Rousseau's positions anticipate later insights concerning not only the inefficacy, but also the active injuries and harms of deliberation, particularly the domination and symbolic violence it inflicts. This apprehension towards deliberation is paralleled by a deep-running and longstanding historical suspicion as to the manipulative effects of rhetorical and oratorical modes of political speech in particular. Remer, for example, details how historical instances of ostensibly deliberative exercises such as the ratification of the United States Constitution—while supposedly characterised by egalitarian reciprocity and sincerity—actually resembled 'oratory' more than 'deliberation', proving agonistic, emotive and a-rational, and prizing eloquence over the reasoned argument celebrated by Habermas.[47] In general terms, Rousseau anticipates a later branch

---

[44] Against the Kantian idea that 'emotion is manipulative while reasoned discourse is not', thinkers 'like James Bohman, Iris Marion Young, Henry Richardson, and Bryan Garsten have attempted to rehabilitate rhetoric as a legitimate component of deliberation': Chambers, above n 30, 326.

[45] See generally Shawn Rosenberg, 'Rethinking Democratic Deliberation: The Limits and Potential of Citizen Participation' (2007) 39 *Polity* 335, 348.

[46] ibid.

[47] Gary Remer, 'Two Models of Deliberation: Oratory and Conversation in Ratifying the Constitution' (2000) 8 *The Journal of Political Philosophy* 68.

of critical linguistics that 'sought to explore and expose how language is used as a tool for power, a means of concealment and method of marginalisation.'[48] More specifically, he presages later theorists such as Pierre Bourdieu in affirming the highly *embodied* and *performative* nature of deliberative technique, and especially, the understanding that deliberative capacities and merits are evaluated based not on cognitive or rational criteria, but rather, based on *habitus* and on 'articulatory style'—encompassing factors as ostensibly mundane as 'accents, gestures, intonations, and other bodily techniques for speaking.'[49] And like Bourdieu, he appreciates the often imperceptible, even invisible nature of those inequalities and hierarchies that are encoded both in performative and corporeal social techniques: he notes 'the devouring ambition ... the desire to place oneself above others, inspiring ... a surreptitious envy *which is all the more dangerous for the fact that it is often masked as benevolent.*'[50] This anticipates Bourdieu's argument that symbolic distinctions are efficacious because 'they function below the level of consciousness and language, beyond the reach of introspective scrutiny.'[51] While Rousseau's concern is that we identify natural authority in refined and manners dispositions—that arbitrary distinctions and hierarchies are mistaken as natural and innocent—Bourdieu similarly suggests that 'dominated agents ... tend to attribute to themselves what the distribution [of value and status] attributes to them, reproducing in their verdict on themselves the verdict [pronounced] on them.'[52] Similarly, Rousseau's understanding of discourse as a specialised social activity, with techniques and competences specific to particular micro-societies, echoes Foucault's understanding of discourse as a site of power that itself conditions and disciplines subjects.[53]

For Bourdieu, deliberative competence lies in the ability to command attention, to be *listened to* in a linguistic 'market'.[54] We are evaluated as deliberators based not on how we reason, but rather how we *speak*. Indeed, Hayward has demonstrated that the persuasiveness of political speech depends on its 'form and style', that are linked to the dominant *habitus*—and that this inequality cannot be remedied or overcome by the standard safeguards proposed by deliberative-democracy theorists.[55] Deliberative capacity is assessed in reality based on 'social dynamics',

---

[48] Alan Finlayson, 'Critique and Political Argumentation' (2013) 13 *Political Studies Review* 313.
[49] ibid 359.
[50] *Second Discourse*, above n 31, 140, emphasis added.
[51] Pierre Bourdieu, *Distinction: a Social Critique of the Judgement of Taste* (R Nice trans, Cambridge MA, Harvard University Press, 1987) 466.
[52] ibid 452.
[53] Dryzek notes: 'followers of Michel Foucault often treat discourses as power/knowledge formations that condition—to the extent of imprisoning—human subjects. If so, then, it is hard to be a Foucauldian and a deliberative democrat because deliberation across discourses is hard to imagine.': Dryzek, above n 29, 658.
[54] Bourdieu, above n 40, 29.
[55] Clarissa Hayward, 'Doxa and Deliberation' (2004) 7 Critical Review of International Social and Political Philosophy 1.

not 'abstract cognitive and communicative capability'.[56] And this in turns entails insidious forms of domination: as Olson argues, 'people of dominant identities are ascribed greater competence than others, and not coincidentally those people are more likely to have political opinions and feel entitled to express them'.[57] Those unwilling or indisposed to deliberate may lack the requisite *habitus* or the social/cultural capital necessary to participate, or may be unwilling to affect the necessary competences and strategies: 'persons lacking the linguistic competences valorized in particular social and institutional domains are de facto excluded from participation in them'.[58]

Thus, while deliberative-democratic theorists offer certain explanations as to how deliberative inequalities can be remedied—such that, in particular, citizens have roughly equal resources and opportunities permitting them to participate[59]— Rousseau offers a more sceptical perspective as to how meaningful deliberative equality could ever be realised in a competitive linguistic marketplace. Even where formal avenues are maintained, the problem is that our 'linguistic-bodily competence' can constitute a 'practical barrier to *authoritative* political speech' within ostensibly egalitarian speech fora. Relatedly, the problem is not so much that the capabilities necessary for deliberative participation are unequally shared or distributed, but rather that these required competences have an essentially arbitrary value outside the context of a particular speech-culture. Thus the factors that determine *legitimate* political speech—for example those insinuated in bodily technique—are simply dependent on the peculiar *habitus* operating in the relevant 'linguistic market'.[60] And consequently, marginalised voices may struggle to find adequate expression through conventional idiom[61]—especially since 'moral grievances … are systematically obstructed by received linguistic and epistemic practices'.[62]

Since Rousseau, like Bourdieu, understands that the social validity of speech acts is determined by arbitrary symbolic and social classifications rather than by any yardstick of rationality, he is sceptical as to how deliberation can offer a mechanism of political and social emancipation. Relatedly, his insight concerning the

---

[56] Kevin Olson, 'Legitimate Speech and Hegemonic Idiom: The Limits of Deliberative Democracy in the Diversity of its Voices' (2011) 59 *Political Studies* 527, 536. Echoing Rousseau's concerns on social differentiation and language, Bourdieu argues that in late-modern societies domination occurs as 'esoteric discourses … undergo a kind of automatic universalization' outside the boundaries of a specialised 'field'.: Bourdieu, above n 40, 41.

[57] Olson, ibid 535.

[58] Topper, above n 17, 354.

[59] See, eg, Amy Gutmann and Dennis Thompson, *Why Deliberative Democracy?* (Princeton NJ, Princeton University Press, 2004).

[60] Topper, above n 17, 354–55.

[61] Bosworth, above n 39.

[62] Congdon argues: 'situations of injustice arise in which an individual or a group is left without adequate and authoritative expressive resources.' Congdon has argued that epistemic injustice of this kind occurs where, within the 'moral vocabulary' that already exists, 'some inchoate sense of injury or harm is registered yet remains socially inarticulable.': Matthew Congdon, 'Wronged beyond Words: On the Publicity and Repression of Moral Injury' (2016) 42 *Philosophy and Social Criticism* 815, 816.

domination that is intrinsic to language offers a critical response to Habermas' conception of communicative rationality as conferring legitimacy on political authority.[63] While Habermas posits an ideal speech situation, free of confusion and manipulation, as a regulative benchmark for politics, Bourdieu contests Habermas' conception of an ideal speech situation in which the 'rational character of communicative action would be unhindered by social constraints'—because 'whatever power of force speech acts possess is … ascribed to them by the social institution of the utterance of which the speech act is part.'[64] Similarly, Rousseau implicitly understands that communicative rationality cannot serve as a normative benchmark for political freedom because symbolic domination and befuddlement are intrinsic to language, not aberrational or accidental features. Language has no pure form—even hypothetically—outside of social power relations,[65] meaning that no hypothetical speech situation can offer a useful benchmark for political freedom.[66] While Connolly has noted that conventional language entails 'institutionalized structure of meanings that channels political thought and action in certain directions',[67] this problem is a more or less intractable one. Or, to repurpose Iris Marion Young's argument, there is no hard and fast distinction between *what* political speech says, and *how* it is said or communicated—between substance and style.[68]

Therefore, deception and domination are not anomalous or abusive, but rather intrinsic to language. And similarly, by extension, the problem of political speech is not that of rational discourse being 'hijacked' by rhetorical or other manipulative modes of speech; rather, the problem is that since political speech is intrinsically a social rather than a cognitive competence, the (social) *authority* of political speech is inevitably, and by necessity, somewhat arbitrary.

Thus on the one hand, a common critique of deliberative democracy suggests that deliberative reasoning tends to be ineffective in overcoming prior biases and interests, because psychologically, humans perceive and assimilate new

---

[63] See Bourdieu's critique of Habermas; above n 40, 10.
[64] ibid, Editor's introduction, 10.
[65] Margaret Kohn, 'Language, Power, Persuasion: Towards a Critique of Deliberative Democracy' (2000) 7 *Constellations* 408.
[66] Finlayson notes: 'The Kantian tradition is primarily concerned with setting limits to what will be considered reasonable language, and with policing the borders of linguistic legitimacy. This results in a normative concern with the institutions and processes of deliberation and debate, and in the design of principles with which to evaluate them—particularly in terms of their inclusivity and rationality. In contrast, a Wittgensteinian tradition has been concerned with language in use. This has issued in rich studies of political language understood not as descriptions or representations but as "tools and weapons of ideological debate". A third tradition derives from varied blends of Marxism, phenomenology and continental theories of language. One strand conceptualises discourses as structures within which identities are shaped and reshaped, and examines how the force of meaning is contained or deployed within and through political action, another emphasises the productivity and excess of language.': Finlayson, above n 48, 313–14 (internal citations omitted).
[67] William Connolly, *The Terms of Political Discourse* (Lexington MA, DC Heath, 1974).
[68] Iris Marion Young, *Inclusion and Democracy* (Oxford, Oxford University Press, 2000).

'information in ways that are unintentionally biased to protect our prior commitments and social identities', such that even sincerely motivated interlocutors are 'highly unlikely to change their minds as a result of deliberation'.[69] Thus whereas self-interested claims can be universalised and promoted under the guise of shared rationality, this seems relatively intractable in particular because it is unconscious. This refers to the post-hoc or insidiously partisan nature of sincere reasoning processes—a problem which Rousseau and others at least allude to. However, the Rousseauan insight runs deeper and refers not only to the indeterminacy and manipulability of rational argument, but also that of language itself, thus anticipating and pre-empting the Habermasian ideal. Like Bourdieu, Rousseau understands that language cannot be understood prior to or outside its communicative context. His insight is that deliberation or discourse generally occurs not as a propositional or rational activity but rather as a 'speech culture',[70] with relations of power insinuated in its specific symbols and rituals. And the Rousseauan critique of deliberation, specifically, is especially salient because unlike other modes of political speech—especially rhetoric—deliberation is characterised by an ostensible innocence, a commitment to reciprocity and rationality and a disavowal of manipulative distortions.

Arguably, Rousseau is distinct from other republican thinkers because he is relatively unconcerned with the *form* or mode of political speech—whether it assumes the form say, of deliberation or rhetoric. Madison, for example, worried that 'irregular passions'—or the 'artful misrepresentations of interested men'—might prevail over the 'cool and deliberate sense of the community' (represented by institutions like the Senate).[71] And Plato, amongst others, was concerned to defend the dialogic as opposed to the demagogic format of political speech.[72] But the Rousseauan perspective is that the ostensibly rational and egalitarian form of deliberative exercises is especially insidious as it obscures the domination encoded within deliberative language itself—language that is ostensibly innocent. His apprehension of political discourse extends from obviously asymmetric and manipulative

---

[69] Bagg notes: 'even given maximally optimistic levels of deliberative norm enforcement in mini-publics and the broader public sphere, we are unlikely to achieve power-neutralising deliberative conversions with substantially greater regularity than we already observe. Powerful citizens are unlikely to recognise their agendas as "selfish", or as illegitimately perpetuating their own concentrated power at the expense of others. Nor will their allies recognise this, so long as that alliance is grounded in their own forms of social identification. Because our "reason" is constitutively shaped by our identity, much of the "selfishness" we exhibit is unintentional and even invisible to us; unconsciously woven into the fabric of our moral experience.': Bagg, above n 24, 2.

[70] This phrase is borrowed from Jensen Sass and John Dryzek, 'Deliberative Cultures' (2014) 42 *Political Theory* 3.

[71] Madison et al, above n 2, no 10.

[72] Chambers notes: 'Plato's attack on rhetoric is an attack on democratic politics because Plato assumes that, as the rule of the many, democracy must proceed through speeches that seek to persuade the many. But he questions whether oratory can ever be brought in line with reason. In contrast to the speech, Plato, especially in the figure of Socrates, champions an ideal of communication that is pursued by a small group of individuals.': Chambers, above n 30, 328.

forms of speech to embrace the insidious violence that is equally embedded in ostensibly reasonable and rational alternatives. In short, he rejects the idea that the problem of political speech can be understood in terms of dichotomies between artifice and sincerity, passion and reason.[73] The real source of domination in political speech is not the degeneration from a legitimate to an illegitimate mode or form—that is, from deliberation to rhetoric—but rather the deception and symbolic violence rooted in the legitimate form itself. (Indeed, Rousseau *must* reject this distinction, partly because as I have explored, the Republic must 'persuade' as well as 'convince'). And this anticipates, in part, the critical insights of scholars like Iris Marion Young, who argue that ostensibly dispassionate modes of speech may serve both to universalise and obscure the culturally dominant idiom.[74] Indeed it has been observed that 'the groups regularly identified as lacking sufficient neutrality in speech have been overwhelmingly drawn from the marginalized or less powerful in society.'[75]

In this light, Rousseau's stated aim of excluding complex political discourse from the public sphere can be understood as aiming at a kind of social transparency— and thus as an extension of the politics of austerity outlined in previous chapters. Just as republican austerity in general foils the domination embedded in complex social practices, the eschewal of complex political speech, and of deliberative practices in particular, precludes the domination latent in the performative complexities of political speech. Of course, this begs the question as to what form political communication and political discourse *can* assume under republican austerity— and how this enables the general will to be discerned and realised in practical forms.

V. Deliberation under Republican Austerity

In one sense, Rousseau's civic ritualism—ceremonies, oaths, festivals and the like—can be understood as an alternative form of political communication that largely supplants, or obviates, the need for linguistic and propositional forms of discourse.[76] By contrast, deliberative-democratic theorists have understood nonrational persuasion as coercive and illegitimate.[77] Rousseau's conjecture, in part,

---

[73] On this distinction see Chambers, ibid.
[74] Young, above n 68.
[75] Chambers, above n 30, 326.
[76] Dryzek and Sass note: 'For Sanders and Young, political deliberation is not a basic feature of human societies, but rather a practice limited to particular classes of people in certain countries during a short period of history.': Dryzek and Sass, above n 70, 3.
[77] Remer notes: 'theorists of deliberative democracy seek to "set conditions such that only rational, that is, argumentative, convincing is allowed to take place" ... Nonrational persuasion, meanwhile, becomes equated with coercion ... For deliberative democrats, coercion is not limited to "threats and bribes," but includes "rhetorical manipulation," which consists chiefly of appeals to the passions.' Remer, above n 15, 50–51, internal citations omitted.

is that political community can, and is perhaps more likely to flourish, based on quite different forms of communication (or communion).[78] This strategy stems partly from Rousseau's sense of the *limits* of linguistic, rational or propositional discourse in the absence of emotional and affective connection amongst citizens (indeed, contemporary theorists of agonistic politics contend that deliberation is ineffective because it is too constraining in the kind of communication it allows).[79] He implicitly recognises that deliberation presupposes a certain division of political labour that tends towards aristocracy and inequality, perhaps because of the reciprocity and mutual sincerity, and thus the intimacy it requires. And indeed, modern political scientists have observed that mass participation and political equality necessarily require sacrifices to deliberative culture and quality.[80]

But as I have noted, Rousseau is concerned not only with the inefficacy, but also with the positive injuries, that is, the domination and violence that is actively (albeit insidiously) imposed within deliberative practices—and understands that language is never a neutral communicative medium, but rather a social practice which reflects and reproduces social hierarchies—'a weapon to leave individuals in a state of befuddled inferiority.'[81] While Arendt and others view political speech as potentially emancipatory in that it permits individuals to insert themselves in public space, offering a kind of self-actualisation through intersubjective recognition, Rousseau views it, more sceptically, as a highly corruptible tool of social distinction and thus as an insidious site of domination. Thus his preference for ritualism both reflects the limits of language itself, while supplanting and foiling the complexity—and thus the domination—that is inherent in deliberation as a specialised social technique. This explains why, for Rousseau, political liberty requires not only a commonly avowable set of public norms, but a shared symbolic universe which foils the symbolic violence—and domination—that are latent in complex social practices.

While Rousseau's apprehension towards deliberation is consistent with his wider social politics, it leaves open the question as to how, then, the general will is to be discerned and legislated in this austere social world. Through what kinds of political communication, specifically, is a non-dominating republican politics to be

---

[78] Sass and Dryzek note: 'in their study of the social order of a public bar in Buffalo, New York, [Eliasoph and Lichterman discovered a group culture that was strongly egalitarian and yet antideliberative. While patrons of this bar were strongly committed to civic life, and while they promoted equal relations between all patrons, they shared the presupposition that to talk about politics with one another was not democratic or egalitarian but hierarchical and elitist, a form of grandstanding that was potentially antagonistic.': Sass and Dryzek, above n 70, 15. See also Nina Eliasoph and Paul Lichterman, 'Culture in Interaction' (2003) 108 *American Journal of Sociology* 735.

[79] John Dryzek, 'Deliberative Democracy in Divided Societies: Alternatives to Agonism and Analgesia' (2005) 33 *Political Theory* 218.

[80] See generally James Fishkin, 'Deliberative Democracy and Constitutions' (2011) 28 *Social Philosophy and Policy* 242. Also Chambers notes: 'contemporary deliberative theory appears to doubt that the mass public sphere can be deliberative': Chambers, above n 30, 324.

[81] J Patrick Dobel, 'The Role of Langauge in Rousseau's Political Thought' (1986) 18 *Polity* 638, 655.

conducted? It is clear, on the one hand, that the common good cannot be realised through political deliberation, in its typical sense of the reciprocal exchange and consideration of reasons, in an otherwise fragmented social universe. But equally is it unclear, on the other hand, how experiential and ritual forms of political communication can achieve this. In some accounts, the content of the general will is not pre-given—as something to be discovered—but rather, counter-intuitively, is discerned *through* deliberative practices. On this view, the general will has no fixed content—in the sense of an objective or transcendent account of the common good—but rather equates to a set of decisions formulated through a deliberative procedure which filters out sectional and personal interests.[82] Sreenivisan, for example, argues the general will is 'the totality of unrescinded decisions made by a community ... *when its deliberation is subject to certain restraints*.'[83] These deliberative constraints give expression to citizens' moral and contractual equality and mark the passage from natural to moral freedom. Alternatively, if instead the general will encompasses fixed common interests that precede any democratic procedure, it can still be argued that these transcendent interests can only be discerned through a form of deliberation (subject to similar constraints).

Of course, this contradicts Rousseau's stated rejection of deliberative practices. What it suggests, in effect, is that his ostensibly strident rejection of political deliberation must be qualified (especially when we bear in mind his sometimes hyperbolic style). On the one hand, we must bear in mind that, in the *Social Contract*, Rousseau rejects deliberation in a very specific context—that of the plenary legislative assembly where the entirety of citizens exercise sovereignty through legislation. In *Poland* (where he concedes the inevitability of a certain kind of political representation), he notes that whereas a plenary citizen legislature 'is impossible to corrupt but easy to deceive', a representative assembly is 'hard to deceive, but easy to corrupt.'[84] What this suggests, arguably, is that Rousseau's apparent aversion to deliberation stems from a fear of demagoguery and manipulation in the context of asymmetrical communication between rhetoricians and mass audience, and that it may not extent to all contexts of political discourse. His concern, in this light, is that deliberation degenerates into more manipulative modes of speech. Arguably, then, it is comparable, for example, to the suspicion of referendums that is quite commonplace today.[85]

---

[82] For Rawls, the general will is 'a form of deliberative reason that each citizen shares with all other citizens in virtue of their sharing a conception of their common good.': John Rawls, *Lectures on the History of Political Philosophy* (Cambridge MA, Harvard University Press, 2007) 224.

[83] Gopal Sreenivasan, 'What is the General Will?' (2000) 109 *The Philosophical Review* 54, emphasis added.

[84] Jean-Jacques Rousseau, *Considérations sur le Gouvernement de Pologne et sur sa réforme projetée* in *Collection complète des oeuvres* (Genève, 1780–89) vol 1 Ch IV; for a translation see 'Considerations on the Government of Poland' in Frederick Watkins, *Jean-Jacques Rousseau: Political Writings* (New York, Thomas Yelsen, 1953) Chapter 7. Nonetheless, he says: 'To save precious time in the diets, you should try to rid these assemblies of useless discussions which are merely time-consuming'.

[85] See generally Fishkin, 'Deliberative Democracy and Constitutions', also Eoin Daly, 'A Republican Defence of the Constitutional Referendum' (2015) 35 *Legal Studies* 30.

Of course, Rousseau cannot only be concerned about the degeneration of rational political discourse towards manipulative demagoguery, because as I have argued, part of this insight is that the apparent rationalism and reasonableness of ostensibly effective deliberative exercises can itself harbour hierarchy and symbolic violence. And certainly, Rousseau is concerned that sophisticated political discourse may effectuate a sort of symbolic violence by excluding and duping those without access to the relevant techniques and terminologies. He understands, in particular, that where deliberation assumes the form of a specialised social technique with its own internal logic—that is, with its peculiar norms, classifications, symbols and rituals and so on—it will more likely obscure than illuminate, and offer befuddlement and confusion, rather than mutual enlightenment, to the various interlocutors. But if 'deliberation' is to occur at all in the Rousseauan constitutional schema, crucially it will occur only in a social context of austerity—that can stem the esotericism and obscurity of deliberative practices.

For all Rousseau's aversion to 'deliberation' both in its degenerate and ostensibly legitimate forms, arguably the general will is discerned 'deliberatively', at least in quite a specific sense. In its widest sense, deliberation entails a weighing up of preferences and reasons with a disposition towards revision and adaptation.[86] To legislate the general will requires that individuals reflectively evaluate their preferences and opinions with reference to the common good of their community—that is, to reason from the abstract standpoint of the citizen, filtering out their own particular interests. This is, quintessentially, a deliberative model of public reason. And in turn, Rousseau's conjecture is that this specific form of public reason can be fostered not by endowing citizens with specific deliberative skills, but rather through the austerity which he believes can offer transparency—and foil symbolic domination—in social practice generally. This is what he alludes to, essentially, where he suggests the general will is discernible 'only through good sense'—figuratively, by 'peasants gathered under an oak'.[87] Therefore he does not seek to eliminate deliberation, or eschew political speech altogether.[88] Nor does he even intend, necessarily, that individual citizens' reasoning should be untainted by communication or discussion. Instead he is simply concerned that political discourse should not become a specialised social ritual with insidiously exclusionary terminologies and techniques, of the sort that tends to mystify the uninitiated and obscure social hierarchies. His concern, then, is that deliberation should occur in a social context where it will not likely inflict the sorts of insidious domination with

---

[86] Chambers: 'classically, deliberation refers to the weighing of factors relevant for choosing a course of action': Chambers, above n 30, 332.

[87] *Social Contract*, above n 3, Bk IV, Ch 1.

[88] Sass and Dryzek note that deliberation can assume non-rational forms: 'rhetoric, silence, gossip, humor'. Equally they point out: 'Rather than take Western practices as a yardstick of democratic performance, we should examine democratic potential wherever it appears, even (perhaps especially) in seemingly unpromising contexts such as the Islamic revival in Egypt. Democratic potential is widespread—not limited to democratic polities—because it can be located in diverse expressions of the universal human capacity to deliberate collectively.': Sass and Dryzek, above n 70, 6.

which he is concerned. This perhaps explains why he suggests 'simple and upright men' cannot be 'duped' by sophistry or 'refined flourishes': the dominating effects of sophisticated deliberation are foiled in the context of an austere society.

In turn, while it might appear that Rousseau's ritualism is intended to *substitute* linguistic and propositional discourse—offering a more transparent outlet for political expression—alternatively we can say that ritualism *aids* 'deliberation' in the sense outlined, by giving citizens concrete experiential and visual representation for 'public meanings'.[89] Deliberation, and political discourse generally, are more likely to fulfil their aims—and to remain benign—within a common symbolic universe. On the one hand, republican citizenship is partly deliberative in nature, but this is meaningful only in the context of a common ritual and symbolic life, bereft of the kind of complex symbolic distinctions discussed in chapter three in particular. In short, therefore, it is impossible to understand Rousseau's critique of deliberation considered apart from the kind of austere social universe that I discussed in the previous chapters. Only in this sort of austere society, egalitarian and fraternal, can the appropriate deliberative virtues be fostered.

VI. Deliberation and Difference

While I have argued that there is scope for deliberation in Rousseau's social and political universe at least in a limited and specific way, there will, in one sense, be less need for deliberation under republican austerity—simply because the *differences* that are usually thought of as necessitating deliberation will be erased. While deliberation is often presented as a response to deep-seated social differences,[90] correspondingly the cultural homogeneity outlined in chapter two removes, in part, much of the need to deliberate. And such deliberation as might exist in the austere republic cannot be aimed at reconciling such differences, simply because Rousseau understands the formation (and perception) of such differences as expressing a corrupted *amour-propre*. As Gauthier puts it, he aims to see 'self and other united in a single whole.'[91] The more we 'deliberate' based on an understanding of our difference that stems from a corrupted *amour-propre*, the more we are distanced figuratively from the austere peasants deliberating under the 'oak tree'. While theorists of agonistic politics argue that deliberative democracy is 'incapable of processing deep difference',[92] Rousseau is focused more on the arbitrariness and contingency of identity itself—viewing differentiation itself as an expression

---

[89] Dobel, above n 81, 650.
[90] Dryzek, above n 79.
[91] David Gauthier, *Rousseau: the Sentiment of Existence* (Cambridge, Cambridge University Press, 2006) 65.
[92] Dryzek, above n 79, 220.

of corruption. Like Pierre Bourdieu then, Rousseau understands that the main barrier to effective political deliberation is not differential identity, but rather differential *habitus*. He understands that differentiating techniques and discursive signifiers, whether corporeal or symbolic, are not simply markers of differentiated group identity that are antecedent to deliberation itself. Rather, these determine the legitimacy and authority of deliberative inputs based on factors as arbitrary and mundane as accent, intonation or bodily poise—that is, the 'embodied character of speech'.[93]

Thus Rousseau sounds a cautionary note concerning the role of communication or discourse in response to difference, as he brings into question both the relevant concept of difference, as well as the emancipatory effects of deliberation itself. For Arendt, 'the problem of politics is not when people are different, but when they are unable to communicate'.[94] But Rousseau, like Bourdieu, focuses on how political communication itself inflicts domination. Therefore, the central problem of politics is not our inability to communicate, but rather the befuddlement and alienation produced by ostensibly innocent forms of communication. Arendt celebrates the pleasure and spontaneity of political action, '*the joy and gratification that arise out of being in company with our peers*, out of acting together and appearing in public, out of inserting ourselves into the world by word and deed.'[95] However, while for Arendt political voice is the cornerstone of the just political community, for Rousseau it threatens to undermine it, and so on the one hand, he prefers ritual and symbolic affirmations of commonality that foreclose much of the supposed need for deliberative engagement. On the other hand, such deliberation as occurs is to be disciplined by republican austerity. For Arendt, politics is largely 'a matter of individual distinction and identity.'[96] And while her sense of republican citizenship is not simply a matter of crude 'self-display'—or a mechanism for disclosing pre-determined identities,[97] nonetheless, it is this very feature of political expression—our dependency on external recognition for our sense of self—which for Rousseau, harbours and inflicts domination.

Similarly, Topper argues that while Arendt focuses on the political consequences of citizens' 'loss of voice', Bourdieu is more centrally concerned by 'the often inconspicuous ways in which language itself becomes a mechanism of silencing, domination, or exclusion.'[98] Arendt, Topper suggests, overlooks the political significance of 'social distinctions embodied in and expressed through speech.'[99] Bourdieu, in contrast, shows that 'domination and exclusion are enacted through concrete

---

[93] Olson, above n 56, 533.
[94] Iseult Honohan, *Civic Republicanism* (Abingdon, Taylor and Francis, 2002) 124.
[95] Hannah Arendt, *Between Past and Future* (Harmondsworth, Penguin 1977) 263, emphasis added.
[96] Honohan, above n 94, 123.
[97] Thus 'citizens interactively define what their collective ends might be, rather than implementing previously determined ... ends': ibid.
[98] Topper, above n 17, 354.
[99] ibid 357.

linguistic exchanges'.[100] Thus political discourse potentially harbours 'gentle' and 'inconspicuous'[101] violence in which status-hierarchies are unconsciously enforced and reproduced. While people suffer domination where they lack 'the linguistic competences valorised in a particular social or institutional domain',[102] encompassing bodily and symbolic techniques—political speech constitutes its own self-referential competences which inflict befuddlement and exclusion—and ultimately help secure the 'domestication of the dominated'.[103] Far from erasing or reconciling differences, deliberation constitutes fresh and insidious axes of social distinction.

For Rousseau, like Bourdieu, political expression cannot be conceptualised primarily as a form of 'identity disclosure',[104] because we do not use political speech primarily to disclose our identities in the Arendtian sense, but rather to *distinguish* ourselves. Both share the insight, described by Kohn, that 'miscommunication and manipulation are not accidental ... but part of the nature of language itself'.[105] Thus 'while Arendt extols the way that words and public speech bond and constitute political communities, Bourdieu explores the ways in which they quietly wound and dissolve them.'[106] This questions 'the basis on which any shared or authorized language is constituted and hence the basis of politics itself'.[107]

VII. Neo-republican Blindspots

In general, I have argued that Rousseau's communitarian politics—his commitment to austerity—can be interpreted in large part as a response to the intractability of domination in the social practices of liberal societies. In this concluding section, I will argue that Rousseau's scepticism concerning the subversive and potentially dominating effects of deliberation help to illustrate certain blindspots in contemporary, neo-republican thought concerning the source and structure of domination itself.

While republicans have emphasised the emancipatory potential of political deliberation, they have, I argued, paid insufficient heed to the possibility that political deliberation itself may harbour insidious forms of domination. While most republican theorists value deliberation for its role in a politics aimed at stemming public and private domination across a range of interpersonal, communal

---

[100] ibid 358.
[101] ibid 355.
[102] ibid 360.
[103] Bourdieu, above n 40, 167.
[104] Topper, above n 17, 359.
[105] Kohn, above n 65, 410.
[106] Topper, above n 17, 358.
[107] ibid 360.

and political relationships, they generally under-account for the forms of domination embedded in deliberative practice itself.

Neo-republicans understand unfreedom, roughly speaking, as the subjection of individual choice to alien will. Domination may occur in private relationships marked by disparities of bargaining power, even where no actual interference occurs; alternatively, public coercion dominates unless it is subject to an equally shared system of control, complemented by avenues of individual contestation.[108] Correspondingly, neo-republicans assume public and private domination can be minimised through appropriate systems of rule of law and democratic control which track 'commonly avowed interests'.

Crucially, as discussed, republicans ascribe a central role to political deliberation as a criterion for non-domination in public coercion. For Pettit, public interference is non-dominating where, rather than being exercised at the pleasure of or with impunity by the interfering agent, it is subject to an equally accessible system of control by its subjects which functions such as to track their commonly avowable interests. This requires a procedure for determining what counts as 'commonly avowable interests', and in turn this necessitates some form of public deliberation in which citizens' interests and voices are given at least roughly equal weight and opportunity for articulation.

From both the Rousseauan and the Bourdieusian perspectives, this ignores or at least significantly underestimates the symbolic violence latent in political discourse and thus, the potentially dominating nature of political deliberation itself. First, for both Rousseau and Bourdieu domination cannot be understood primarily in terms of alien interference, or control over individual choice. Compared to the neo-republicans, Rousseau views domination as more intractably embedded in the production and exchange of symbolic, cultural and social capital. As discussed in Chapter 1, it stems partly from the need for external recognition which 'natural' man experiences once he enters society and develops *amour-propre*. As Gauthier notes, Rousseau's insight is essentially that 'dependence on another person is … not simply dependence on his power; most deeply, it is *dependence on his recognition*.'[109] Thus domination is exercised and experienced through 'positional goods'[110]—in hierarchies constituted by taste, bodily dispositions and techniques, and the know-how needed to negotiate complex symbolic codes.

This essentially highlights the commonality of Rousseau's understanding with Bourdieu's theory of symbolic power. For both, domination is irreducible to our subjection to others' powers of interference, as per the neo-republican account. Rather, it stems fundamentally from the fact that our sense of self is dependent on symbolic classifications determined by arbitrary external forces. We are dominated partly because (for Rousseau at least) our choices and identities lack authenticity

---

[108] Pettit, above n 23, Chs 4–5.
[109] Gauthier, above n 91, 30, emphasis added.
[110] ibid 19.

where they are the product of social competition for symbolic capital, and thus, of corrupted *amour-propre*. For example, we are forced to feign behaviours which attract status and legitimacy. Therefore unfreedom cannot be understood as the subjection of choice to alien will, if 'choice' itself stems from a fundamental sort of corruption, which is itself dominating. Thus Bourdieu's analysis shows that 'by merely focusing on the intentional constraints of other agents, we leave out a whole variety of ways in which [agents] might adjust to [their] subordinate position in society independent of the intentional interference of others.'[111]

However, Rousseau's thought is distinct from Bourdieu's because he seeks to devise a specific political and constitutional project in which this domination is erased through the sources of symbolic distinction being rendered common and transparent. His sense of the intractability of domination in symbolic and ritual form means his prescription, compared to the neo-republicans, is correspondingly more drastic; indeed, his politics of austerity would seem to risk engendering equally potent forms of domination, 'transform[ing] personal dependence into dependence on the Republic.'[112] Just as subjection to the general will substitute dependence on the whole for dependence on capricious individual wills, subjection to the transparent symbolic power of the republican state is preferable, he conjectures, to the symbolic violence wrought by the encoded private rituals of more complex, differentiated societies. Of course, while Rousseauan austerity might prevent dependency on capricious, esoteric and obscures nexuses of recognition, citizens will still be subject to the arbiters of symbolic legitimacy in republican society.

Second, Pettit under-accounts for symbolic domination in the range of 'choices' that are understood as being necessary to safeguard from domination. He notes 'the possible modes of subjection are many and diverse',[113] and insists the republican state must guard against domination only 'in respect of certain choices' which are deemed significant—particularly those choices pertaining to the traditional domain of the 'basic liberties'.[114] This delineation (perhaps any delineation) of the choices most deserving of non-domination arbitrarily discounts the significance of symbolic and linguistic power—particularly in respect of culture and taste—as potentially important aspects of domination in liberal society. It overlooks the role of status hierarchies embedded in habitus and cultural practice—inequalities which may represent both an important source of interpersonal domination, while undermining the deliberation thought necessary in a non-dominating politics. This neglect is all the more remarkable given Pettit's emphasis on a 'status' citizenship which should, intuitively, account for the importance of recognition.

---

[111] Daniel Savery, 'Power to the People: Freedom as Non-domination, Disabling Constraints and the Eyeball Test' (2015) 8 *Journal of Political Power* 363, 377.
[112] Frederick Neuhouser, 'Freedom, Dependence and the General Will' (1993) 102 *Philosophical Review* 363, 390.
[113] Pettit, above n 23, 2.
[114] ibid 83.

Undominated citizens will, he says, 'walk tall, live without shame or indignity, and look one another in the eye without any reason for fear or deference.'[115] Consequently it seems odd to discount those forms of dependency and domination which stem from the differential distribution of symbolic capital. His theory of freedom appeals to a social world in which, far from the classical liberal society, citizens 'do not have to bow or scrape, toady or kowtow, fawn or flatter', where they are 'their own men and women.'[116]

Pettit suggests an 'eyeball test' as a criterion for social non-domination—that is, whether, given our relative resources and powers, we can look our fellows in the eye without need for ingratiation or deference.[117] However he insists this test cannot account for us being able to look others in the eye based simply on our timidity or natural deference, as opposed to real obstacles stemming from others' powers of interference. From the Bourdieusian perspective, this naturalises dispositions of 'timidity'—ignoring the befuddlement and exclusion which stems from unequal distributions of symbolic capital and which structure our seemingly inane interactions.[118] People may decline to deliberatively participate simply because since they are not 'native' practitioners of the 'hegemonic idiom'; they may both 'seem less competent to others' and 'internalise this incompetence' in their attitudes to politics.[119] Indeed Bourdieu's perspective is that the 'ordinary violences' of social practice are 'inconspicuous and gentle' and that 'they defy the standard liberal dichotomies of freedom and constraint, will and coercion.'[120]

Third, and relatedly, neo-republicans' attempt to understand domination in terms of alien control of choice, takes 'choice' itself, somewhat uncritically, at face value. In Pettit's analysis, for a given choice to be dominated it is necessary either that it is subject to 'interference' (of particular kinds) or the apprehension thereof. This ignores how a given choice—although undominated in this sense—may, in the Bourdieusian (or indeed Rousseauan) perspective, be the product of an agent's requirement for recognition and capital in the competitive 'fields' of liberal society. It is a concern for this deeper dimension of domination that underlies Rousseau's politics of austerity—and it is this very 'communitarian' bent which leads neo-republicans to reject Rousseau's legacy.[121] Yet these critics largely ignore those

---

[115] ibid 3.
[116] ibid 82.
[117] ibid 84–85.
[118] For Pettit, non-domination obtains we can look our fellow citizens 'in the eye' without need for ingratiation or deference. However he insists this test cannot account for us being able to look others in the eye based simply on our timidity or natural deference. Similarly, he insists that whereas popular 'control' over government must be equally or jointly shared, this merely requires '*equal access* to the system of popular influence' and not equal input since 'some individuals *may choose not to play their part in the system*.' See Pettit, above n 23, 84–85, 169, emphasis added.
[119] Olson, above n 56, 538.
[120] Topper, above n 17, 355.
[121] Pettit, above n 23, Ch 3.

forms of domination against which his 'communitarian' strategies are directed. Pettit effectively naturalises 'choice', failing to sufficiently consider how choice itself—the unimpeachable bedrock of non-domination—may be in some important respects a function of dominating social structures.

Fourth, the Rousseauan perspective seem to undermine the idea that appropriate deliberative practices can render public power non-dominating by orienting it towards commonly avowed interests. In Pettit's analysis, the role of deliberation is both to define 'common avowable interests' and thus to undergird an 'equally accessible' form of popular influence and control.[122] He argues that a republican model of democratic control requires not only popular influence, but also popular *direction* of government. This requires him to argue, against most standard analyses of democracy, that the people can form a set of objectives or interests which give government this *directive* influence.

The Rousseauan perspective—with its focus on the gentle violence that is latent in political discourse—challenges this neo-republican conception of public deliberation as the bedrock of non-dominating state power. For Rousseau, the common interest should be clear in the austere, fraternal and undifferentiated society; complex deliberative practices only serve to obscure it. Chantal Mouffe, and other contemporary critical theorists, argue that since deliberation is 'committed ... to rationalistic denial of passion and the pursuit of consensus', in practice it 'both masks and serves power.'[123] Similarly, cognisant of how, in a complex differentiated society, political deliberation will represent a sort of competitive, symbolically encoded game, Rousseau also views the very *differences* which make deliberation necessary as themselves being the product of dominating social structures. This does not mean that he embraces cultural or non-political solidarities as a precondition for a more authentic republican deliberation. Rather, his insight is simply that, at least in what we can roughly term a liberal society, political discourse will be too beset by symbolic complexity to host a deliberative politics that can meaningfully be said to define and articulate common interests. Unlike many contemporary republicans, Rousseau realises that domination cannot be understood simply in terms of the external control of individual *choice*—where 'choice' itself is taken as a given.

---

[122] ibid 22.
[123] Dryzek, above n 79, 220, in reference to Chantal Mouffe, 'Deliberative Democracy or Agonistic Pluralism?' (1999) 66 *Social Research* 745; Chantal Mouffe, *The Democratic Paradox* (London, Verso, 2000).

5

The Constitution of Judgment

> a Man of an ordinary capacity ... very well understands a text of a Law ... til he consults an Expositor, [who] makes the Words signifie either nothing at all, or what he pleases.[1]

I. Introduction

While Rousseau is a celebrated theorist of legislative power, his views on judicial power—and its relation to legislation—are less well understood. And on the face of things, his comments on judges and adjudication are confused and contradictory. On the one hand, Rousseau's quintessentially modern understanding of law itself—both as assuming legislative form and as an emanation of sovereign power—should suggest quite a modest conception of judicial power, based on the mechanical uncreative application of legislative rules, similar to the conception that prevailed in continental Europe following the French revolution. On the other hand, however, Rousseau also advocates a very terse, open-textured style of legislation, and so concedes, almost blithely, that judges will enjoy a good deal of freedom and discretion in interpreting and developing the law—appealing, mysteriously, to their 'good sense'. And crucially, this, in turn, seems to undermine the supremacy of legislative power and thus, of the general will itself. It introduces a further puzzle as to how the general will is actualised and instantiated.

In this chapter, I will consider possible explanations to this apparent paradox. In doing so, I aim to locate Rousseau's views on judicial power within the wider history of legal thought. I will argue that the apparent paradox—that of judicial creativity subverting legislative supremacy—cannot, on the one hand, be resolved through any understanding of judges as engaging in principled, discursive reasoning, as per our contemporary liberal understanding. By necessity, Rousseau rejects any concept of legal reasoning as a specialised, expert or esoteric practice. Instead, judicial power is disciplined and constrained by the

---

[1] John Locke, *An Essay Concerning Human Understanding* (New York, Dover Publications, 1959) Bk 3, Ch X, para 9.

austerity of republican society. The broader argument, then, is that Rousseau's peculiar understanding of the division of labour between legislative and judicial power must be viewed in light of his broader apprehension towards social differentiation and specialisation as insidious sources of domination and symbolic violence. Thus Rousseau's views on judicial power offer an insight into his wider apprehension of esoteric discourses and social practices as important sources of domination.

II. Legislation and Judgment in Rousseau's Constitutional Projects

In the *Social Contract*, Rousseau addresses legislative power in rather abstract terms. He considers legislation mostly as an expression of popular sovereignty and of the general will, but says virtually nothing about the role of judges in interpreting or adjudicating legislation. And while he says a good deal about the legislative power and process, he says little about the form it takes—in particular its drafting style, its detail, and its relation to other kinds of law. However, in *Government of Poland*, in particular, Rousseau gives rather more detailed consideration to the specific form and style of legislation in the republican state—and to the role of judges in expounding legislative provisions.

The most striking practical recommendation Rousseau makes concerning legislation relates to its terse and general form. In the *Social Contract*, Rousseau suggests, almost in passing, that a well-governed state 'needs very few laws',[2] but says little about the statecraft of legislation. In *Poland*, however, he elaborates in more detail on the form and style of legislation. He insists not only that laws should be few, but also that legislation should be drafted in a terse and general, rather than a precise and detailed style: he suggests 'it is possible, *with a few clear and simple laws* ... to have justice well administered.'[3] Crucially, then, he recommends that legislation should be sparse not only in its volume—as one might expect in an eighteenth century state—but more pertinently, also, terse in its style. And specifically, he recommends the Poles adopt three legislative codes—covering 'constitutional', civil and criminal law—and that these should be as 'short' and 'clear' as possible.[4] In short, then, he eschews the detailed, 'precise' style of legislative drafting associated with the English common-law tradition, in favour of the terser, 'concise' style that later became associated with French and continental

---

[2] Jean-Jacques Rousseau, *Du Contrat Social* (Paris, ENAG, 1988/1762), (hereinafter *Social Contact*) Bk IV, Ch 1.

[3] Jean-Jacques Rousseau, *Considérations sur le Gouvernement de Pologne et sur sa réforme projetée* in *Collection complète des oeuvres* (Genève, 1780–89, vol 1) (hereinafter *Poland*) Ch 10, emphasis added; for a translation see 'Considerations on the Government of Poland' in Frederick Watkins, *Jean-Jacques Rousseau: Political Writings* (New York, Thomas Yelsen, 1953).

[4] ibid, Ch 10.

civil-law culture.⁵ Indeed, Rousseau's recommendations presage the terse, elegant style that later became associated with the influential French *Code Civil* of 1804.⁶ In fact, he specifically derides the English style of legislative drafting:

> Nothing could be more puerile than the precautions taken by the English on this point. To avoid arbitrary judgments, they have subjected themselves to a thousand judgments which are iniquitous, even absurd. They are devoured by multitudes of lawyers, consumed by endless lawsuits; and with the mad idea of trying to foresee every eventuality, they have turned their laws into an immense labyrinth where memory and reason alike are lost.⁷

This disparaging reference to English legal culture is revealing. In decrying English lawyers' 'mad idea of trying to provide for every eventuality', Rousseau is likely referring to the classically precise style of legislative drafting associated with English law, which is traditionally juxtaposed with a terse style, preferred by the French, and that is focused on general principles rather than fact-specific provisions. In England, legislative detail—and specifically, the practice of providing specifically for various fact situations in the 'catalogue' style—was favoured, historically, on the grounds that it would minimise uncertainty and judicial discretion (particularly in criminal law) and thus enhance certainty and predictability as components of the rule of law.⁸ However, Rousseau rejects this approach partly, we can assume, because it undermines the symbolic and didactic function of legislation (as elaborated on below), but partly also, on more practical grounds. In particular, he is concerned that attempts at legislative precision will in fact accentuate uncertainty: 'masses' of legislative provisions risk confusion, and thus 'arbitrary judgments'.⁹ And of course, complex statutes will require more lawyers to interpret them.¹⁰

Thus Rousseau rejects the most obvious strategies for containing and structuring judicial power—whether, say, a literal approach to statutory interpretation, or a precise style of drafting. And perhaps the main implication of legislation of this kind is, crucially, the interpretive power that accrues to judges (or perhaps administrators) as a result of vague or general provisions—or, put more simply, the general divestment of decision-making power from the legislature to lower

---

⁵ See generally John Merryman and Rogelio Pérez-Perdomo, *The Civil Law Tradition: An Introduction to the Legal Systems of Europe and Latin America* 3rd edn (Stanford, Stanford University Press, 2007).
⁶ The original, somewhat utopian intendment of the Napoleonic code was that it could be consulted without the aid of lawyers. Merryman and Pérez-Perdomo, ibid 29.
⁷ *Poland*, above n 3, Ch 10.
⁸ For a comparison between English and French styles of legislative drafting, see Eva Steiner, *French Law: a Comparative Approach* (Oxford, Oxford University Press, 2008) Ch 3.
⁹ *Poland*, above n 3, Ch 10. Echoing Rousseau's apprehension of judge-made law, Richard Ekins states: 'the structure of the legislative act is directed towards positing law in the best form possible, by way of a public, canonical text.': Richard Ekins, *The Nature of Legislative Intent* (Oxford, Oxford University Press, 2012) 123, 125.
¹⁰ Morriss has noted that in the nineteenth century US, proponents of codification accused their opponents of wishing to keep the law obscure in order to preserve lawyers' income. Andrew Morriss 'Codes and Right Answers' (1999) 74 *Chicago-Kent Law Review* 355, 375.

authorities. Indeed, Rousseau acknowledges that the open-textured legislative style he recommends will entail something approximating judicial discretion. Inevitably, vague legislative principles must be developed by judges, in a manner that is irreducible to legislative intent.[11]

Yet surprisingly, Rousseau is blithely accepting of this power. He says that legislation will 'leave the judges with power to interpret the laws, and when necessary to supplement them in the light of natural justice and common sense.'[12] Moreover, he suggests legislative ambiguities should be resolved using judges' 'good sense [*bon sens*] and integrity.'[13] Thus something of a puzzle emerges, because despite Rousseau's insistence on the supremacy of legislation as the expression of the general will, it appears that the form legislation assumes will enable judges to creatively develop, supplement or possibly to subvert legislative intent. Or, at least, a good deal of autonomy will be divested from the legislature to the judges. In short, it seems that legislation of the sort Rousseau recommends can instantiate the general will only in a highly compounded and compromised form.

III. The Paradox of Judicial Power under the General Will

Rousseau's account of judicial power—which follows in part from his understanding of legislation—points to an apparent paradox. While legislation is understood as an exercise of popular sovereignty and as an expression of the general will, the *indeterminacy* of legislation—which allows judges to supplement or develop legislative provisions—seems to undermine the authority of the general will in practice. In short, judicial power, of the kind Rousseau contemplates, seems to undercut the capacity of legislation to effectuate the general will as the cornerstone of a republican concept of political freedom.

In the *Social Contract* itself, at least, Rousseau says nothing about this problem. He insists that since the general will is an expression or 'act' of sovereignty properly understood, it is 'general' in its object as well as its authorship and so cannot speak 'to some particular and determinate object', or 'pronounce on a man or a fact.'[14] The same applies to legislation: when the 'whole people' legislates in relation to the 'whole people', 'it is considering only itself'; then, the law 'considers

---

[11] It is worth noting, in general, a more skeptical view towards the entire concept of legislative intent. Waldron argues: 'there is no question of our being able to attribute to the legislature as such any thoughts, intentions beliefs of purposes beyond the meaning embodied conventionally in the text of the statutes.': Jeremy Waldron, *The Dignity of Legislation* (Cambridge, Cambridge University Press, 1999) 27. For the opposite view, see Ekins, above n 9.
[12] *Poland*, above n 3, Ch 10.
[13] ibid.
[14] *Social Contract*, above n 2, Bk II, Ch 4.

subjects *en masse* and actions in the abstract, and never a particular person or action';[15] similarly, 'no function which has a particular object belongs to the legislative power'.[16] Thus he insists legislation must be 'general' in its object as well as its authorship;[17] 'true' legislation 'unites universality of will with universality of object'.[18] And since legislation must 'come from all and apply to all',[19] 'magistrates' (executive agents) can in no sense exercise legislative power, as theirs is a 'particular' will,[20] applied to particular objects, being 'general' in neither object nor authorship. Only the 'will of the body of the people' can exercise sovereignty, whereas a ruling by 'only a part of it' represents an exercise of 'magistracy'.[21] This analysis of magistracy would equally seem to extend to judicial power, as judicial rulings are 'general' neither in authorship nor object. Since Rousseau insists the general will cannot be discerned 'save when the people is assembled' as a plenary legislature, this obviously precludes any subordinate or delegated legislatures: 'the people, being subject to the laws, must be their author.'[22] And since only 'authentic acts of the general will' can create legislation,[23] his theory of popular sovereignty cannot accommodate any conception of judges as deputy legislators, or of their function as being in any sense quasi-legislative.

The problem lies, in part, in the contradiction between legislation's supposed political *authority* and the indeterminacy that stems from its general *form*. Legislation must effectuate the general will partly so that it can become socially and politically authoritative—so that it actually *rules*. However, the acts, decisions and judgments through which legislation is interpreted, executed and applied are not expressions of the general will because, as explained, they cannot be considered 'general' in either object or authorship. Yet it is only through, and indeed *in* such acts that the general will can actually be instantiated and that it can rule. While such adjudicative and executive acts are necessary for the general will to be realised—and while, indeed, they determine the *character and content* of its realisation—they equally compromise its 'general' nature. Then, it appears that legislation can successfully effectuate the general will only until it is actually adjudicated upon and applied—the very point at which its 'general' character is lost, yet equally the only point where it can become authoritative and assume its full content. Legislation, then, only becomes authoritative through acts of 'particular' will.[24] Indeed Rousseau's paradox is, arguably, only one expression of a wider

---

[15] ibid, Bk II, Ch 6.
[16] ibid, Bk II, Ch 6.
[17] ibid.
[18] ibid.
[19] ibid, Bk II, Ch 4.
[20] ibid, Bk II, Ch 2.
[21] ibid, Bk II, Ch 11.
[22] ibid, Bk II, Ch 6.
[23] ibid, Bk III, Ch 12.
[24] Indeed this highlights a broader question of how legislation of *any* form—not just terse, vague legislation—can successfully effectuate the general will. Indeed the paradox of Rousseauan adjudication is perhaps simply a corollary of a broader conundrum: legislation's form, particularly

conundrum as to how the limiting form of legislation can be reconciled with its supposed political authority, and specifically, the role it is assigned in expressing a political *will* (of *whatever* kind).

Of course, some degree of indeterminacy is pervasive in all legislation, given the instability or indeterminacy of language itself. But the problem is particularly acute in Rousseau's thought, given the contradiction between the open-textured style of legislation on the one hand, and its central political status on the other. Moreover, the problem seems particularly intractable given that this concept of legislation is not some kind of quirk, but rather, is an inevitable corollary of Rousseau's core political commitments. On the one hand, law must have motivational as well as prescriptive force—it must be internalised and accepted by citizens as capturing their common good. And Rousseau recognises that this precludes excessive legislative volume and complexity. Instead, legislative minimalism will shore up state authority: 'We want few laws, but … well enforced.'[25] Moreover Rousseau suggests: 'it is necessary for all citizens … to be taught the positive laws of their own country, and the particular rules by which they are governed. They will find them in the codes they are to study.'[26] Indeed historically, republicans in particular understood legislation as having a civic-educative or exhortatory purpose, fostering virtues of citizenship rather than demanding mere compliance. In particular, the French Civil Code was originally envisaged as having a didactic purpose, even as being similar to (or perhaps substituting) the 'family bible'[27]—and, given its elegant readability, as being accessible to citizens without the need for legal advice.[28] And while it now seems unfeasible or indeed utopian, this belief that legislative codes should be universally comprehensible is also found, in particular, in certain nineteenth century American states.[29]

And yet it was this same simple, accessible style, Portalis suggested, which would necessitate judicial interpretation and development of legislative codes.[30] This would confound, in turn, one of the core orthodoxies of post-revolutionary

---

its generality, limits the extent to which it can instantiate the sovereign will as a dispositive and authoritative framework for political and social life.

[25] *Poland*, above n 3, Ch 10. Rousseau is accordingly insistent that arcane and redundant laws should be formally repealed even if they are benign.

[26] *Poland*, above n 3, Ch 10.

[27] Merryman and Pérez-Perdomo, above n 5, 39. Morriss notes a similar view amongst certain figures in some of the nineteenth century American states, such as Montana, that attempted codification. Morriss, above n 10, 384. 'Lawyers preferred the law to be obscure, code proponents suggested, because its obscurity increased demand for their services.' ibid 375.

[28] Merryman and Pérez-Perdomo, above n 5, 39. For example, see Art 1382 of the French civil code, which defines civil liability: 'Tout fait quelconque de l'homme, qui cause à autrui un dommage, oblige celui par la faute duquel il est arrivé à le réparer' (Any act of man, which causes harm to another, obliges he whose by fault it occurred to compensate it).

[29] Morriss, above n 10, 376.

[30] Indeed 'the drafters of the Civil Code, Napoléon in particular, intended only to set general principles, leaving it up to judges to apply the principles to the circumstances of cases.': Claire Germain, 'Approaches to Statutory Interpretation and Legislative History in France" (2003) *Duke Journal of Comparative & International Law* 195.

French legal thought, which had previously insisted on eliminating or minimalising judicial interpretation—based both on a concern to eliminate the judicial abuses of the *ancien régime* as well as a strict theory of the separation of powers.[31] That kind of thinking—premised on strict legislative supremacy, but which proved unworkable in practice—had been reflected, for example, in the Prussian Civil Code of 1794. With its 17,000 articles, it had attempted (unsuccessfully) to preclude any judicial discretion by specifically addressing every plausible fact situation that might arise.[32] Furthermore, the aim of legislative codes in eighteenth and nineteenth century Europe was not only to clarify and simplify the law, but also to supplant non-legislative sources of law, such as custom, judicial precedent or Roman law. To achieve this, legislation needed to be exhaustive and comprehensive in scope, and therefore, terse and general in style, in order to cover all possible controversies.[33] This, in turn, inevitably enhanced the role of judicial interpretation—despite the republican aversion to judge-made law.

Accordingly, the great codification projects of the nineteenth century were motivated by two aims that were both quintessentially 'republican' but also quite incompatible. Codification aimed, first, to provide lay citizens with an intelligible and authoritative account of the framework of rules and standards by which the state ordered their relationships, and second, to supplant supra-national, sub-national and judge-made law with an exhaustive legislative framework that would confine judges to a narrow and mechanistic role centred on deductive and syllogistic reasoning.[34] However, these aims suggested rather opposite styles as well as concepts of legislation. In a sense then, Rousseau's apparent paradox is simply the intellectual history of European codification, writ large.

IV. Principled Adjudication and the General Will

One possible explanation for the paradox I have outlined is that despite Rousseau advocating open-ended and indeterminate legislation, this does not entail judicial law-making as such—at least in a way that undermines the authority of

---

[31] Merryman and Pérez-Perdomo, above n 5, 30–31. Portalis said: 'The function of statutes is to establish through a broad view the general maxims of the law; to establish principles rich in consequences, and not to descend to the details of question, which would arise on every question. It is for the judge and the jurist imbued with the general spirit of the laws, to direct their applications.' Cited in Gerard Carney, 'Comparative Approaches to Statutory Interpretation in Common Law and Civil Law Jurisdictions' (2015) 36 *Statute Law Review* 46, 50.
[32] Merryman and Pérez-Perdomo, above n 5, 39.
[33] See Morriss, above n 10.
[34] Schauer notes: 'When François Gény celebrated the judge as a creative law maker in cases where the civil code did not indicate an outcome, he departed from his civilian predecessors who believed that substantially constrained logical or linguistic operations enabled interpreters of the code to identify uniquely correct results even when the code did not explicitly cover a particular *situation*.' Frederick Schauer, 'Legal Realism Untamed' (2013) 91 *Texas Law Review* 749, 763.

the general will. HLA Hart argued that in 'penumbral' cases where legal rules are silent, indecisive, indeterminate or unclear, judges effectively fill the gap by exercising a secondary legislative power, using extra-legal or policy norms. However, Ronald Dworkin famously argued, against Hart, that in such cases, judges need never legislate afresh as such, or reach *beyond* the law at all. Instead they fill any gaps or indeterminacies using deeper 'principles'—drawn from the political-moral identity of the polity—that are part of the 'law' in its broad sense, despite never having been formally enacted.[35] In short, legislative indeterminacy does not entail judicial law-making, or even wide judicial discretion, because judges can refer to the principled or normative context of legislation. Critically, in turn, Dworkin's account of adjudication—as a kind of a principled discourse—might help to explain how Rousseau's general will can be successfully instantiated despite the problem of legislative indeterminacy and the limits of legislative form. In this view, legislation gives an inevitably provisional and limited expression to the general will, but through principled reasoning, judges can nonetheless preserve the integrity of the general will in particularised rulings.

Indeed, Nordahl suggests that Dworkin's 'principles' bear strong resemblance to Rousseau's general will, as each emanates from, and defines, the normative identity of the political community as a corporate person.[36] Certainly, of course, Dworkin's principled adjudication has a more elite flavour. Whereas the general will emanates from the deliberations of virtuous citizens, principle—although emerging from the historical practices of a political community—is ultimately discerned and pronounced by judges.[37] Nonetheless, both concepts appeal to the normative identity of a *corporate* political community that transcends any aggregation of private or individual interest. For Dworkin, the will of the community is the will of its citizens, but 'taken in the collective sense as an expression of [their] integrated practices, not as a simple summation of their individual wills';[38] similarly, Rousseau distinguishes the general will from any aggregation of individual wills, or the 'will of all.'[39]

More pertinently, Dworkin's theory helps to explain how the general will might 'survive' the particularised nature of judicial rulings. Nordahl points out that for Dworkin, 'principle' gives legitimacy to judicial review, even where it overrules transient majority opinion, by linking judicial rulings to the background political culture of the community in question. Thus 'judges are expressing the general will of their community, even when their rulings are contrary to the views of the

---

[35] Ronald Dworkin, *A Matter of Principle* (Oxford, Oxford University Press, 1985).
[36] Richard Nordahl, 'Rousseau in Dworkin: Judicial Rulings as Expressions of the General Will' (1997) 3 *Legal Theory* 317.
[37] Nordahl, ibid, 326. Dworkin states: 'judges should decide hard cases by interpreting the political structure of their community in the following, perhaps special way: by trying to find the best justification they can find, in principles of political morality, for the structure as a whole.': Ronald Dworkin, *Law's Empire* (Cambridge MA, Harvard University Press, 1986) 165.
[38] Nordahl, ibid 325.
[39] *Social Contract*, above n 2, Bk II, Ch 4.

majority of citizens.'⁴⁰ Although it does not produce 'right answers' in the manner of logical syllogisms, principle nonetheless has a 'disciplining and integrative'⁴¹ effect on judicial power, because it significantly constrains the range of possible outcomes. In short, then, 'principle' conserves the link between judicial rulings and the moral identity of the political community in contexts where judges ostensibly enjoy discretion by virtue of legislative ambiguity. Although Rousseau insists that only citizens, in legislating, can discern the general will, this account of judicial reasoning as a principled discourse helps to explain how the general will survives the particularised application of legislation. In contrast, if legislative indeterminacy entails judicial discretion or a secondary legislative power, the link between judicial rulings and the general will is broken: as Rousseau insists, whatever a man 'commands of *his own motion* cannot be a law'.⁴²

V. Adjudication under Republican Austerity

The dilemma I have posed is how, within Rousseau's scheme, the general will can be effectuated through the indeterminate, open-ended form of legislation that he advocates, despite the wide judicial creativity it seems to entail. I have considered perhaps the most obvious response—that a 'principled' style of adjudication can preserve the authority of the general will, obviating the apparent problems of legislative indeterminacy and judicial discretion.⁴³ However, I argue that Dworkin's liberal theory of adjudication cannot provide a satisfactory response to this problem. In particular, it presupposes an institutional, and indeed a social division of labour—between legislative and judicial roles—that is inconsistent with the austere and undifferentiated social universe that Rousseau contemplates. More generally, Rousseau's comments on judicial virtue and judicial reasoning can only make sense when viewed as an extension of his wider project of austerity. Indeed this dovetails with the fact that while Rousseau understands legislation itself as an expression of popular sovereignty, in fact his overwhelming emphasis

---

⁴⁰ Nordahl, above n 36, 345.
⁴¹ ibid.
⁴² *Social Contract*, above n 2, Bk II, Ch 6, emphasis added.
⁴³ There is a further, possible explanation. Colón-Ríos and others argue that the 'legislation' created by the sovereign embraces only fundamental or foundational laws, and that confusingly, much of what is now understood as 'legislation' is, in Rousseau's thought, created by the 'government' rather than the people as the sovereign. This would mean there was no contradiction in judges exercising law-making power in the broad sense. And indeed, many routine, unremarkable statutes—or even code provisions—are not, arguably, properly 'general' in the strict sense Rousseau envisages, because they refer to specific social or economic sectors rather than the body of the citizenry as a whole. However, while I see merit in Colón-Ríos' argument, Rousseau in *Poland* refers to legislative codes as encompassing 'civil' and 'criminal' as well as constitutional law—hardly meeting the sense of fundamental or foundational law—and so the problem remains. See Joel Colón-Ríos, 'Rousseau, Theorist of Constituent Power' (2016) *Oxford Journal of Legal Studies*, Advance Access, published 12 June 2016, http://ojls.oxfordjournals.org/content/early/2016/06/11/ojls.gqw012.full.

is, counter-intuitively, the clarity and transparency of legislation as a *form*, rather than its virtues as a political *process*. Any specific *art* or science of legislating (as distinct from *legislation*) is seen suspiciously as a source or intrigue and mystification—and essentially, the same applies to adjudication and judgment.

On the one hand, republican austerity necessarily precludes any account of adjudication or of judicial reasoning as a specialised, expert endeavour. The very point of Dworkin's liberal account, in part, is to effectuate a kind of division of labour, both institutional and cognitive, between lay reasoning, on the one hand—suited to the rough and tumble of ordinary political debate—and judicial reasoning on the other, which requires particular skill and training, albeit not of a particularly technical kind. For Dworkin, principled legal reasoning is distinct from virtuous 'lay' reasoning; he assumes judges have the necessary skill to draw out 'principle' from the traditions and political morality of the community; they are better placed than ordinary citizens to do this partly because of their dispassionate distance and intellectual discipline.[44] Judges, he suggests, are 'the most authoritative, and the most responsible, practitioners of the interpretive enterprise concerning rights.'[45] In the contemporary liberal account that Dworkin has championed, adjudication, then, is not a science or a skill, but rather a *discourse*, albeit one engaged in by those assumed or imagined as enjoying particular, and superior insights on the grand horizons—if not the minutiae—of politics.[46] And as explored in previous chapters, it is precisely such kinds of specialised social and cultural practices—in the vein of say, cultural performance or even intellectual debate—that Rousseau regards as insidious sources of social domination. Specialised discourses obscure, and exclude.

While republican austerity precludes any esotericised account of judicial reasoning as a specialised or expert endeavour, equally it provides a response of its own to the apparent problems of legal indeterminacy and judicial discretion. In the first instance, we cannot assume that any response to the problem of judicial legitimacy, in general, lies in institutional safeguards—or, indeed in any style, theory or philosophy of adjudication. Rather, the question of whether judicial power is in some sense subversive of democratic and republican norms cannot be considered apart from the social environment—and specifically, the universe of symbolic classifications and meanings—within which adjudication will occur. And in this light, Rousseau's apparently wide-ranging understanding of judicial power cannot be understood apart from the austere social environment within which it is envisaged as operating. Judicial power will be disciplined and constrained by the

---

[44] Dworkin, above n 37, Ch 6.

[45] Nordahl, above n 36, 329.

[46] As Balkin argues in response to Dworkin, 'judges are socially situated individuals who interpret the law for a particular purpose and bring a particular set of sociological and ideological predispositions to their understanding ... so hermetically sealed is Dworkin's [legal] universe that it becomes impossible to object that the concerns of judges occupy only one rather limited portion in the constellation of legal reality and the forms of legal understanding.': Jack Balkin, 'Understanding Legal Understanding: The Legal Subject and the Problem of Legal Coherence' (1993) 103 *Yale Law Journal* 105, 134.

transparency and holism of republican austerity, of the kind considered in earlier chapters.[47] It is precisely this social transparency, as I will explain, that will prevent the law from developing as a specialised, esoteric discourse that mystifies—and thus dominates—those without access to the requisite forms of social capital, the vocabulary and discursive techniques, and so on. (Indeed, Rousseau echoes a wider tradition of intellectual scepticism towards lawyerly artifice and contrivance[48]— Locke, in particular, complained of lawyers' 'multiplied curious Distinctions, and acute niceties').[49]

Indeed in *Poland*, Rousseau, as discussed earlier, explicitly acknowledges the problem of legislative indeterminacy, and accepts the inevitability of judges interpreting open-ended legislative provisions. He suggests that terse, general legislation should be interpreted using 'rectitude' [*droiture*] and 'good sense',[50] and that ambiguities should resolved using 'common sense [*bon sens*] and integrity.'[51] He also rejects the idea that legislation could be supplemented by customary or Roman law, asserting: 'the rules of natural law are better inscribed in men's hearts than in all Justinian's nonsense.'[52] On the face of things, this seems either to permit judicial discretion—as in 'common sense'—or to trust, alternatively, in a kind of principled discourse ('integrity') that will preserve the integrity of the general will.

Indeed, what is striking about Rousseau's legal thinking is that while it is quintessentially *modern* in its insistence on the primacy and centrality of legislation, ostensibly it also appears to appeal, simultaneously, to an ancient concept of the

---

[47] Roughly speaking, transparency refers to an idea that the grounds and the justification of public decisions are reasonably accessible. And arguably, this is why Rousseau, in particular, understands legislative transparency not only as an instrument of republican didacticism, but also as a foil against the mystifying and dominating esotericism of archaic pre-revolutionary laws.

[48] Waldron notes: 'Jurisprudence has always been dogged by populist suspicion of lawyers and legalism and by a demand that the law of the land should be such as to be easily known and understood by ordinary folk. The more complex and technical law is, the more plausible the reproach that it is an alien imposition on the people by those who care only for their exploitation and submission. Certainly there seems to be something particularly offensive to democratic jurisprudence in systematic opacity or mystification.': Jeremy Waldron 'Can there be a Democratic Jurisprudence'' (2008–09) 58 *Emory Law Journal* 675, 708. See also Duncan Kennedy, *A Critique of Adjudication [fin de siècle]* (Cambridge MA, Harvard University Press, 1998); William Edmundson, 'Transparency and Indeterminacy in the Liberal Critique of Critical Legal Studies' (1993) 24 *Seton Hall Law Review* 557. Kennedy argues: 'Adjudication has at least three ideological effects. First, the diffusion of law-making power reduces the power of ideologically organized majorities, whether liberal or conservative, to bring about significant change in any subject-matter area heavily governed by law. It empowers the legal fractions of intelligentsias to decide the outcomes of ideological conflict among themselves, outside the legislative process. And it increases the appearance of naturalness, necessity, and relative justice of the status quo, whatever it may be, over what would prevail under a more transparent regime. In each case, adjudication functions to secure both particular ideological and general class interests of the intelligentsia in the social and economic status quo.': ibid 1.

[49] Locke, above n 1.
[50] *Poland*, above n 3, Ch 10.
[51] ibid.
[52] ibid.

rule of law that is predicated on the authority of aristocratic judicial wisdom rather than the mechanical and impartial application of legislative rules.[53] This is apparent in his simultaneous appeal to legislative supremacy as well as judicial rectitude or 'good sense'. And yet, the concept of judicial virtue he appeals to can hardly be the quasi-Aristotelian notion of aristocratic wisdom that prevailed before the ascendancy of a more mechanical, and quintessentially modern, understanding of judicial power in the eighteenth and nineteenth centuries. Instead, I argue that Rousseau's vision appeals not to any peculiar vision of judicial *wisdom*, in this sense—nor of expertise—but rather to the kinds of virtues that will be secured by republican austerity generally.

Effectively then, judicial power is to be disciplined by the virtues of republican austerity, which will permeate social and institutional life generally as well as the domain of law. The idea of virtue per se as constraining judicial power is hardly distinctive: it is present, for example, in Dworkin's metaphor of Judge 'Hercules', the virtuous judge who is tasked with upholding individual rights against majority interests—and with resisting 'politics' in the name of 'principle'.[54] But this is a kind of virtue that is specific to judges, and presupposes dispositions and styles of reasoning that, it is assumed, other citizens do not have. By contrast, it seems that Rousseau's account of judicial virtue is simply an extension of his broader account of citizen virtue. What Rousseau rejects, then—as emphasised in chapter four—is essentially any division of labour, or indeed, any specialisation in political reasoning broadly speaking. And by the same measure, judicial virtues are neither aristocratic virtues of judicial wisdom, nor esoteric skills of legal science, but much the same as those virtues that permit the general will to be discerned and legislated in the first instance. It is perhaps in this spirit that Rousseau suggests to the Poles: 'Make men honest and virtuous ... and they will know enough law.'[55] Thus there can be no distinction, such as Dworkin observes, between the discourse of ordinary politics, based on competing reasons of 'policy', and 'principled' discourse, treated as an intellectual specialisation. While the suggestion that judges use 'good sense' ostensibly seems like an endorsement of discretion, in fact it bears remarkable similarity with Rousseau's account of how the general will is discerned at the legislative stage—expressed in the metaphor of peasants 'deliberating under an oak'. And indeed, this dovetails with Rousseau's rejection of the value of complex or eloquent discourse more generally. It closely reflects his idea that sophisticated, 'principled' discourse will tend simply to mask sentiment, interest and prejudice—obscuring the real grounds of decision.

---

[53] Martin Loughlin, *Sword and Scales: An Examination of the Relationship between Law and Politics* (Oxford, Hart Publishing, 2000) 67–70.
[54] Dworkin, above n 37, Ch 6.
[55] *Poland*, above n 3, Ch 10.

VI. Complexity, Differentiation and Symbolic Power

In this final section, I will suggest that Rousseau's apparent rejection of adjudication, as an expert or specialised exercise, can be understood as an extension of his wider view of social and political domination—and particularly, his view of domination as being embedded in social complexity and differentiation.

What does it mean, in practical terms, to reject the division of labour in law? On the one hand, it implicitly rejects the view that the reasoning processes involved in legislating and adjudicating are, necessarily, radically different, or that the *grounds* of decision are hermetically separate and distinct. On the other hand, more pertinently, the division of labour that is to be rejected is *institutional* and thus social as much as *cognitive*. Since, in Rousseau's scheme, judicial reasoning is not a specialised endeavour—but rather requires the same virtues that apply to legislation itself—this suggests that judges will not be very much different from other citizens. Indeed, in one of his few institutional recommendations concerning judges, Rousseau, echoing ancient Roman ideas, suggests that the judiciary should be non-professional.[56] Judicial office, he says, should be 'a temporary employment through which the nation can test and evaluate the merit and probity of a citizen, in order to raise him afterwards to those more important positions of which he has been found capable.'[57]

Under republican austerity, judicial reasoning cannot operate as an independent, discrete mode of reason because it is precisely this kind of social specialisation—or in this context, an intellectual division of labour—that leads to befuddlement, alienation and ultimately domination. In Chapter 4, I discussed how, for Rousseau, intellectual discourse in general represents a performative social ritual that confers authority and status upon those with access to the requisite forms of social and symbolic capital, and how, in turn, specialised discourses operate as sites of social domination. By the same measure, we can say that legal discourse—whether of the formalistic kind traditionally favoured in continental Europe or the open-ended, principled style more familiar to American liberals—relies largely on stylistic and idiomatic methods and techniques, that it confers distinction and recognition on those inducted in the requisite techniques, and simultaneously, that it is portrayed and interpreted, outwardly and in society, as having natural legitimacy. Legal discourse does not operate, then, simply as a means of discovering valid legal truths, but rather as an instrument for producing and conferring status and distinction. That is to say, it must be understood in performative rather than propositional terms. Claims or utterances of legal discourse are valid, that is, based on their competence within the symbolic classifications and norms of that field. There can

---

[56] ibid. Montesqueieu makes a similar recommendation. Charles-Louis Montesquieu, *Spirit of the Laws* (Cambridge, Cambridge University Press, 1748/1989) Bk 11, Ch 6.
[57] *Poland*, above n 3, Ch 10.

be no concept of legal *truth*, or of truth and validity in legal argument, considered apart from the social dynamics of legal practice.

On the one hand, principled discourse generally—and by extension, legal discourse—is an exercise in symbolic power, providing a source of distinction or positional capital for those inducted in the requisite techniques, linguistic and corporeal. It is often an esoteric practice, requiring mastery of certain styles and idioms. Thus it is not primarily a cognitive, but rather a social competence, requiring mastery of techniques that are legitimate within a given, contingent social field. In turn, then, it will befuddle, exclude and ultimately dominate those lacking such techniques. While political and legal discourse may have the air of an erudite parlour game—a ritual in which competent participants please and win recognition from one other—it can also have an insidiously manipulative, deceptive aspect. It particular, it may inflict subtle forms of domination upon those lacking the correct *habitus*—understood as a set of social techniques that are contextually legitimate or efficacious—and who misrecognise such techniques as having intrinsic value, thus potentially internalising their inferiority. From the Rousseauan perspective, then, 'principled' judicial discourse cannot link judicial rulings to the general will in part because, in reality, such specialised discourses invariably operate as exercises of positional capital and performances of symbolic power. And crucially, this also means that Rousseau's advocacy of legislative simplicity cannot stem only from a concern for accessibility—it can also be read as excluding contrived complexity, as a source of mystification and domination, from legal discourse. Law, as I will argue, can be dominating not only because it is inaccessible or incomprehensible, but also because it is *esoteric*.

On the other hand, principled discourse—which may be more or less specialised in style and register—may also serve simply as a façade for injustice, as an elaborate mechanism through which status hierarchies are eloquently rationalised, legitimated or obscured. Many critical thinkers have derided Dworkin's idea that 'principle' can have a unifying, disciplining and constraining effect on judicial power, and thus resolve the problem of legal indeterminacy, or indeed the ideological conflicts that legal language obscure. 'Principles', they argue—equality, liberty, fraternity and the rest—are as flexible and manipulable as rules, but additionally, they are insidiously ideological.[58] Whereas Dworkin appeals to principles that are authoritative and dispositive and that supposedly transcend the ideological conflicts within law, instead they are contested, flexible and easily manipulated.[59]

---

[58] Andrew Altman, 'Legal Realism, Critical Legal Studies, and Dworkin' (1986) 15 *Philosophy and Public Affairs* 205; Jack Balkin, 'Taking Ideology Seriously: Ronald Dworkin and the CLS Critique" (1987) 55 *UMKC Law Review* 392.

[59] Dworkin's understanding of interpretivist adjudication requires judges 'so far as this is possible, to treat our present system of public standards as expressing and respecting a coherent set of principles.' Dworkin, above n 37, 217. Similarly, 'Judges ... decide hard cases by trying to find, in some coherent set of principles about people's rights and duties, the best constructive interpretation of the political structure and legal doctrine of their community.': ibid.

Similarly, while Rousseau understands that the general will can be subverted not only by naked factionalism and self-interest, but also by alluring deliberative sophistry that clothes factional interests in the terminology of public reason, this applies equally to legal as much as political discourse. Just as the techniques of political discourse serve to confuse private interest and the common good, the meaningless doctrinal flourishes of legal discourse will obscure the real interests at stake. Public reason, whether deployed in 'political' or 'legal' contexts, is first and foremost a social competence, constructed and evaluated with reference to a particular, rather arbitrary set of symbolic classifications and linguistic idioms. Although Bourdieu, in *The Force of Law*, focuses on a more formalistic style of legal reasoning familiar in civil-law countries, 'principled' or rights-based legal discourse can equally be understood both as being partly ideological in content—as reflecting agendas and concerns external to the law itself—but simultaneously as the exercise of a practical and social competence. Constitutional jurisprudence offers an example *par excellence* of a specialised discourse operating amongst a relatively autonomous field of practitioners that are inducted in the requisite participatory techniques.

The distinctiveness of Rousseau's view, then, lies not in his understanding of adjudicative reasoning as indeterminate or even as inaccessible due purely to its intricacy, but rather as quintessentially *esoteric*. In effect, its complexity performs a social function in its own right—that of distinction and differentiation within a social universe constructed around symbolic power. And principled adjudication is an insidious source of domination, then, not only because of the *interests* and ideologies it obscures—those external to or antecedent to law—but also those classifications and distinctions, with the attendant mystification and obscurity, that are generated within the discourse or practice itself. Symbolic domination in law occurs as much through the arbitrary content of legal discourse being misrecognised as such, as through the interests and hierarchies it insidiously upholds. As Pierre Bourdieu puts it:

> [A]s the quintessential form of legitimized discourse, the law can exercise its specific power only to the extent that it attains recognition, that is, to the extent that the element of arbitrariness at the heart of its functioning ... remains unrecognized.[60]

Like Bourdieu, again, Rousseau views law neither as an autonomous system of rational rules and principles that excludes open-ended normative considerations—as many republican contemporaries were inclined to do—nor, however, does he accept that legal discourse simply projects and pursues interests that are external to the field of law itself.[61] That is to say, he accepts neither a formalist nor an instrumentalist position. Legal reasoning is neither independent of politics in the broad sense, nor is it crudely ideological. Rather,

---

[60] ibid 843.
[61] See Mauricio García Villegas, 'On Pierre Bourdieu's Legal Thought' (2004) 56 *Droit et société* 57.

law, in liberal society, generates its own specific forms of capital, its own semi-autonomous set of symbolic and social classifications, that are influenced by, yet irreducible to antecedent or external interests.[62] Bourdieu, similarly, argues that legal doctrine operates according to a logic that is 'relatively independent of exterior constraint';[63] thus, the 'juridical field' is 'an entire social universe which is in practice relatively independent of external determinations and pressures.'[64] The juristic 'field' is a site of 'symbolic production';[65] accordingly, 'the social practices of the law are in fact the product of the specific power relations which give it its structure.'[66] And while law, through its esoteric character, produces forms of capital and power that are irreducible to antecedent interests, economic or otherwise, it is externally represented as innocent and naturally legitimate. Thus 'when esoteric discourses are diffused outside the restricted field', they 'undergo a kind of automatic universalization, ceasing to be merely the utterances of dominant agents within specific fields and becoming statements valid for all dominating or dominated individuals.'[67]

Just as Bourdieu understands that the basis for modern law, as a specialised social practice, lies in a 'division of labour'[68]—that is, the allocation and designation of participatory competences—Rousseau's eighteenth century institutional prescriptions are informed by his understanding of the mystifying and dominating function that such classifications perform. Fundamentally, he understands that this process of specialisation, with the insidious domination and symbolic violence it entails, is destructive to republican goals.

VII. Conclusion

As I have argued, Rousseau understands judicial virtue as an extension of the civic virtue that prevails in a radically austere and undifferentiated republican society. On the one hand, this gives us a greater insight as to his broader critique of liberal institutions and liberal society. It further illustrates his sense—presaging later critical theory—of how domination becomes insinuated in the ostensibly benign

---

[62] Of course the semi-autonomous nature of the legal field does not preclude legal practitioners from 'imposing an official representation of the social world which sustains their own world view and favors their interests':. Pierre Bourdieu, 'The Force of Law: Towards a Sociology of the Juridical Field' (1987) 38 *Hastings Law Journal* 805, 848.
[63] Bourdieu, ibid 815.
[64] ibid 816.
[65] ibid.
[66] ibid.
[67] Pierre Bourdieu, *Language and Symbolic Power* (J Thompson ed, Cambridge MA, Harvard University Press, 1999) 41.
[68] Bourdieu, above n 62, 817.

patterns of intellectual and cultural life, in the social division of labour and in the distribution of human capital. As seen in chapter four, Rousseau's sceptical attitude towards political deliberation is explained by his fear that eloquence and subterfuge will clothe sectional interest and domination in the guise of the common interest. Yet his comments on legal discourse, while containing similar insights, give more specific insight into his apprehension towards social differentiation or specialisation. Compared to political deliberation, legal reason is perhaps a more dramatic example of a highly performative, and indeed an esoteric discourse that obscures affect, interest and ideology in an ostensibly benign and refined form, because while it operates at a greater distance from 'lay' discourses about rights, it cannot transcend sentiment, affect, ideology or substantive politics, and so on. And this is equally true whether law is understood in technical and formalistic terms, or as a principled discourse that is framed as distinct from ordinary political reason.

On the other hand, Rousseau's writings on law also underline how, more generally, his constitutional prescriptions cannot be considered apart from a social framework of austerity, which underscores the relevant forms of discipline, cohesion and motivation that will bring republican liberty to life. Whereas Rousseau's concern is to ensure that law should not develop as a mystifying expert discourse, this can be understood, in one sense, simply as an extension of his politics of radical transparency to the domain of law.

BIBLIOGRAPHY

Books

Ackerman, Bruce, *We the People 1: Foundations* (Cambridge MA, Harvard University Press, 1991)
——, *We the People 1: Tranformations* (Cambridge MA, Harvard University Press, 1998)
Arendt, Hannah, *Between Past and Future* (Harmondsworth, Penguin 1977)
Bagehot, Walter, *The English Constitution* (London, 1873)
Baron, Hans, *In Search of Florentine Civic Humanism* (Princeton NJ, Princeton University Press, 1988)
Bellamy, Richard, *Liberalism and Modern Society* (Philadelphia, Pennsylvania State University Press, 1992)
——, *Political Constitutionalism* (Cambridge, Cambridge University Press, 2007)
Berlin, Isaiah, *Two Concepts of Liberty* (Oxford, Clarendon, 1958)
Besson, Samantha and Marti, José-Luis, *Legal Republicanism: National and International Perspectives* (Oxford, Oxford University Press, 2009)
Boswell, James, *An Account of Corsica, the Journal of a Tour to That Island, and Memoirs of Pascal Paoli* (Bolton and McLoughlin eds, Oxford, Oxford University Press, 2006)
Bourdieu, Pierre, *Distinction: a Social Critique of the Judgement of Taste* (Richard Nice trans, Cambridge MA, Harvard University Press, 1987)
——, *Language and Symbolic Power* (J Thompson ed, Cambridge MA, Harvard University Press, 1999)
Cerulo, Karen A, *Identity Designs: The Sights and Sounds of a Nation* (New Brunswick NJ, Rutgers University Press, 1995)
Charvet, John, *The Social Problem in the Philosophy of Rousseau* (Cambridge, Cambridge University Press, 1974)
Cicero, *On Duties* (Cambridge, Cambridge University Press, 1999).
Cohen, Joshua, *Rousseau: A Free Community of Equals* (Oxford, Oxford University Press, 2010)
Connolly, William, *The Terms of Political Discourse* (Lexington MA, DC Heath, 1974)
Constant, Benjamin, *Ecrits Politiques* (Paris, Gallimard/Folio, 1997)
Copp, David, Hampton, Jean and Roemer, John, *The Idea of Democracy* (Cambridge, Cambridge University Press, 1993)
Dagger, Richard, *Civic Virtues: Rights, Citizenship and Republican Liberalism* (Oxford, Oxford University Press, 1997)
Dalisson, Rémi, *Célébrer la nation. Les fêtes nationales en France de 1789 à nos jours* (Paris, Nouveau monde éditions, 2009)
Dent, Nicholas, *Rousseau* (London, Taylor and Francis, 2005)
Douglass, Robin, *Rousseau and Hobbes: Nature, Free Will and the Passions* (Oxford, Oxford University Press, 2016)
Dworkin, Ronald, *A Matter of Principle* (Oxford, Oxford University Press, 1985)

——, *Law's Empire* (Cambridge MA, Harvard University Press, 1986)
Ekins, Richard, *The Nature of Legislative Intent* (Oxford, Oxford University Press, 2012)
Ferguson, Adam, *An Essay on the History of Civil Society* (New Brunswick, Transaction Books, 1980)
Freeman, Samuel, *Justice and the Social Contract: Essays in Rawlsian Political Philosophy* (Oxford, Oxford University Press, 2007)
Galligan, Dennis and Versteeg, Milla (eds), *Social and Political Foundations of Constitutions* (Cambridge, Cambridge University Press, 2013)
Gauthier, David, *Rousseau: the Sentiment of Existence* (Cambridge, Cambridge University Press, 2006)
Grace, Eve and Kelly, Christopher, *The Challenge of Rousseau* (Cambridge, Cambridge University Press, 2013)
Gutmann, Amy and Thompson, Dennis, *Why Deliberative Democracy?* (Princeton NJ, Princeton University Press, 2004)
Habermas, Jurgen, *Between Facts and Norms: Contributions to a Discourse Theory of Law and Democracy* (Cambridge, MIT Press, 1996)
——, *The Theory of Communicative Action: Volumes 1 and 2* (Boston, Beacon, 1984/1987)
Hall, Thadd E, *The Development of Enlightenment Interest in Eighteenth-century Corsica* 'Studies on Voltaire and the Eighteenth Century' vol 64 (Geneva, Institut et Musee Voltaire, 1968)
Harrington, James, *The Commonwealth of Oceana* (Pocock ed, Cambridge, Cambridge University Press, 1992)
Hobbes, Thomas, *Leviathan: Or the Matter, Forme, and Power of a Common-Wealth Ecclesiasticall and Civill* (Ian Shapiro ed, Yale, Yale University Press, 2010)
Honohan, Iseult, and Jennings, Jeremy (eds), *Republicanism in Theory and Practice* (London, Routledge, 2015)
Honohan, Iseult, *Civic Republicanism* (London, Routledge, 2002)
Hume, David, *Essays: Political and Moral* (Edinburgh, Fleming, 1777)
Hylland Eriksen, Thomas and Jenkins, Richard, *Flag, Nation and Symbolism in Europe and America* (London, Routledge, 2007)
Kalyvas, Andreas and Katznelson, Ira, *Liberal Beginnings: Making a Republic for the Moderns* (Cambridge, Cambridge University Press, 2008)
Kennedy, Duncan, *A Critique of Adjudication [fin de siècle]* (Cambridge MA, Harvard University Press, 1998)
Kingston, Rebecca, *Public Passion. Rethinking the Grounds for Political Justice* (Montreal and Kingston, McGill-Queen's University Press, 2011)
Kymlicka, Will, *Politics in the Vernacular: Nationalism, Multiculturalism, and Citizenship* (Oxford, Oxford University Press, 2001
Laborde, Cécile and Maynor, John, *Republicanism and Political Theory* (London, Blackwell, 2008)
Locke, John, *An Essay Concerning Human Understanding* (New York, Dover Publications, 1959)
Loughlin, Martin, *Sword and Scales: An Examination of the Relationship between Law and Politics* (Oxford, Hart Publishing, 2000)
Madison, James, Hamilton, Alexander and Jay, John, *The Federalist Papers* (I Kramnik ed, London, Penguin, 1987)
McIlwain, Charles, *Constitutionalism Ancient and Modern* (Liberty Press, 2010, first published 1940)

Merryman, John and Pérez-Perdomo, Rogelio, *The Civil Law Tradition: An Introduction to the Legal Systems of Europe and Latin America* 3rd edn (Stanford, Stanford University Press, 2007)
Mill, John Stuart, *On Liberty* (London, John Parker and Son, 1859)
Montesquieu, Charles-Louis, *Spirit of the Laws* (Cambridge, Cambridge University Press, 1748/1989)
Mouffe, Chantal, *The Democratic Paradox* (London, Verso, 2000)
Neuhouser, Frederick, *Rousseau's Theodicy of Self-Love: Evil, Rationality and the Drive for Recognition* (Oxford, Oxford University Press, 2010)
Newman, William, *The Politics of Aristotle* (Oxford, Oxford University Press, 1902)
Nussbaum, Martha, *Political Emotions* (Cambridge MA, Harvard University Press, 2013)
Ozouf, Mona, *Festivals and the French Revolution* (Alan Sheridan trans, Cambridge MA, Harvard University Press, 1988)
Peden, William, *The Selected Writings of John and John Quincy Adams* (New York, Knopf, 1946)
Pettit, Philip, *On the People's Terms: a Republican Theory and Model of Democracy* (Cambridge, Cambridge University Press, 2013).
——, *Republicanism: A Theory of Freedom and Government* (Oxford, Clarendon Press, 1997)
Rawls, John, *Lectures on the History of Political Philosophy* (Cambridge MA, Harvard University Press, 2007)
——, *Political Liberalism* (Cambridge MA, Harvard University Press, 1996)
——, *Political Liberalism* (New York, Columbia University Press, 1996)
Rousseau, Jean-Jacques, *Considérations sur le Gouvernement de Pologne et sur sa réforme projetée* in *Collection complète des oeuvres* (Genève, 1780–89) vol 1 Ch XI; for a translation see 'Considerations on the Government of Poland' in Frederick Watkins, *Jean-Jacques Rousseau: Political Writings* (New York, Thomas Yelsen, 1953)
——, *Discourse on Political Economy* (1755) in Jean-Jacques Rousseau, *Discourse on Political Economy and On the Social Contract* (Christopher Betts trans, Oxford, Oxford University Press, 2009)
——, *Discours sur les sciences et les arts* (Paris, Livres de Poche, 2012/1751)
——, *Discours sur l'origine et les fondements de l'inégalité parmi les hommes* (Paris, Flammarion, 1755/2008)
——, *Du Contrat Social: Principes de Droit Politique* (first published 1762, Paris, ENAG, 1988)
——, *Emile or On Education* (A Bloom trans, New York, Basic Books, 1979)
——, *Julie ou la Nouvelle Héloïse* (Paris, Ornée de Gravures, 1819)
——, *Lettre à d'Alembert* (1758). See Allan Bloom, Charles Butterworth and Christopher Kelly, *Rousseau: Letter to d'Alembert and Writings for the Theatre* (Lebanon NH, University Press of New England, 2004)
——, Preface to '*Narcisse: or Lover of Himself*' (1752), see translation and introduction in Benjamin Barber and Janice Forman, 'Jean-Jacques Rousseau's "Preface to *Narcisse*"' (1978) 6 *Political Theory* 537
——, *Projet de Constitution pour la Corse* (Paris, Nautilus, 2000)
Sandel, Michael, *Liberalism and the Limits of Justice* (Cambridge, Cambridge University Press, 1998)
Saul, John Ralston, *Voltaire's Bastards* (New York, Vintage, 1993)

Sellers, Mortimer, *The Sacred Fire of Liberty: Republicanism, Liberalism and the Law* (New York, Macmillan and NYU Press, 1998)
Shklar, Judith, *Men and Citizens: a Study of Rousseau's Social Theory* (Cambridge, Cambridge University Press, 1969)
Skinner, Quentin, *Liberty before Liberalism* (Cambridge, Cambridge University Press, 1998)
——, *The Foundations of Modern Political Thought* Vol 1 (Cambridge, Cambridge University Press, 1979)
Smith, Adam, *Lectures on Jurisprudence* (Indianopolis, Liberty Press, 1982)
——, *Theory of Moral Sentiments* (Edinburgh, Strathan, 1759)
Starobinksi, Jean, *Jean-Jacques Rousseau: Transparency and Obstruction* (Chicago, University of Chicago Press, 1988)
Steiner, Eva, *French Law: a Comparative Approach* (Oxford, Oxford University Press, 2008)
Strong, Tracy, *Rousseau: the Politics of the Ordinary* (London, Sage, 1994)
Tocqueville, Alexis de, *Democracy in America* (Kramnick ed, Bevan trans, London, Penguin, 2003)
Tuck, Richard, *The Sleeping Sovereign: The Invention of Modern Democracy* (Cambridge, Cambridge University Press, 2008)
Viroli, Maurizio, *Republicanism* (New York, Hill and Wang, 2002)
Waldron, Jeremy, *The Dignity of Legislation* (Cambridge, Cambridge University Press, 1999)
Walzer, Michael, *Politics and Passion: Towards a more Egalitarian Liberalism* (New Haven CT, Yale University Press, 2006)
Webb, Jen, Shirato, Tony and Danaher, Geoff, *Understanding Bourdieu* (London, Sage, 2002)
Webster, Noah, *An Examination of the Leading Principles of the Federal Constitution* (Philadelphia, 1787)
West, HR, *An Introduction to Mill's Utilitarian Ethics* (Cambridge, Cambridge University Press, 2004)
Wokler, Robert (ed), *Rousseau and Liberty* (Manchester, Manchester University Press, 1995)
Young, Iris Marion, *Inclusion and Democracy* (Oxford, Oxford University Press, 2000)

Articles

Affeldt, Steven, 'The Force of Freedom: Rousseau on Forcing to be Free' (1999) 27 *Political Theory* 299
Altman, Andrew, 'Legal Realism, Critical Legal Studies, and Dworkin' (1986) 15 *Philosophy and Public Affairs* 205
Bagg, Samuel, 'Can Deliberation Neutralize Power?' (2015) *European Journal of Political Theory*, published online before print, 20 October 2015, http://ept.sagepub.com/content/early/2015/10/19/1474885115610542.abstract
Balkin, Jack, 'Taking Ideology Seriously: Ronald Dworkin and the CLS Critique' (1987) 55 *UMKC Law Review* 392
—— 'Understanding Legal Understanding: The Legal Subject and the Problem of Legal Coherence' (1993) 103 *Yale Law Journal* 105
Bellamy, Richard, 'Democracy as Public Law' (2013) 14 *German Law Journal* 1
Bellhouse, Mary L, 'Femininity & Commerce in the Eighteenth Century: Rousseau's Criticism of a Literary Ruse by Montesquieu' (1980) 13 *Polity* 285
Ben-Amos, Avner, 'The Sacred Centre of Power: Paris and Republican State Funerals' (1991) 22 *The Journal of Interdisciplinary History* 27
Boswell, John, 'How and why Narrative Matters in Deliberative Systems' (2013) 61 *Political Studies* 620

Bosworth, William, 'An Interpretation of Political Argument' (2016) *European Journal of Political Theory*, published online before print, 7 September 2016

Bourdieu, Pierre, 'The Force of Law: Towards a Sociology of the Juridical Field' (1987) 38 *Hastings Law Journal* 805

Brint, ME, 'Jean-Jacques Rousseau and Benjamin Constant: A Dialogue on Freedom and Tyranny' (1985) 47 *The Review of Politics* 323

Burtt, Shelley, 'The Good Citizen's Psyche: on the Psychology of Civic Virtue' (1990) 23 *Polity* 10

Canovan, Margaret, 'Arendt, Rousseau, and Human Plurality in Politics' (1983) 45 *Journal of Politics* 286

Carrington, Dorothy, 'The Corsican Constitution of Pasquale Paoli' (1973) 88 *The English Historical Review* 481

Chambers, Simone, 'Rhetoric and the Public Sphere: Has Deliberative Democracy Abandoned Mass Democracy?' (2009) 37 *Political Theory* 323

——, 'Deliberative Democratic Theory' (2003) 6 *Annual Review of Political Science* 307

Cohen, William, 'Symbols of Power: Statutes in Nineteenth-Century Provincial France' (1989) 31 *Comparative Studies in History and Society* 491

Colón-Ríos, Joel, 'Rousseau, Theorist of Constituent Power' (2016) *Oxford Journal of Legal Studies*, Advance Access, published 12 June 2016, http://ojls.oxfordjournals.org/content/early/2016/06/11/ojls.gqw012.full

Congdon, Matthew, 'Wronged beyond Words: On the Publicity and Repression of Moral Injury' (2016) 42 *Philosophy and Social Criticism* 815

Daly, Eoin 'A Republican Defence of the Constitutional Referendum' (2015) 35 *Legal Studies* 30

Dobel, J Patrick, "The Role of Language in Rousseau's Political Thought' (1986) 18 *Polity* 638, 640.

Downing, Lyle and Thigpen, Robert, 'Virtue and the Common Good in Liberal Theory' (1993) 55 *Journal of Politics* 1046

Doyle, William, 'An Account of Corsica, the Journal of a Tour to That Island, and Memoirs of Pascal Paoli (review)' (2007) 61 *French Studies: A Quarterly Review* 227

Dryzek, John and Sass, Jensen, 'Deliberative Cultures' (2014) 42 *Political Theory* 3

Dryzek, John, 'Legitimacy and Economy in Deliberative Democracy' (2001) 29 *Political Theory* 651

Edmundson, William, 'Transparency and Indeterminacy in the Liberal Critique of Critical Legal Studies' (1993) 24 *Seton Hall Law Review* 557

Eisgruber, Christopher, 'Civic Virtue and the Limits of Constitutionalism' (2001) 69 *Fordham Law Review* 2131

Eliasoph, Nina and Lichterman, Paul, 'Culture in Interaction' (2003) 108 *American Journal of Sociology* 735

Ellison, Charles, 'Rousseau and the Modern City: The Politics of Speech and Dress' (1985) 13 *Political Theory* 497

Finlayson, Alan 'Critique and Political Argumentation' (2013) 13 *Political Studies Review* 313

Fishkin, Joseph and Forebath, William, 'Reclaiming Constitutional Political Economy: An Introduction to the Symposium on the Constitution and Economic Inequality' (2015–16) 94 *Texas Law Review* 1287

France, Peter, 'Primitivism and Enlightenment: Rousseau and the Scots' (1985) 15 *The Yearbook of English Studies* 64

Germain, Claire, 'Approaches to Statutory Interpretation and Legislative History in France' (2003) Duke Journal of Comparative & International Law 195

Gibbs, Alun Howard, 'The Horizons of the Constitution: Politeia, the Political Regime and the Good' (2016) 27 Law and Critique 83

Goodin, Robert, 'Folie Républicaine' (2003) 6 Annual Review of Political Science 55

Grey, Thomas, 'The Constitution as Scripture' (1984) 37 Stanford Law Review 1

Grimm, Dieter, 'Integration by Constitution' (2005) 3 International Journal of Constitutional Law 193

Hanley, Ryan, 'Commerce and Corruption: Rousseau's Diagnosis and Adam Smith's Cure' (2008) 7 European Journal of Political Theory 137

Hayward, Clarissa, 'Doxa and Deliberation' (2004) 7 Critical Review of International Social and Political Philosophy 1

Hénaff, Marcel (Roxanne Lapidus trans), 'Cannibalistic City: Rousseau, Large Numbers, and the Abuse of the Social Bond' (1992) 21 SubStance 3

Horowitz, Asher, '"Laws and Customs Thrust Us Back into Infancy": Rousseau's Historical Anthropology' (1990) 52 The Review of Politics 215

Janara, Laura, 'Commercial Capitalism and the Democratic Psyche: The Threat to Tocquevillian Citizenship' (2001) 22 History of Political Thought 317

Jubb, Robert, 'Rawls and Rousseau: Amour-propre and the Strains of Commitment' (2011) 17 Res Publica 245

Kohn, Margaret, 'Homo Spectator: Public Space in the Age of the Spectacle' (2008) 34 Philosophy and Social Criticism 467

——, 'Language, Power, Persuasion: Towards a Critique of Deliberative Democracy' (2000) 7 Constellations 408

Kuhn, William, 'Ceremony and Politics: the British Monarchy 1871–1872' (1987) 26 Journal of British Studies 133

Laborde, Cecile, 'On Republican Toleration' (2002) 9 Constellations 167

Laden, Anthony, 'Republican Moments in Political Liberalism' (2006) 237 Revue internationale de philosophie 341

Larmore, Charles, 'A Critique of Philip Pettit's Republicanism' (2001) 11 Philosophical Issues 229

Lukes, Steven, 'Political Ritual and Social Integration' (1975) 9 Sociology

Marks, Jonathan, 'Jean-Jacques Rousseau, Michael Sandel and the Politics of Transparency' (2001) 4 Polity 619

Maynor, John, 'Without Regret: The Comprehensive Nature of Non-domination' (2002) 22 The Review of Politics 51

McCormick, John, '"Keep the Public Rich, but the Citizens Poor": Economic and Political Inequality in Constitutions, Ancient and Modern' (2013) 34 Cardozo Law Review 879

McLendon, Michael Locke, 'Rousseau and the Minimal Self: A Solution to the Problem of Amour-propre' (2014) 13 European Journal of Political Theory 341

Morriss, Andrew, 'Codes and Right Answers' (1999) 74 Chicago-Kent Law Review 355

Mouffe, Chantal, 'Deliberative Democracy or Agonistic Pluralism?' (1999) 66 Social Research 745

Nederman, Cary, 'Commercial Society and Republican Government in the Latin Middle Ages: The Economic Dimensions of Brunetto Latini's Republicanism' (2003) 31 Political Theory 644

Neuhouser, Frederick, 'Freedom, Dependence and the General Will' (19993) 102 Philosophical Review 363

Nielsen, Wendy C, 'Staging Rousseau's Republic: French Revolutionary Festivals and Olympe de Gouges' (2002) 43 *The Eighteenth Century* 268

Niemeyer, Simon, "The Emancipatory Effect of Deliberation: Empirical Lessons from Mini-publics' (2011) 39(1) *Politics and Society* 103

Nisbet, Robert, 'Rousseau and Totalitarianism' (1943) 5 *The Journal of Politics* 93

Nordahl, Richard, 'Rousseau in Dworkin: Judicial Rulings as Expressions of the General Will' (1997) 3 *Legal Theory* 317

Olson, Kevin, 'Epistemologies of Rebellion: the Tricolor Cockade and the Problem of Subaltern Speech' (2015) 43 *Political Theory* 730

——, 'Legitimate Speech and Hegemonic Idiom: The Limits of Deliberative democracy in the Diversity of its Voices' (2011) 59 *Political Studies* 527

Peled, Yoav, 'Rousseau's Inhibited Radicalism: An Analysis of His Political Thought in Light of His Economic Ideas' (1980) 74 *American Political Science Review* 1034

Pettit, Philip, 'The Tree of Liberty: Republicanism, American, French and Irish' (2005) 1 *Field Day Review* 30

Pocock, JGA, 'Virtues, Rights, and Manners: A Model for Historians of Political Thought' (1981) 9 *Political Theory* 353

Posner, Eric A, 'Symbols, Signals, and Social Norms in Politics and Law' (1998) 27 *Journal of Legal Studies* 765

Putterman, Ethan, 'Realism and Reform in Rousseau's Constitutional Projects for Corsica and Poland' (2001) 49 *Political Studies* 481

Rearick, Charles, 'Festivals in Modern France: The Experience of the Third Republic' (1977) 12 *The Journal of Contemporary History* 435

Reisert, Joseph, 'Authenticity, Justice and Virtue in Taylor and Rousseau' (2000) 33 *Polity* 305

Remer, Gary, 'Political Oratory and Conversation: Cicero versus Deliberative Democracy' (1999) 27 *Political Theory* 39

——, 'Two Models of Deliberation: Oratory and Conversation in Ratifying the Constitution' (2000) 8 *The Journal of Political Philosophy* 68

Riley, Patrick, 'A Possible Explanation of Rousseau's General Will' (1970) 64 *American Political Science Review* 86

Rosenberg, Shawn, 'Rethinking Democratic Deliberation: The Limits and Potential of Citizen Participation' (2007) 39 *Polity* 335

Savery, Daniel, 'Power to the People: Freedom as Non-domination, Disabling Constraints and the Eyeball Test' (2015) 8 *Journal of Political Power* 363

Schauer, Frederick, 'Legal Realism Untamed' (2013) 91 *Texas Law Review* 749

Scott, John, 'Politics as the Imitation of the Divine in Rousseau's "Social Contract"' (1994) 26 *Polity* 473

Sitaraman, Ganesh, 'Economic Structure and Constitutional Structure: an Intellectual History' (2015–16) 94 *Texas Law Review* 1301

Skillen, Anthony, 'Rousseau and the Fall of Social Man' (1985) 60 *Philosophy* 105

Sreenivasan, Gopal 'What is the General Will?' (2000) 109 *The Philosophical Review* 54

Steinberger, Peter, 'Hobbes, Rousseau and the Modern Conception of the State' (2008) 70 *The Journal of Politics* 595

Strong, Tracy, 'Theatricality, Public Space and Music in Rousseau' (1996) 25 *SubStance* 110

Topper, Keith, 'Arendt and Bourdieu between Word and Deed' (2011) 39 *Political Theory* 352

Turner, Brandon, 'Mandeville against Luxury' (2016) 44 *Political Theory* 26

Tushnet, Mark, 'Varieties of Constitutionalism' (Editorial) (2016) 14 *International Journal of Constitutional Law* 1

Villegas, Mauricio García, 'On Pierre Bourdieu's Legal Thought' (2004) 56 *Droit et société* 57

Waldron, Jeremy, 'Can there be a Democratic Jurisprudence' (2008–09) 58 *Emory Law Journal* 675

Walker, Graham 'The Constitutional Good: Constitutionalism's Equivocal Moral Imperative' (1993) 26 *Polity* 91

Weithman, Paul, 'Political Republicanism and Perfectionist Republicanism' (2004) 66 *The Review of Politics* 294

Contributions to Edited Collections

Brooke, Christopher, 'Isaiah Berlin and the Origins of the "Totalitarian" Rousseau' in Ritchie Robertson and Laurence Brockliss (eds), *Isaiah Berlin and the Enlightenment* (Oxford, Oxford University Pres, 2016)

Bryan, Dominic, 'Between the National and the Civic' in Thomas Hylland Eriksen and Rickard Jenkins (eds), *Flag, Nation and Symbolism in Europe and America* (London, Routledge, 2007)

Fulcher, Jane, 'Symbolic Domination and Contestation in French Music: Shifting the Paradigm from Adorno to Bourdieu' in Victoria Johson, Jane Fulcher and Thomas Ertman, *Opera and Society in Italy and France from Monteverdi to Bourdieu* (Cambrdige, Cambridge University Press, 2007)

Hardin, Russell, 'Why a Constitution?' in Dennis Galligan and Milla Versteeg (eds), *Social and Political Foundations of Constitutions* (Cambridge, Cambridge University Press, 2013)

Honohan, Iseult 'Educating Citizens' in Iseult Honohan and Jeremy Jennings (eds), *Republicanism in Theory and Practice* (London, Routledge, 2015)

Jarman, Neil, 'Pride and Possession, Display and Destruction' in Thomas Hylland Eriksen and Richard Jenkins (eds), *Flag, Nation and Symbolism in Europe and America* (London, Routledge, 2007)

Kramer, Matt, 'Liberty and Domination' in Cécile Laborde and John Maynor, *Republicanism and Political Theory* (London, Blackwell, 2008)

Mason, John Hope, 'Forced to be Free' in Robert Wokler (ed), *Rousseau and Liberty* (Manchester, Manchester University Press, 1995)

Pettit, Philip, 'Law and Liberty' in Samantha Besson and José-Luis Marti, *Legal Republicanism: National and International Perspectives* (Oxford, Oxford University Press, 2009)

——, 'Deliberative Democracy, the Discursive Dilemma and Republican Theory' in James Fishkin and Peter Laslett (eds), *Philosophy, Politics and Society* Vol 7 (New York, Cambridge University Press, 2003)

Skinner, Quentin, 'Liberty and Rights' in Michael Rosen and Jonathan Wolff, *Political Thought* (Oxford, Oxford University Press, 1999)

INDEX

Note: Alphabetical arrangement is word-by-word, where a group of letters followed by a space is filed before the same group of letters followed by a letter, eg 'free speech will appear before 'freedom'. In determining alphabetical arrangement, initial articles and prepositions are ignored.

a-rational kinds of political communication, 82
abnegation of self-interest, 67
absentee ownership of land, Corsica, 41
absolute sovereignty, 31
absolutism, 16, 18, 35
abstract cognitive capability, 116
abstract political ideals, 68
abuse, political speech, 113
accent, 112
Adams, John, 65
adjudication, 131
  as discourse, 140
  principled, 137–39, 145
  under republican austerity, 139–42
  rule of law, 142
adjudicative acts, 135
adjudicative reasoning, 145
aesthetic distinction, 85
aesthetic processes, 80
affective connection amongst citizens, 120
affective dimensions of citizenship, 82
affective forms, domination and social power in, 85
affective resources, republican self-government, 70–71
Affeldt, Steven, 93
agents, dominated, 115
agonistic politics, 120, 123
agrarian austerity, 67
agrarian egalitarianism, 56–57
agrarian political economy, 43
agrarian social order, 59
agrarian society, 53
agrarianism, 39, 40, 42, 59
alien control of choices, 128
alien interference, 126
alien others, 23, 24
alien will, 26, 32, 34, 126, 127
alienation, 20, 31, 59, 124, 143
allocative functions of Constitutions, 74
altruism, 56
altruistic devotion to community of citizens, 65
ambiguity, rituals, 102

ambition, 89, 115
amour de soi, 18–19, 23
amour-propre, 4, 14, 19–20, 21, 23, 26, 33, 36
  commerce and, 57
  consummation in benign forms, 87
  corrupted, 67, 85, 86, 123, 127
  cultural practices, 85, 86–87, 112
  dependency, engendering, 23
  education, 98
  expression of, 112
  insidious forms of, 57–58
  leisure practices as expression of, 112
  manipulating, 96
  positively harnessed, 95
  as potentially destructive passion, 56
  reorientating, 96
  runaway, 60
  taming, 98
  untamed forms of, 57–58, 60
ancient ritualism, 52
antecedent interests, law, 146
anthems, 75, 84, 92
anti-liberal constitutionalism, 66, 71
anti-oligarchic imperatives, 70
anti-structural force providing rituals, 102
apolitical practices, 61
approbation, 23, 58
approved behaviours, exaltation of, 82
approved dispositions, exaltation of, 82
arbitrariness, 31, 117
arbitrary authority, 30
arbitrary cultural practices, 88
arbitrary forms of social distinction, 58
arbitrary interference, 28
arbitrary judgment, 133
arbitrary powers, 26, 30, 32, 35, 51
arbitrary social practices, 88
ardour, 64
Arendt, Hannah, 108–109, 120, 124–25
argument, rational, 118
aristocracy, 120
aristocratic judicial wisdom, 142
Aristotle, 32, 56, 67

Index

array of evils, 20
art:
   as domination source, 85, 89
   as power source, 89
   as social distinction source, 85
   social inequality source, 85
   social power site of, 86
art of legislating, 140
art of statecraft, 77
articulatory style, deliberation, 115
artistic progress, 3
arts, 57, 86
aspirants, Corsica, 40–1
assemblies:
   formal, 90
   legislative, 42, 121
   representative, 121
assimilation, brute, 69
asymmetrical dependency, 26
asymmetries, powers, 26
athletic festivals, 90
Atlanticist republicanism, 69
atomisation, 70
attention, commanding, 115
austere agrarianism, 59
austere social politics, 5
austere society, 129
austerian constitutionalism, 10
austerity, 2–4, 5
   adjudication under, 139–42
   aesthetics under, 90–96
   agrarian, 67
   Corsica, 68
   cultural, 9
   culture under, 90–96
   deliberation under, 119–23
   domination, 71, 87
   dour, 61
   economic, 9
   general will and, 107
   holism, 140–41
   introspective, 61
   judicial power disciplined and constrained by, 131–32, 140–41
   laws, reconciliation purpose, 84
   Poland, 68
   politics of, 119, 127, 128
   public ritualism realisation, 87
   purpose, 87
   social, 9
   as social framework for republican politics, 34
   social hierarchies, stemming, 87
   as social horizon of republican freedom, 5
   spectacles, 90
   stability and, 68
   transparency, 122, 140–41
   virtues, 142

autarky, 37–8
   citizens, 55–56
   commerce in Corsica and Poland, 38–44
   conclusion, 71
   constitution of, 37–71
   Corsica, 8, 38–44, 63
   economic, 55
   in Poland, 39, 44
   political economy, 40, 42, 43, 59
   politics, 68
   projects, 87
   between realism and utopia, 66–71
   Rousseau's concept of constitutionalism, 62–66
   between utopia and realism, 66–71
   virtue and corruption and, 44–47
      destructive force of commercial society, 53–62
      morality of commerce, constitutional translations, republican adaptations, 49–51
      republican compromise with commerce, Rousseau's rejection of, 52–53
      republican politics for moderns, 47–49
   virtuous, 61
authentic acts of general will, 135
authentic private interests, 67
authoritarian shades of civic ritualism, 97
authoritative political speech, 116
authority:
   arbitrary, 30
   of general will, 137–38, 139
   political, 81
autonomy, 17
   individual, 50, 67
   judges, 134
   private, 70
awards, 82

Bagehot, Walter, 101
Baron, Frans, 47
basic liberties, 22, 127
befuddlement, 3, 117, 122, 124, 125, 128, 143, 144
beguilery, 79
behaviours:
   approved, exaltation of, 82
   attracting status and legitimacy, 127
Bellamy, Richard, 17, 27–8, 49, 64
Ben-Amos, Avner, 99
Bentham, Jeremy, 16, 28
bodily dispositions, 126
Bourdieu, Pierre, 82, 88, 89, 98, 112, 114, 116–18, 124–28, 145–46
bourgeois, 46, 58
bracing realism, 61
brute assimilation, 69

Burtt, Shelley, 50–51, 96, 103
Buttafoco, 7

capability, communicative, 116
capacity, deliberation, 115
capital:
    economic, competition for, 58
    exchange of, domination embedded in, 33
    forms, law generating, 146
    positional, 113, 144
    production of, domination embedded in, 33
    see also cultural capital; social capital; symbolic capital
capital cities, 39–40
capitalism, 51, 97
capitalist democracies, 100–101
celebrations, 78
ceremonials, 90, 91, 93
    see also feasts; festivals: pageantry
ceremonies, 74–75, 77, 79, 81, 87
certainty, rule of law, 133
chaos, 18
characters, citizens, 65
checks and balances, 29, 31
Chesnais, Robert, 39
choices:
    alien control of, 128
    dominating social structures, 129
    domination, to safeguard from, 127
    external control of, 32
    individual, 3, 126, 129
    subjection to alien will, 34, 127
    symbolic domination in, 127
Cicero, 32, 50
circumstances of politics, 28
citizens, 15
    affective connection amongst, 120
    altruistic devotion to community of, 65
    autarky, 55–56
    characters, 65
    common projects and concerns, 110
    Corsica, 40–1
    emotional connections, 82, 120
    integration, 97
    legislature, plenary, 121
    life plans, 65
    loss of voice, 124
    militia, Corsica, 42
    other, integrity of, 82
    political engagement, 61
    political power, contesting or participation in, 32
    private interests, preoccupation with, 55
    undominated, 128
    will, 138
citizenship:
    affective dimensions of, 82
    eligibility in autarkic political economy, 40

good, 75
non-rational dimensions of, 82
oaths, Corsica, 78
ranks, Corsica, 40–1
republican, 65, 69, 77
rituals and, 79
under rule of law, freedom as, 30
status, 127
civic belonging, 52
civic ceremonials, 93
civic decay, 106, 107
civic-educative purpose, legislation, 136
civic humanism, 56
civic-republican philosophy, 52
civic revelry, 95
civic rites, 77
civic ritualism, 52, 73–74, 87, 90, 91
    as alternative form of political communication, 119–20
    authoritarian shades, 97
    constitutional design and, contemporary problems, 96–102
    egalitarian vision of, 101
    neo-Durkheimian interpretations, 100–101
    orchestrating, 100
    radical scope of, 83–85
    spectacles of modern liberal republics and, 98
civic sentiment, 75, 84
civic socialisation, 99
civic solidarity, 114
civic stimuli, 84
civic virtues, 44–47, 52, 60, 65, 66, 69
    corruption and, 61
    Corsica, 76
    flourishing, 61
    Poland, 76
    rural basis, 53
    wealth and, inconsistencies, 59
civil freedom, 23, 24
civil-law culture, 132–33
civil religion, 77
claims, self-interested, 118
clarity legislation, 140
classes:
    conflict, 49
    interests and, equilibrium of creative tension between, 67
    stratification, 91
classic virtues, revival, 47
classical concept of constitutionalism, 63
classical liberalism, 16, 29
classical republican politics, 55
classifications:
    domination, based on, 26
    legitimacy, 113
    merit, 113
    social, 34, 89

symbolic, 146
symbols, 98
value, 113
codes, symbolic, 126
coercion, 16, 17, 28, 84, 126, 128
cognition, political, 79–81
cognitive capability, abstract, 116
cognitive division of labour, 143
cohesion, 109
cohesive social order, 61
collective emancipation, 4
collective self-government, 30
collectiveness, 63
commanding attention, 115
commemorations, military, 81
commerce, 2
  competitive nature of, 56
  corrupting effect of, 46
  in Corsica, autarky, 38–44
  destructive, 58–59
  development of, disincentivising, 40
  moral effects of commercial society, 52
  morality of, constitutional translations, republican adaptations, 49–51
  ostensible vices of commercial life, 48
  parasitic nature of, 56
  in Poland, autarky, 38–44
  practices reconciled with public morality, 47
  republican compromise with, Rousseau's rejection of, 52–53
  republican politics and, 47, 59
  suppression, 40
  transactional world of, 35
  undermining republican virtues, 60
commercial activities, Corsica, 39
commercial life, virtues and, 53
commercial society, 53–62
commercial virtues, 49
commodity exchange, Corsica, 41
common good, 54, 55, 68, 77, 97, 107, 121, 136, 145
common interests, 54, 109, 121, 129
common-law culture, 132–33
common projects and concerns, citizens, 110
common sense, 134
commonality, 124
commonly avowed interests, 32, 126, 129
commons, 41, 53
communication:
  difference, role in response to, 124
  political, *see* political communication
communicative capability, 116
communicative context of language, 118
communicative rationality, 117
communitarian philosophy, 2
communitarianism, 30, 32, 33, 34, 128–29
community, political, *see* political community
community will, 138

competence, deliberation, 115
competing interests, 52
competing rights claims, 64
competition, 58, 98
competitive nature of commerce, 56
competitive social fields, 88
competitive social practice, deliberation as, 113–14
competitiveness, 58
complex political speech, 119
complex private social practices, 34
complexity:
  encoded, 90
  social, *see* social complexity
  symbolic, 129
comprehensibility, legislative codes, 136
comprehension of political concepts, 80
comprehensive doctrines, 3
compulsion to duty, 96
concealment, language as means of, 115
concentrations, excessive powers, 59
concrete images, 80
conflicts, ethnic and cultural, 76
conformism, social, 69
confusion, 122
Connolly, William, 117
consciousness, 88, 89
consensus, overlapping, 68–69, 82
consent, legitimacy through, 16
conservatism, social, 30
consideration, desire for, 56
Considerations on the Government of Poland (Rousseau, 1772), 5, 9, 39, 63, 66, 77, 86, 90, 101, 121, 132, 141
Constant, Benjamin, 30–31, 45, 55, 70
constituting freedom, 21–6
constitutional design, 3, 96–102
constitutional jurisprudence, 145
constitutional law, 132
constitutional political economy, 70
constitutional politics, 76
Constitutional Project for Corsica (Rousseau, 1772), 5, 8, 38, 40, 54–57, 66–67, 77, 90
constitutional projects, 4–10
constitutional respectability, 74
constitutional theories, 4
constitutional theorist, 1–4
constitutional translations, 49–51
constitutionalising freedom, 36
constitutionalism:
  anti-liberal, 66, 71
  austerian, 10
  classical concept, 63
  directive, 71
  economic structures and, link between, 66
  as idea of government, 1
  legal, 28
  liberal, 62

liberal-democratic, 4, 5
  Rousseau's concept of, 62–66
  socially-directive, 2, 5, 10, 62
constitutions, 1
  of autarky, 37–71
  as conscious formulation of fundamental law, 62
  cultural conditions, fostering, 5
  cultural focus, 2
  of deliberation, 105–29
  economic conditions, fostering, 5
  of freedom, 13–36
  as institutional coordination of governance, 62
  of judgment, 131–47
  as master-law, 62
  as political code, 62
  as recognition of private rights, 62
  republican, 4
  of ritual, 73–103
  social conditions, fostering, 5
  socio-economic focus, 2
  of symbol, 73–103
  symbolic focus, 2
  United States, 70
constraining language, 113
constraints, 75, 128
contemporary constitutional thought, 74–76
contestation, 110, 126
control:
  of choices, alien, 128
  democratic, 109
  over individual choice, 126
  popular, 109
coordinating functions of Constitutions, 74
corporate will of political communities, 25
corrupted *amour-propre*, 123, 127
corrupting effect of wealth, 46, 54, 55
corrupting effect of commerce, 46
corruption, 60
  autarky, *see* autarky: virtue and corruption and
  civic virtues flourishing in absence of, 61
  cultural activities as, 85
  differentiation as expression of, 123
  political debate as harbinger of, 106
Corsica, 1–2, 5, 6–8
  agrarianism, 39, 40, 42
  austerity, 68
  autarky in, 38–44, 63
  citizenship oaths, 78
  civic ritualism, 91
  civic virtue, 76
  commerce in, 38–44
  egalitarian temperament of people, 56–57
  honorary citizenship, 78
  isolation, 68

land redistribution, 53, 59
political economy, 42, 43
public reason, 76
republic without financiers, 41
republican politics, as fortuitous for, 38
rituals, 76–78
rusticity, 68
symbols, 76–78
vices contracted during servitude, 63
see also Constitutional Project for Corsica
cosmopolitanism, 2
cosmopolitans, leisured, 87
counter-cultural force providing rituals, 102
creativity, 102, 131
criminal law, 132
critical discourse theory, 114–19
cruelty, 20
crystallising shared interests, deliberation, 109–10
cultural activities, 85
cultural austerity, 9
cultural capital, 3, 33, 58, 60, 74, 86, 87–88, 111, 126
cultural concerns, 5
cultural conditions, 5
cultural conflicts, 76
cultural expression, 87
cultural focus of Constitutions, 2
cultural pluralism, 93
cultural plurality, 67
cultural politics, 75
cultural practices, 88, 89, 112
cultural progress, 3
cultural solidarity, 109
culturally dominant idiom, 119
culture, 3, 64
  distinction, instrument of, 88
  as domination source, 85
  in early-modern world, 85–89
  rights, 28
  sceptical view of, 86
  as social distinction source, 85, 87
  social inequality source, 85
  sophisticated, growth, 57
currency abolition, Corsica, 41
customary law, 141

debate, political, 106
  see also deliberation
debauchery, 58
decay, civic, 106, 107
decentralised government, 43
decentralised power, Corsica, 43
deception intrinsic to language, 117
decision-making powers, 133–34
decisions:
  grounds, 143
  unrescinded, general will as totally of, 121

decorum, 81, 87
deeper dimension of domination, 128
delegated legislature, 135
deliberation, 105–106
　as antidote to domination, 110
　articulatory style, 115
　capacity, 115
　common interests, discerning and articulating, 109
　competence, 115
　as competitive social practice, 113–14
　constitution of, 105–29
　critical discourse theory, 114–19
　crystallising shared interests, 109–10
　degeneration into manipulative modes of speech, 121
　difference and, 123–6
　dissensus, dissent and, 106–108
　as domination, 111–19
　embodied nature of, 115
　harms of, 114
　inefficacy, 114
　inequalities, 116
　injuries of, 114
　neo-republican blind spots, 125–9
　non-domination and, 108–11
　participation in, 112
　performative nature of, 115
　political, *see* political deliberation
　as political domination source, 111
　as potentially destructive social practice, 106
　public power, rendering non-dominating, 129
　under republican austerity, 119–23
　ritualism aiding, 123
　role, 109
　in social context of austerity, 122
　social distinction, constituting, 125
　as specialised social technique, 122
　as speech culture, 118
　as symbolic and social domination source, 105
　symbolic violence inflicted by, 114, 120
　as virtuous political action form, 108
deliberative capacity, 115
deliberative competence, 115
deliberative democracy, 105, 117–18, 123
deliberative-democracy theory, 108, 110, 115–16, 119
deliberative discernment, 122
deliberative engagement, 109
deliberative politics, 129
delights, rich sensual, 78
demagogic form of political speech, 118
demagoguery, 121, 122
demeanour, 112

democracy:
　deliberative, 105, 117–18, 123
　direct, 2
　freedom and, 16
　mass, 110
　representative, Poland, 44
democratic absolutism, 35
democratic contestation, 110
democratic control, 32, 109
democratic government, 28
dependency, 14
　amour-propre engendering, 23
　asymmetrical, 26
　economic, 23
　on esteem, 23
　intractable nature, 22, 34
　loss of freedom through onset of, 24
　material, 23
　mutual, 26
　on nature, 23
　on others, 25
　on personal will, 23
　pervasive nature, 22, 34
　within political relationships, 20
　reciprocal, 26
　on recognition, 23, 33
　on recognition of others, liberation from, 93
　in social relationships, 20, 34
　unfreedom consisting of, 30
design, constitutional, 3, 96–102
despotic spectacles, 81
destructive commerce, 58–59
destructive force of commercial society, 53–62
destructive vices, Corsica, 57
determinism, social, 64, 66
devouring ambition, 115
dialogic form of political speech, 118
didactic spectacles, 92
Diderot, Denis, 79
difference, 123–6, 129
differential distributions, symbolic capital, 128
differentiation, 5, 45, 123, 143–46
　see also social differentiation
dignity, national, 4
direct democracy, 2
direct popular legislation, 2
directive constitutionalism, 71
directive influence of government, 129
discernment, general will, 107, 120, 122
discipline, 94
disclosure, identity, 125
discontinuity, 30
discord, 31–2
discourse:
　adjudication as, 140
　difference, role in response to, 124
　as domination source, 89

Index 163

legal, 143–5
linguistic, 119, 120
political, *see* political discourse
as power source, 89
principled, 138, 142
propositional forms of, 119
social power site, 86
as specialised social activity, 115
as speech culture, 118
violence, harbouring, 125
Discourse on Political Economy (Rousseau, 1755), 54, 57
Discourse on the Origin and Basis of Inequality Among Men (Rousseau, 1754), 18, 20, 22, 56, 71, 85, 86, 89, 112
Discourse on the Sciences and Arts (Rousseau, 1750), 8, 80, 85, 86, 89, 92
Discourses, 3, 4, 9
discretion, judicial, 134, 139
disgust, 98
disparities, social power, 110
dispassionate modes of speech, 119
dispositional resources, 70–71
dispositions, 82
dissensus, deliberation and, 106–108
dissent, deliberation and, 106–108
distinction:
  aesthetic, 85
  culture as instrument of, 88
  by decorum, 87
  desire for, 86
  esoteric sources of, 58
  frenzy for, propertied society as, 86
  individual, 88
  individual, politics, 124
  individual procured and conferred by social practices, 88
  know-how, based on arbitrary forms of, 113
  legal discourse, conferring, 143
  principled discourse as source, 144
  in pursuit of wealth, 48
  seeking, 23
  social, *see* social distinction
  sources of, 58
  symbolic, 115
  symbols, 98
  of talent, inequalities introduced by, 89
  taste as instrument of, 88
  through virtue, 87
diversity, 31–2, 97
divided societies, 58
division, economic, 66
division of labour, 45, 142
  as basis for law, 146
  cognitive, 143
  domination, leading to, 143
  institutional, 143
  intellectual, 143

judicial and legislative power, 132
judicial reasoning and lay reasoning, 140
legislative and judicial power, 132
rejection, 143
social, 143
social differentiation ills and, 57
Dobel, J Patrick, 78, 80, 84, 89
doctrines, comprehensive, 3
domestication of the dominated, 125
dominant identities, 116
dominated agents, 115
dominating political communication, 83
dominating social structures, 129
domination, 1–2
  in affective forms, 85
  art as source of, 85, 89
  austerity combating, 71
  austerity stemming forms of, 87
  choices
    external control of, 32
    to safeguard from, 127
  classifications, based on, 26
  complex private social practices, arising in, 34
  in cultural capital production and exchange, 126
  culture as source of, 85
  deeper dimension, 128
  deliberation as, 111–19
  discourse as source of, 89
  division of labour leading to, 143
  domestication of the dominated, 125
  in early-modern world, 85–89
  economic, 39, 69
  economic inequality and, 54
  embedded in production and exchange of capital, 33
  enactment through concrete linguistic exchanges, 124–25
  equated with unfreedom or servitude, 2–3
  forms, 33
  at foundational social level, 4
  freedom as absence of, 15, 17, 109
  government sources, 26
  in Hobbes and Rousseau, 18–21
  insidious forms, foiling, 3–4
  insidious kinds of, 113
  insidious nature, 69
  interpersonal, 127
  intractability, 23, 32, 34, 69, 127
  invisible kinds of, 113
  irreversible, 23
  language as instrument of, 89
  language as mechanism of, 124
  language, intrinsic to, 117
  law, 144
  legal discourse, 144
  in liberal traditions, 14–21

in material forms, 85
music as source of, 89
neo-republican blind spots, 125–29
oligarchic, 70
'people' as source of, 31
pervasiveness, 32, 34, 35
perversive character in social life concerns, 5
political, 3, 59, 60, 111
political communication inflicting, 124
political deliberation, 112, 125
political discourse, 126
political speech as site of, 120
positional goods, exercise and experience through, 33
potential for, 82
principled adjudication as source, 145
principled discourse, 144
private, 32
private social practices, arising in, 34
private sources, 26, 29
public, 32
recognition, dependency on, 87
in republican traditions, 14–21
in ritual form, 127
seeds sown by need for recognition, 22
slavery as, 30
social, *see* social domination
in social capital production and exchange, 126
social complexity as source, 57
social differentiation as source, 132
social hierarchies, based on, 26
social practices and, 9, 34, 63
in social relationships, 34
social structure choices, 129
sources, 5
specialisation as source, 132
statist, 69
symbolic, *see* symbolic domination
unfreedom consisting of, 30
Douglass, Robin, 19, 60
doux commerce, 49
dowries, land, Corsica, 41
doxa, 88
drafting legislation, 133
duty:
  compulsion to, 96
  inculcation of, 50
Dworkin, Ronald, 64, 138, 139–40, 142, 144
dynamics, social, 115–16

early-modern liberalism, 71
economic austerity, 9
economic autarky, 55
economic capital, competition for, 58
economic complexity, 57
economic concerns, 5
economic conditions, 5

economic dependency, 23
economic division, 66
economic domination, 39, 69
economic equality, 70
economic inequality, 54, 59
economic interests, 53
economic projects, 65
economic structures, 66, 71
education, 77–81, 92, 96
egalitarian imperatives, 70
egalitarian temperament of people, Corsica, 56–57
egalitarian vision of civic ritualism, 101
egotistic competition, 98
Eisgruber, Christopher, 65
elites, divestment of powers to, 43
eloquence, 114
emancipation, 4, 22
emancipatory potential of political speech, 114, 120
embodied character of speech, 124
embodied nature of deliberation, 115
Emile, or on Education (Rousseau, 1762), 81
emotional connections, citizens, 82, 120
emotional kinds of political communication, 82
emotional processes, 80
emotions, 74, 80, 83, 92, 98
empathy, 65
enchantment, 79
encoded complexity, 90
engagement, deliberative, 109
England, law and legislation, 132–33
Enlightenment, 3, 4, 92
envy, 89, 98, 115
equality, economic, 70
equilibrium between competing interests, 52
esoteric character of law, 144, 146
esoteric nature of adjudicative reasoning, 145
esoteric sources of distinction, 58
establishment of rights, 27
esteem, 22, 23, 56
ethical pluralism, 64
ethical plurality, 67
ethnic conflicts, 76
ethno-national politics, 75
Europe, legislative codes, 137
evils, array of, 20
excess wealth, possession of, 56
exchange, transactional world of, 35
exchanges, rituals and symbols, 80
exclusion, 124–25, 128, 144
execution, legislation, 135
executive:
  acts, 135
  legislature and, separation, 8
exhortatory purpose of legislation, 136
existence, sentiment of, 21, 26

experiential forms of political education, 78–79, 80
experiential forms of political communication, 121
experiential forms of moral education, 92
experiential spectacles, 92
experiential stimuli, 80
expression, political, 124
expressive individuality, 93
external approbation, 23
external interests, law, 146
external recognition, 3, 22, 126
extravagance, pompous, 81
eyeball test, 128

factional concerns, 54
factional interests, competing, 55
factionalism, 106, 107, 145
factions, 106
fall of man, 20
false consciousness, 88
families, Corsica, 40, 41
feasibility questions, 68
feasts, 73, 90
federalism, 50, 51
Federalist Papers (Madison, Hamilton and Jay), 105
Ferguson, Adam, 37, 45, 48–49, 70
festivals, 73, 74–75, 78, 81, 95, 99
festivities, 97, 99
Fête de la Fédération (Monet), 100
financiers, 41
fine arts, 57, 86
flags, 74–75, 76, 79, 92
forbearance, 56, 94
formal ceremonies or assemblies, 90
Foucault, Michel, 115
foundational laws, legislation as, 44
foundational social level, servitude and domination at, 4
fractured societies, 58
fragmentation, 57
France:
 Code Civil (1804), 133, 136
 legal thought, 137
 republican tradition, 65
 revolutionary festivals, 102
 Third Republic, 91, 99–100
 tricolor, 102
France, Peter, 39
fraternal society, 129
fraternalism, 85
free political institutions, 70
free speech, 97
freedom:
 as absence of domination, 15, 17, 109
 Bentham, 16
 as citizenship under rule of law, 30
 civil, 23, 24
 coercion through law constituting, 28
 constitution of, 13–36
 constitutionalising, 36
 defined in liberal sense, 16
 democracy and, 16
 democratic government and, connection between, 28
 government and, 16
 guaranteed through citizenship under rule of law, 32
 Hobbes, 16
 in Hobbes and Rousseau, 18–21
 individual, 32
 liberal dichotomies of, 128
 in liberal traditions, 14–21
 loss through onset of dependency, 24
 moral, 23
 natural, 21, 23, 24, 25, 31
 negative, 22, 32
 as non-domination, 34, 50
 as non-interference, 15, 16–17
 participation in sovereignty, 31
 political, 1, 15, 23, 25, 28, 95
 political self-rule, identification with, 28
 politics and, relationship between, 27
 private, security and protection of, 35
 promoting, 71
 radical republican ideas around, 68
 (re)constituting, 21–6
 recovery, 95
 republican, 9, 29, 34, 35
 republican concept of, 44
 in republican traditions, 14–21
 as security from arbitrary power, 51
 as self-rule in political community, 25
 situating, 27–9
 sovereignty, participation in, 31
 status, 29
 theories, 2, 4
 understandings of, 4
 wealth and, incompatibility, 55
fundamental law, 62
futility, rituals and symbols, 73–74

games, 78
Gauthier, David, 33, 87, 96, 123, 126
general interest, 58
general will, 25–6, 31, 35, 54, 55, 60–61, 67, 76–77
 austerity and, 107
 authentic acts of, 135
 authority of, 137–38, 139
 deliberative discernment, 122
 discernible through good sense, 61
 discernment, 107, 120, 122
 discovery of, 107
 encompassing fixed common interests, 121

expressing itself, 106
expression of sovereignty, 134
factionalism, subversion by, 145
good sense, discernible only through, 107, 122
individual wills, distinguished from aggregation of, 138
integrity, judges preserving, 138
judges expressing, 138–39
judicial power under, 134–37
legislation as expression, 134
legislation creation by authentic acts of, 135
legislation effectuation, 135
limited expression, legislation giving, 138
principled adjudication and, 137–39
private identities and interests, reconciliation to, 84
provisional expression, legislation giving, 138
realisation, 135
self-interest, subversion by, 145
sovereignty, act of, 134
subjection to, 127
subversion, 145
surviving judicial rulings, 138
as totally of unrescinded decisions, 121
transparency, 95
wealth and virtues, incompatibility, 55
will of all, distinguished from, 138
genuine private interests, 93
good citizenship, 75
good sense, 107, 122, 131, 134, 141
goods, positional, 33, 88, 126
governance, 62
government:
    constitutionalism as idea of, 1
    decentralised, 43
    directive influence, 129
    domination sources, 26
    freedom and, 16
    mixed, republican model of, 30
    non-democratic, 28
    non-dominating form, 87
    popular direction of, 129
    popular, highly centralised and undivided, 43
    representative, Poland, 9
    sovereigns' delegation to, 44
    theatrical elements of, 101
    undivided, 35
    unitary, 43
    see also self-government
Gracchus, Tiberius and Gaius, 59
gravity, 81
grievances, moral, 116

Habermas, Jurgen, 82, 110, 114, 117, 118
habitus, 88, 112, 113, 115, 116, 124, 144

Hanley, Ryan, 54, 56, 71
harmony, 67
harms of deliberation, 114
Harrington, James, 15, 42, 51
Hart, HLA, 138
Hayward, Clarissa, 115
Hazareesingh, Sudhir, 100
hegemonic idiom, 128
heterogeneity, 45
hierarchies, 59, 74
    bodily dispositions, constituted by, 126
    insidious, 86
    social, see social hierarchies
    status, 35, 125, 127, 144
    taste, constituted by, 126
historical genealogy of unfreedom, 13–14
Hobbes, Thomas, 16, 18–21, 30, 31
holism, austerity, 140–41
holistic social order, 61
honesty, 49
honorary citizenship, Corsica, 78
honour, mechanisms of, 82
human capital, 33
human diversity and independence, 97
human excellence, 71
human flourishing, 64, 66, 71
human motivation, 19
humanism, civic, 56
humans in pre-social state, 18
Hume, David, 37, 48, 53
hypocrisy, 73–74, 91

ideal republics, 1
ideas manipulation, 113
identities, 108, 116, 124, 125
ideologies, 145
idiom, 112
idleness, 40, 55, 56
illiberal forces, 98
images, concrete, 80
immunities, 31
improvisation, 102
inane vanity, 58
inauthentic social and cultural practices, 88
incompetence, 128
inculcation of duty, 50
Independence Days, 84
independence, human, 97
indeterminacy, 118, 134, 135, 136, 138, 139, 141, 144
individual autonomy, 50, 67
individual choices, 3, 126, 129
individual contestation, 126
individual distinction, 88
individual freedom, 32
individual rights, 31
individual self-expression, 94

individual wills, 138
individualism, 49, 61
individuality, 30, 93
individuals:
  arbitrary power of, 26
  personal will of, 26
  sovereign power, subjection to, 35
  state power over, limitation, 4
indivisible sovereignty, 43
industrial development, Corsica, 41
industrial society, 48
industrialisation, 91
industriousness, 56, 64
industry, 49
inefficacy, 73–74, 114, 120
inequality, 70, 120
  deliberation, 116
  distinction of talent, introduced by, 89
  economic, 54, 59
  relations of, 20
  social, 85
  wealth, mitigation, 54
influence, popular, 129
injuries of deliberation, 114
injustice, 144
innocent spectacles, 94
insidious forms of domination, foiling, 3–4
insidious nature of domination, 69
insidious violence, 118–19
instability, 31–2, 102
institutional division of labour, 143
institutional influences, 18
integration, 24, 97
integrity, 134, 138
intellectual comprehension, 81–82
intellectual division of labour, 143
intellectual life, 113
intellectual practices, 89
intellectual scepticism, 141
interdependence, social, 95
interdependency, 14
interested men, 118
interests:
  antecedent, law, 146
  classes and, equilibrium of creative tension between, 67
  common, 54, 109, 121, 129
  commonly avowed, 32, 126, 129
  external, law, 146
  factional, competing, 55
  principled adjudication obscuring, 145
  private, *see* private interests
  public, 50–51
  real, legal discourse obscuring, 145
  see also self-interest
interference, 15, 17, 28, 126, 128
interpersonal domination, 127

interpretation:
  judicial, 136–37
  legislation, 135, 141
intersubjective recognition, 120
intractability, 22, 23, 32, 34, 69, 127
introspective scrutiny, 89
invisible kinds of domination, 113
irregular passions, 118
irreversible domination, 23
isolation, Corsica, 68
Italian-Atlantic republicanism, 69

Jefferson, Thomas, 42
judge-made law, 137
judges:
  autonomy, 134
  general will, expressing, 138–39
  good sense, 131, 134
  integrity, 134
  legal reasoning, 140
  legislature, autonomy divested to, 134
  power to interpret law, 134
judgment, 131–3
  adjudication:
    principled, and general will, 137–39
    under republican austerity, 139–42
  arbitrary, 133
  complexity, differentiation and symbolic power, 143–46
  conclusion, 146–47
  constitution of, 131–47
  judicial power under general will, 134–37
  legislation and, 132–34
judicial creativity, 131
judicial development, 136–37
judicial discretion, 134, 139
judicial interpretation, 136–37
judicial law-making, 138
judicial legitimacy, 140
judicial power:
  constrained by austerity, 131–32, 140–41
  constrained by principle, 144
  containing, 133
  disciplined by austerity, 131–32, 140–41
  disciplined by principle, 144
  disciplining effect of principle on, 139
  division of labour, 132
  integrative effect of principle on, 139
  legislation and, 134
  structuring, 133
  subversiveness, 140
  unified by principle, 144
judicial reasoning, 140, 143
judicial rectitude, 142
judicial reviews, 138–39
judicial rulings, 138
judicial virtue, 142
judicial wisdom, 142

juridical field, 146
jurisprudence, constitutional, 145
juristic field, 146
justice, 64, 68, 83, 98, 134

Kant, Immanuel, 24
know-how for complex symbolic codes, 126
Kohn, Margaret, 92, 125

Laborde, Cecile, 65
labour:
    division of, *see* division of labour
    political, 120
    vices tempered by, 40
land, 41, 42, 53, 59
landlord–peasant relationships, Corsica, 41
language:
    communicative context, 118
    as concealment means, 115
    constraining, 113
    deception intrinsic to, 117
    domination intrinsic to, 117
    as instrument of social power, 113
    as instrument of domination and power, 89
    as marginalisation method, 115
    as mechanism of silencing, domination or exclusion, 124
    misuse, 113
    as power tool, 115
    shaping, 113
    as social practice, 120
    symbolic domination and befuddlement, 117
    symbolic social classifications functioning below level of, 89
    see also entries beginning with linguistic
law:
    actions in abstract, 135
    antecedent interests, 146
    capital forms, generating, 146
    civil, 132
    constitutional, 132
    criminal, 132
    customary, 141
    division of labour as basis for, 146
    domination, 144
    England, 132–33
    esoteric character, 144, 146
    external interests, 146
    inaccessibility, domination through, 144
    incomprehensiveness, domination through, 144
    interpretation, judges' power, 134
    judge-made, 137
    judges' power to interpret, 134
    judicial law-making, 138
    legislative form, 131
    motivational force, 136
    natural, 141
    prescriptive force, 136
    Roman, 141
    rule of, 32, 126, 133, 142
    secure acceptance of, 84
    social classifications, generating, 146
    social practices of, 146
    sovereign power emanation, 131
    subjects *en masse*, 134–5
    sub-national, 137
    supra-national, 137
    symbolic classifications, generating, 146
    symbolic domination in, 145
lay reasoning, division of labour, 140
legal concepts, 80
legal constitutionalism, 28
legal discourse, 143–5
legal foundations for autarkic political economy, 40
legal indeterminacy, 144
legal interference, 28
legal reasoning, 140
legal science, 142
legalised rights, 28
legislation:
    application, 135
    authoritative, becoming, 135
    civic-educative purpose, 136
    clarity, 140
    creation by authentic acts of general will, 135
    direct popular, 2
    drafting, 133
    England, 132–33
    execution, 135
    exhortatory purpose, 136
    form, 131, 135, 138, 140
    as foundational laws, 44
    general nature in object and authorship, 135
    general will, 134, 135, 138
    good sense, 141
    indeterminacy, 134, 135, 136
    interpretation, 135, 141
    judgment and, 132–34
    judicial power and, 134
    limiting form, 136
    particular will and, 135
    political authority, 135, 136
    political will, expressing, 136
    popular sovereignty exercise, 134
    rectitude in interpretation, 141
    sparsity, 132
    statecraft, 132
    terseness, 132
    transparency, 140
    uniting universality of will with universality of object, 135

Index

legislative assemblies, 42, 121
legislative codes, 136–37
legislative indeterminacy, 138, 139, 141
legislative minimalism, 136
legislative power, 43, 132, 138
legislative supremacy, 131, 142
legislators' roles, rituals, 79
legislature:
   autonomy divested to judges, 134
   delegated, 135
   executive and, separation, 8
   plenary, 135
   plenary citizen, 9, 121
   subordinate, 135
legitimacy, 16, 33, 113, 127, 140
legitimate political speech, 116
leisure practices, 112
leisure pursuits, 100
leisured cosmopolitans, 87
Letter to d'Alembert (Rousseau, 1758), 9, 29, 46, 90–91, 92, 94, 101
liberal constitutionalism, 62
liberal cosmopolitanism, 86
liberal democracies, ceremonials, 84
liberal democratic constitutional thought, 64
liberal-democratic constitutionalism, 4, 5, 74
liberal dichotomies of freedom, 128
liberal dichotomies of constraint, 128
liberal dichotomies of coercion, 128
liberal dichotomies of will, 128
liberal individualism, 61
liberal institutions, 65
liberal principles of justice, 83
liberal republics, 52
liberal social orders, 3, 69, 71
liberal society, 52, 87, 113
liberal tastes and social practices, 57
liberal traditions, 14–21
liberalism, 2, 68, 82
   classical, 16, 29
   early-modern, 71
   republicanism distinguished, 14–15
   social, 16
liberties, basic, 127
liberty, 98, 120
   see also freedom
licence, 15
life plans, citizens, 65
limits of politics, 27
linguistic discourse, 119, 120
linguistic exchanges, 124–25
linguistic power, 127
Lives of Plutarch (John Ralston Saul, 1993), 7
Locke, John, 25, 141
loss of freedom through onset of dependency, 24
Lukes, Steven, 100–101

luxuries, 20, 39, 40, 57, 81, 86
Lycurgus, 53

Machiavelli, Niccolò, 15, 60, 64, 66
Madison, James, 27, 31, 46, 49–51, 52, 53, 105, 118
magistracy, 135
majesty, 81
majorities, tyranny of, 31
Mandeville, Bernard, 48
manipulability of rational argument, 118
manipulation, 97, 121, 122, 125
marginalisation, 115
marginalised voices, 116
market society, 48
Marx, Karl, 101
Marxism, 88
Mason, John Hope, 84
mass democracy, 110
master-law, constitutions as, 62
material dependency, 23
material forms, 85
materialism, 55
Maynor, John, 65
meaningless forms of social distinction, 58
memorials, public, 84
merit, 33, 89, 113
micro-societies, 113
military commemorations, 81
miscommunication, 125
misidentification of genealogy of servitude, 24
misrecognition, 88
misrepresentations of interested men, 118
misuse, language, 113
mixed government, republican model of, 30
modern republics, 52
monarchical spectacles, 81
Monet, Claude, 100
money, pursuit of, 56
Montesquieu, Charles-Louis, 8, 45, 48, 68
moral costs of political utopias, 67
moral education, 92
moral effects of commercial society, 52
moral freedom, 23
moral grievances, 116
moral pluralism, 64
moral virtues, 65
morality, 47, 48, 49–51, 80, 83
Moses, 77, 79
motivation, human, 19
motivational anchorage, 65
motivational force, law, 136
motivational power, symbols, 98
Mouffe, Chantal, 129
music, 86, 89, 95
mutual dependency, 26
mutual empathy, 65

mutual interdependency, 24, 25
mutual recognition, 113

Narcisse, or Lover of Himself (Rousseau, 1752), 86
national anthems, 84
national dignity, 4
national specificities, 77–78
nationalism, 76, 78
natural freedom, 21, 23, 24, 25, 31
natural humans, 18
natural justice, 134
natural law, 141
natural rights, 35
natural state, 18
natural violence, 18
nature, dependency on, 23
negative freedom, 22, 32
negative rights, 27
neo-Durkheimian interpretations of civic ritualism, 100–101
neo-republican theories of non-domination, 54
neo-republican theories of unfreedom, 33
neo-republican theory, weaknesses in, 69
neo-republicans, 3, 33, 69
   deliberation blind spots, 125–29
   domination blind spots, 125–29
   unfreedom, 126
neo-Roman republicans, 29, 30, 32, 35
neutrality, 65–66
New Zealand, 76
Nielsen, Wendy, 102
non-arbitrary political power, 109
non-arbitrary public power, 109
non-democratic government, 28
non-dependency, 14
non-dominating form of government, 87
non-dominating forms of cultural expression, 87
non-dominating interference, 28
non-dominating public politics, 120–21
non-dominating public power, 109
non-domination, 14
   deliberation and, 108–11
   as economic project, 65
   freedom as, 34, 50
   neo-republican theories of, 54
   in public coercion, political deliberation as criterion for, 126
   republican freedom as, 34
   as social project, 65
   social relations, embracing, 35
non-interference, freedom as, 15, 16–17
non-rational dimensions of citizenship, 82
non-rational persuasion, 119
non-verbal forms of political education, 78–79
non-verbal stimuli, 80

Nordahl, Richard, 138
Northern Ireland, 76
nostalgic utopia, 61
Nouvelle Héloïse (Rousseau, 1761), 43
Numa, 77
Nussbaum, Martha, 83, 97–98

oath swearing, 78
obfuscation, 3
oligarchic domination, 70
oligarchic drift, 70
Olson, Kevin, 102, 116
opinions of others, 22, 48, 112
opulence, 86
oratory, 108, 114
orchestrating civic ritualism, 100
order, 81
Original Sin, 20
ostensible vices of commercial life, 48
ostentation, 40, 81, 86
others:
   alien, 23, 24
   dependence on recognition of, 126
   dependency on, 25
   living in opinions of, 112
   opinions of, 22, 48, 112
   recognition from, 87
   recognition of, 93
   relationships with those perceived as, 23
overlapping consensus, 68–69, 82
ownership of land, 41

pageantry, 73, 78, 79
Paine, Thomas, 1, 27, 50, 53, 62
Paoli, Pascal, 6–8, 39
parades, 78
parasitic nature of commerce, 56
participation:
   in deliberation, 112
   political, 32, 84
participative political education, 80
participative spectacles, 92
particular will, legislation and, 135
passions, 83, 91, 96–98, 112, 118
passive spectacles, 92
passive spectatorship, 92
patrie, 61, 84
patriotism, 75, 79, 92
patriots, Corsica, 40–1
peasant–landlord relationships, Corsica, 41
peculiar rites and ceremonies, 77, 79
'people', domination as source of, 31
performative nature of deliberation, 115
performativity, social, 112
personal security, 31
personal will, 23, 26
persuasion, non-rational, 119
pervasiveness, 22, 32, 34, 35

Pettit, Philip, 15–18, 28–30, 32, 34–35, 69, 109, 126–29
philosophical scope of Rousseau's constitutional project, 66
pictures giving concrete content to words, 80
pièves, Corsica, 41
pitié, 18
Pitt, William (the First), 7
Plato, 118
pleasure, 97
plenary citizen legislature, 9, 121
plenary legislative assemblies, 42, 121
plenary legislature, 135
pluralism, 31, 64, 93
plurality, 67
poise, 112
Poland, 1–2, 8–9
    austerity, 68
    autarky in, 39, 44
    civic virtue, 76
    legislation, 132, 141
    luxury, 81
    public reason, 76
    representative democracy, 44
    rituals, 76–78
    symbols, 76–78
    see also Considerations on the Government of Poland
politeia, 63, 65–66
political action, 84
political authority, 81, 135, 136
political code, constitutions as, 62
political cognition, 79–81
political communication, 3
    a-rational kinds of, 82
    civic ritualism as alternative form of, 119–20
    dominating, 83
    domination, inflicting, 124
    emotional kinds of, 82
    experiential forms, 121
    ritual forms of, 82–83, 121
    signs role, 79
    symbolic kinds of, 82–83
    symbols' role, 79
political communitarianism, 32
political community, 9, 85, 119
    collectiveness as basis for, 63
    corporate will of, 25
    deliberative engagement, 109
    mutual interdependency in, 25
    rituals and, 79
    self-governing, mutual interdependency in, 24
political concepts, 80
political creativity, rituals, 102
political debate, 106
    see also deliberation; political deliberation

political deliberation, 105
    as criterion for non-domination in public coercion, 126
    domination harboured in, 125
    as engendering form of domination, 112
political discourse:
    common good and private interests, confusion, 145
    different modes of, 108
    distinction based on arbitrary forms of know-how, 113
    domination, 126
    insidious violence embraced in, 118–19
    private interests and common good, confusion, 145
    symbolic complexity, 129
    symbolic violence latent in, 126
    violence latent in, 126, 129
political domination, 3, 59, 60, 111
political economy, 40, 42, 43, 59, 70
political education, 78–79, 80
political engagement, citizens, 61
political expression, 124
political force of passions, 97
political freedom, 1, 15, 23, 25, 28, 95
political function of symbols and rituals, 78–83
political horizon of mutual interdependency, 24
political ideals, abstract, 68
political identity, 108
political integration, incompleteness of, 24
political labour, 120
political liberty, 120
political life, economic interests dominance over, 53
political morality, 80, 83
political participation, 32, 84
political power, 32, 109
political reason, rituals and, 79
political relationships, 20
political representation, 50, 51
political rulers, 15
political self-government, 4
political self-rule, 28
political speech, 102, 106
    abuse, 113
    arbitrariness, 117
    authoritative, 116
    complex, 119
    demagogic form, 118
    dialogic form, 118
    as domination site, 120
    emancipatory potential, 114, 120
    as highly specialised pursuit, 113
    legitimate, 116
    oratorical mode of, 114
    refined flourishes of, 112

rhetorical mode of, 114
    as social distinction tool, 120
    substance and style, 117
political stability, 80
political subtleties, 113
political theory, challenge, 3
political utopias, moral costs of, 67
political virtues, 65
political voice, 114, 124
political will, legislation expressing, 136
politics:
    agonistic, 120, 123
    of austerity, 119, 127, 128
    autarky, 68
    central problem, 3
    circumstances of, 28
    cognition, 80
    of common good, 68
    constitutional, 76
    cultural, 75
    deliberative, 129
    emotions, evoking, 80
    ethno-national, 75
    freedom and, relationship between, 27
    individual distinction and identity, 124
    limits of, 27
    passion, role of, 98
    republican, for moderns, 47–49
    social, austere, 5
    social contract theories of, 16
    unfreedom redemption through horizon of, 23
Polock, JGA, 47
pompous extravagance, 81
popular control, 109
popular direction of government, 129
popular government, highly centralised and undivided, 43
popular influence, 129
popular sovereigns, single and indivisible, 43
popular sovereignty, 32, 35, 63, 135
Portalis, Jean-Étienne-Marie, 136
positional capital, 113, 144
positional goods, 33, 88, 126
possessive individualism, 49
potential for domination, 82
potentially destructive social practice, 106
powers:
    arbitrary, *see* arbitrary powers
    art as source of, 89
    asymmetries, 26
    concentrations, excessive, 59
    decentralised, Corsica, 43
    decision-making, 133–34
    discourse as source of, 89
    divestment to elites, 43
    judicial, *see* judicial power
    language as instrument of, 89, 115
    legislative, 43, 132, 138
    linguistic, 127
    motivational, symbols, 98
    music as source of, 89
    political, 32, 109
    prescriptive, republican laws, 82
    public, 42, 109, 129
    relations of, 88
    relative, 29
    separation of, 50, 51, 137
    social, 60
    social, *see* social power
    symbolic, 60, 88, 126, 127, 145
praise, love of, 48
praiseworthiness, love of, 48
pre-existing rights, 27
predictability, rule of law, 133
premiums, land, Corsica, 41
prescriptive force, law, 136
prescriptive power, republican laws, 82
pretentious pleasures, 86
pride, 86
primitive virtues, Corsica, 39
primitivism, 61
principle, 138–39, 144
principled adjudication, 137–39, 145
principled discourse, 138, 144
principled style of adjudication, 139
private autonomy, 70
private distinction, competition for, 58
private domination, 32
private freedom, security and protection of, 35
private identities, reconciliation to general will, 84
private interests:
    authentic, 67
    citizens' preoccupation with, 55
    common good and, 55, 145
    common interests and, 54
    genuine, 93
    potentially destructive, 52
    public interests and, interplay between, 50–51
    reconciliation to general will, 84
    sacrifice, 97
private rights, recognition of, 62
private rituals, 85, 87, 96
private social practices, domination arising in, 34
private sources of domination, 26, 29
private spectacles, 100
private symbols, 85, 87
private virtues, 65
prizes, 82
promoting freedom, 71
propertied society, 86
property, 24, 31, 40, 41, 53–54
propositional content, 102

propositional discourse, 119, 120
protection, private freedom, 35
provisional expression, 138
prudence, 49
Prussian Civil Code (1794), 137
public affect, 74
public awards, 82
public coercion, 126
public conception of justice, 64, 68
public dispositions, 55
public domination, 32
public education, 77
public esteem, 22
public interests, 50–51
public interference, 126
public life, plurality, 67
public meanings, 80, 123
public memorials, 84
public morality, 47, 48
public politics, non-dominating, 120–21
public power, 42, 109, 129
public prizes, 82
public reason, 62, 76, 83, 145
public revenue, Corsica, 41–2
public rituals, 80, 87, 93
public scrutiny, 94
public socialisation, 98
public symbols, 80, 87, 90
public virtues, 55, 65
pursuit of wealth, 56
Putterman, Ethan, 84, 93, 98, 103

quasi-heresy, 40

radical scope of civic ritualism, 83–85
radical transparency, 94
rapaciousness, 20
rational argument, 118
rational discourse, limits, 120
rationality, communicative, 117
Rawls, John, 3, 61–62, 64, 68–69, 82, 83
real interests, legal discourse obscuring, 145
realisation, general will, 135
realism, 61, 66–71
Rearick, Charles, 91, 99–100
reason, 62, 76, 79, 83, 145
reasoning, 118, 140, 143, 145
reciprocal dependency, 26
recognition:
    dependency on, 23, 33
    domination dependency on, 87
    domination seeds sown by need for, 22
    external, 3, 22, 126
    intersubjective, 120
    legal discourse conferring, 143
    mechanisms of, 82
    mutual, 113
    from others, 87
    of others, 93, 126
    social, 88
    social power dependency on, 87
    state-orchestrated nexus of, 93
    symbolic, 95
reconstituting freedom, 21–6
recovery of freedom, 95
rectitude, 141, 142
redemption, 22
redemptive horizon, republican politics, 24
redistribution of land, Corsica, 53, 59
referendums, suspicion of, 121
refined flourishes, 112, 123
relations of power, 88, 111
relationships:
    political, 20
    with others, 23
    social, 4, 20, 34
relative powers, 29
religion, civil, 77
Remer, Gary, 114
representation, political, 50, 51
representative assemblies, 121
representative democracy, Poland, 44
representative government, Poland, 9
republican adaptations, 49–51
republican austerity, *see* austerity
republican citizenship, 65, 69, 77
republican compromise with commerce, Rousseau's rejection of, 52–53
republican concept of freedom, 44
republican constitutions, 4, 44–45
republican freedom, 5, 9, 29, 34, 35
republican ideas, 68
republican laws, 81–82
republican order, 84
republican outlier, Rousseau as, 29–36
republican politics:
    austerity as social framework for, 34
    classical, 55
    commerce and, 47, 59
    Corsica, 38, 39
    for moderns, 47–49
    redemptive horizon, 24
republican ritualism, 90, 91, 92, 93, 95
republican self-government, 70–71
republican spectacles, 90–96
republican states, 1, 127
republican symbolism, 90
republican theatrics, 92
republican thinkers, 3
republican traditions, 14–21
republican values, 81
republican virtues, 45–46, 59, 60
republicanism, 14–15, 65, 69
republicans:
    early Americans, Corsican proposals and, 42
    neo-Roman, 29, 30

rights, position on, 28
  see also neo-republicans; *and entries beginning with* republican
republics, ideal, 1
resources, affective and dispositional, 70–71
respectability, constitutional, 74
revelry, 95
rhetoric, 108, 114, 118, 121
rich sensual delights, 78
rights:
  competing claims, 64
  culture, 28
  establishment, 27
  individual, 31
  legalised, 28
  natural, 35
  negative, 27
  pre-existing, 27
  property, 31
  republican position, 28
rites, 77, 79
  see also ritualism; rituals
ritualism:
  ancient, 52
  civic, *see* civic ritualism
  deliberation, aiding, 123
  see also rites; rituals
rituals, 73–74
  aesthetics and culture under austerity, 90–96
  ambiguity, 102
  anti-structural force, providing, 102
  citizenship and, 79
  civic ritualism, *see* civic ritualism
  conclusion, 102–103
  constitutional importance, 52
  constraints, 75
  in contemporary constitutional thought, 74–76
  in Corsica, 76–78
  counter-cultural force, providing, 102
  creativity source, providing, 102
  culture and aesthetics under austerity, 90–96
  culture and domination in early-modern world, 85–89
  devising, 79
  dimensions, statecraft, 77
  domination and culture in early-modern world, 85–89
  domination in form of, 127
  educative strategy through, 81
  exchanges, 80
  expression of *amour-propre*, 112
  futility, 73–74
  hypocrisy, 73–74
  improvisation source, providing, 102
  inefficacy, 73–74
  instability, 102
  legislators' roles, 79
  national specificities, emphasising, 77–78
  in Poland, 76–78
  political cognition and, 79
  political communication forms, 82–83, 121
  political community and, 79
  political creativity, 102
  political function, 78–83
  political reason and, 79
  private, 85, 87, 96
  public, 80, 87, 93
  republican, 90, 91, 92, 93, 95
  social, 89
  status quo, shoring up and legitimating, 101
  Third French Republic, 99
  visual metaphor of republican values, 81
  see also rites: ritualism: symbols
Roman law, 141
Roman-republicanism, 30, 31, 32
Rosenberg, Shawn, 82, 114
Roy, Jean, 89
rule, 81
rule of law, 32, 126, 133, 142
rulers, political, 15
rural basis of civic virtues, 53
rusticity, Corsica, 68

sacrifice of private interests, 97
safeguards, 31
scepticism, 3, 141
science of legislating, 140
scientific progress, 3
scrutiny, 89, 94
secondary legislative power, 138
security, 31, 32, 35
self-actualisation, 120
self-expression, 94
self-governing political communities, 24
self-government, 4, 30, 68, 70–71
self-interest, 51, 67, 145
self-interested claims, 118
self-love, 3, 19, 48
  see also amour de soi; amour-propre
self-rule in political community, freedom as, 25
sensual delights, 78
sentiments, 21, 26, 75, 84, 98
separation of powers, 50, 51, 137
servitude, 1–2
  equated with domination, 2–3
  experienced and inflicted in ostensibly mundane practices, 22
  at foundational social level, 4
  genealogy, misidentification, 24
  liberalism and, 17
  pervasiveness, 35
  social classifications, expression in, 34
  within social hierarchies, 20

structure, misidentification, 24
theories, 4
shaping, language, 113
shared interests, 109–10
signs:
  political communication role, 79
  see also symbols
silencing, language as mechanism of, 124
simple customs, Corsica, 39
single will, 25
situating freedom, 27–9
situating unfreedom, 27–9
Skinner, Quentin, 15, 30, 46
slavery, 15, 30, 46, 55
smallholding landownership, Corsica, 41
Smith, Adam, 35, 37, 45, 46, 48, 49, 53, 57
social austerity, 9
social capital, 3, 33, 58, 86, 87–88, 111, 126, 141
social classifications, 34, 89
social cohesion, 67
social communitarianism, 32
social complexity, 3–4, 5, 50, 57, 59
social concerns, 5
social conditions, constitutions, fostering, 5
social conformism, 69
social conservatism, 30
social contract, 16, 81
Social Contract (Rousseau, 1762), 1, 2, 6, 38, 39, 42, 43, 54, 61, 68, 76, 106–107, 113, 121, 132, 134
social determinism, 64, 66
social differences, 123
social differentiation, 3, 57, 86, 89, 132
social distinction, 58, 85, 87, 120, 124, 125
social division of labour, 143
social domination, 3, 4, 14, 23, 39, 69, 105, 112, 140
social dynamics, 115–16
social equality, substantive, 62
social fields, competitive, 88
social hierarchies, 26, 85–86, 87, 120
social inequality, 85
social influences, 18
social integration, incompleteness of, 24
social interdependence, 95
social liberalism, 16
social life, 5, 92
social order, 24, 59, 61
  see also liberal social orders
social performativity, 112
social politics, austere, 5
social power, 60
  in affective forms, 85
  art as site of, 86
  cultural practices as source of, 88
  discourse as site of, 86
  disparities, 110
  language as instrument of, 113

in material forms, 85
music as site of, 86
recognition, dependency on, 87
relations, 111
social practices as source of, 88
in symbolic forms, 85
social practices:
  arbitrary, 88
  domination and, relationship between, 9
  domination arising in, 34, 63
  inauthentic, 88
  individual distinction procured and conferred by, 88
  language as, 120
  of law, 146
  of liberal society, 87
  social power source, 88
  transparency, 94–95
social project, non-domination as, 65
social recognition, 88
social relations, 4, 26, 35
social relationships, 4, 20, 34
social rituals, 89
social scope of Rousseau's constitutional project, 66
social structures, 71, 129
social symbols, 88
social transparency, 4, 9, 119, 141
socialisation, 24, 98, 99
socially-directive character of constitutionalism, 2, 5, 10
socially-directive constitutionalism, 62
socially-directive functions of Constitutions, 74
society, 129
socio-economic focus of Constitutions, 2
softness, 58
solidarity, 56, 92, 109, 114
sophistry, 123
sovereign powers, 31, 35, 131
sovereigns, 20, 30, 43, 44
sovereignty, 31, 32, 35, 43, 63, 134, 135
sparsity, legislation, 132
Sparta, 53, 67
specialisation, 57, 132
specialised social activities, 115
spectacles, 90–96, 98, 100
spectatorship, passive, 92
speech:
  culture, deliberation or discourse as, 118
  dispassionate modes, 119
  embodied character of, 124
  free, 97
  manipulative modes of, deliberation degenerating into, 121
  political, *see* political speech
Spitz, Fabien, 46–7
sporadic spectacles, 92

spurious passions, 112
Sreenivisan, Gopal, 121
stability, 68, 69, 80
Starobinski, Jean, 95
state of nature, 18
state-orchestrated ceremonials, 90
state-orchestrated nexus of recognition, 93
state power over individuals, 4
statecraft, 77, 132
states:
  interference to prevent interference, 17
  legitimacy, 97
statist domination, 69
statues, 79, 80
status, 23, 29, 35, 125, 127, 143, 144
status quo, 101
statutory interpretation, 133
stimuli, 80, 84
Strauss, Leo, 63
Strong, Tracy, 79, 94, 95
structure of servitude, misidentification, 24
structuring judicial power, 133
style of political speech, 117
subjection to general will, 127
subjectivity, 88
subjects *en masse*, law, 134–5
subnational law, 137
subordinate legislature, 135
subordination, 20, 70, 97
substance of political speech, 117
substantive social equality, 62
subversion, 67, 145
subversiveness, judicial power, 140
superfluous goods, autarky excluding, 39
supranational law, 137
supremacy, legislative, 131, 142
surplus wealth, taxation of, 57
surreptitious envy, 115
suspicion of referendums, 121
Switzerland, autarky, 56, 58
symbolic affirmations of commonality, 124
symbolic capital, 3, 33, 74, 87–88, 95, 111, 126, 128
symbolic classifications, 146
symbolic codes, 126
symbolic complexity, 129
symbolic dimensions, statecraft, 77
symbolic distinctions, 115
symbolic domination, 85, 88, 89, 105, 117, 127, 145
symbolic exchange, 3
symbolic focus of constitutions, 2
symbolic forms, 85–86
symbolic kinds of political communication, 82–83
symbolic legitimacy, 127
symbolic power, 60, 88, 126, 127, 143–46
symbolic recognition, 95

symbolic social classifications, 89
symbolic universe, 120
symbolic violence, 3, 88, 114, 120, 126
symbolism, republican, 90
symbols, 73–74
  aesthetics and culture under austerity, 90–96
  classifications, 98
  conclusion, 102–103
  constitutional importance, 52
  constraints, 75
  in contemporary constitutional thought, 74–76
  in Corsica, 76–78
  culture and aesthetics under austerity, 90–96
  culture and domination in early-modern world, 85–89
  distinctions, 98
  domination and culture in early-modern world, 85–89
  exchanges, 80
  futility, 73–74
  hypocrisy, 73–74
  inefficacy, 73–74
  motivational power, 98
  national specificities, emphasising, 77–78
  pictures giving concrete content to words, 80
  in Poland, 76–78
  political communication role, 79
  political function, 78–83
  private, 85, 87
  public, 80, 87, 90
  republican symbolism, 90
  social, 88
  visual metaphor of republican values, 81
  see also ritualism, rituals; *and entries beginning with* symbolic

talent, 89
taste, 3, 87, 88, 126
taxation of surplus wealth, 57
temperance, 49, 56, 65
tension, 101–102
terseness, legislation, 132
theatre, 89, 92
theatrical elements of government, 101
theatricality, 88
theatrics, republican, 92
theories:
  constitutional, 76
  freedom, 2, 4
  neo-republican, 33, 54, 69
  servitude, 4
  unfreedom, 2
thrift, 49
timidity, 128
toleration, 15
Topper, Keith, 124
transient emotions, 92

transparency, 4, 9, 94–95, 119, 122, 127, 140–41
tripartite separation of powers, 50
tyranny of majorities, 31

understandings of freedom, 4
undifferentiated society, 129
undivided government, 35
undivided rule, 35
undivided sovereignty, 31, 35
undominated citizens, 128
unequal distributions symbolic capital, 128
unfreedom:
  arbitrary interference, stemming from, 28
  dependency, consisting of, 30
  domination, consisting of, 30
  equated with domination, 2–3
  historical genealogy of, 13–14
  in Hobbes and Rousseau, 18–21
  neo-republicans, 33, 126
  redemption through horizon of politics, 23
  situating, 27–9
  sources, 5
  subjection of choice to alien will, 32, 127
  theories, 2
unhinged competition, 98
unitary government, 43
unitary sovereigns, 30
United States Constitution, 70
unnecessary wealth, possession of, 56
urbanisation, 43, 57, 91
urbanity, corrupting effects, 39–40
utopias:
  nostalgic, 61
  political, moral costs of, 67
  realism and, autarky between, 66–71

vain emotions, 92
values, 50, 81, 89, 113
vanity, 20, 48, 58, 86
vices, 40, 43, 48, 57
violence, 3, 18, 88, 114, 118–20, 125, 126, 129
virtues, 96
  austerity, 142
  autarky, *see* autarky: virtue and corruption and
  civic, *see* civic virtues
  classic, revival, 47
  commercial, 49
  commercial life and, 53
  distinction through, 87
  judicial, 142
  moral, 65
  political, 65
  private, 65
  public, 55, 65
  public reason, 62
  republican, 45–46, 59, 60
virtuous activities, 39
virtuous autarky, 61
virtuous political action form, deliberation as, 108
visual metaphor of republican values, 81
voice:
  loss of, citizens, 124
  marginalised, 116
  political, 114, 124
voting, 108

Walker, Graham, 71
way of being, 91
wealth:
  civic virtues and, inconsistencies, 59
  corrupting effects of, 46, 54, 55
  distinction in pursuit of, 48
  excess, possession of, 56
  freedom and, incompatibility, 55
  general will virtues and, incompatibility, 55
  inequality, mitigation, 54
  pursuit of, 56
  republican virtues and, inconsistencies, 59
  suppression, 40
  surplus, taxation of, 57
  unnecessary, possession of, 56
  vanity in pursuit of, 48
Webster, Noah, 42
Weithman, Paul, 65
West Virginia State Board of Education v Barnette, 75
wholesome tastes, Corsica, 39
will:
  alien, *see* alien will
  of all, general will distinguished from, 138
  of citizens, 138
  of community, 138
  corporate, of political communities, 25
  general, *see* general will
  individual, aggregation, distinguished from general will, 138
  liberal dichotomies of, 128
  particular, legislation and, 135
  personal, 23, 26
  political, legislation expressing, 136
  single, 25
wisdom, judicial, 142

Young, Iris Marion, 117, 119

www.ingramcontent.com/pod-product-compliance
Lightning Source LLC
Chambersburg PA
CBHW061835300426
44115CB00013B/2395